"We're here to arrest you for the murder of Tia Phillips and the attempted murder of Mindy Phillips," Lindquist said.

Priscilla stood stock still and then she threw her purse down on the conference table in disbelief.

"We want to make this difficult situation as easy as possible. If you can act like a lady, we'll take you out of here without handcuffs," Detective Lindquist continued, staring right at her.

"If you consider me a lady, why arrest me here at work, in front of everybody?" Priscilla retorted.

"I never said I consider you a lady." He took her by the arm and walked her out, the two other detectives bunched beside her. The whole world knew what was happening, even without handcuffs.

As they waited for the elevator, Priscilla said quietly, "It's really not your fault that you don't know I'm innocent."

"You're not innocent, Priscilla, and that's why I'm here," Lindquist said, his blue eyes stony.

A MOTHER'S TRIAL

A MOTHER'S TRIAL

Nancy Wright

BANTAM BOOKS
TORONTO • NEW YORK • LONDON • SYDNEY • AUCKLAND

A MOTHER'S TRIAL
A Bantam Book / December 1984

ISBN 0-553-24608-9

Published simultaneously in the United States and Canada

Bantam Books are published by Bantam Books, Inc. Its trademark, consisting of the words "Bantam Books" and the portrayal of a rooster, is Registered in U.S. Patent and Trademark Office and in other countries. Marca Registrada. Bantam Books, Inc., 666 Fifth Avenue, New York, New York 10103.

PRINTED IN THE UNITED STATES OF AMERICA

H   0 9 8 7 6 5 4 3 2 1

For Al, Emily and Philip

You can come to the conclusion that every life event is purely a personal perception. Maybe the essence of it all is that truth is evasive. Maybe there is no such thing as truth: Truth is what you want it to be. And what a large number of people agree upon as truth is truth.

Dr. Michael Applebaum
March 21, 1982

Acknowledgments

Over one hundred people contributed time and effort to this book. Among them were some who are special.

To Ted Lindquist of the San Rafael Police Department; for sacrificing hours of scant free time to help me, asking in return only that I tell the truth (I hope he is not disappointed);

to Evelyn Callas; for poring over Tia's and Mindy's records with me, offering always patient explanations to a pupil whose natural skills and acumen were certainly less than what she was accustomed to; and for resisting pressure from significant forces which preferred she keep silent;

to all the others I interviewed; for freely volunteering enormous amounts of aid and information;

to Dr. Larry Schwartz; for reading the manuscript and making valuable suggestions;

to family and friends; for their editorial assistance; and for bearing with an obsessed personality both patiently and uncritically for over four years;

and most especially to my brother, Tony Ganz; for supporting me and this project from the beginning; for reading the manuscript at various stages with sensitivity and perception; and for encouraging me to keep going on the occasions when it would have been easier to quit:

Thank you.

Author's Note

This is a true story. The events and people—and the scenes involving them—are real.

To protect their privacy, the names of some individuals have been changed.

Prologue

On Wednesday morning, February 22, 1978, Priscilla Phillips angled her car into a marked stall in the parking lot in back of the hillside site occupied by San Rafael's Kaiser Hospital. At eight in the morning, cars were scarce. The clinics would not open for another half an hour, and those doctors arriving early commonly parked by the Emergency entrance. But Priscilla could not wait until eight-thirty. Concerned about Mindy, she had not slept well, tossing with half-framed dreams of anxiety and unfulfilled obligations.

Priscilla, a heavyset woman, with bones too small for the weight she had added in recent years, closed the car door with a thump that sounded hollow in the fog of the February morning.

As the main clinic doors were still locked, Priscilla walked around to the Emergency entrance and started for Five West, the pediatric ward, where her first adopted daughter, Tia, had spent much of her short life.

Priscilla Phillips emerged from the elevator on the fifth floor and turning right, entered the pediatric ward, and walked across to the deserted nurses' station. There was a distant sound of a baby crying. For a moment Priscilla tried to recall who was on duty. She knew all the regular nurses in pediatrics. That had been a godsend when Mindy became sick. Everyone said it was a mistake to adopt a second Korean child so soon after losing Tia. But both she and Steve had insisted, even in the face of the adoption agency's initial resistance to the idea. Just nine months after Tia's death, Mindy was delivered to them. That had been four months ago. Within a few weeks, she, too, fell sick.

Mindy's illness—just like Tia's,—was initially diagnosed as gastroenteritis. She improved and after nine days was discharged. But after only three days at home she was admitted again, at 2:45 A.M. on February sixteenth, with severe diarrhea and vomiting.

In the six days since, her condition had fluctuated, but the diarrhea continued and intravenous therapy was initiated. As Priscilla knew from her experiences with Tia, without an IV a severely dehydrated child could die within fifteen minutes.

The sound of her heels loud in the vacant corridor, Priscilla crossed back to the small utility room where the nurses kept Mindy's Cho-free formula in a refrigerator. There she poured some of the Cho-free from the liter bottle into a baby bottle, stoppered it with a clean nipple, and started for room 503, directly across from the nurses' station. They had put Mindy in the same room Tia had occupied for so many weeks.

Mindy was awake. At thirteen months she was small for her age, although not as small as Tia had been. She wrinkled up her broad nose and squinted up smiling at her mother. Beside her, the IV line rattled slightly as she moved.

Priscilla looked down at her, the light from the window touching and then glancing off Mindy's short black hair. Then she took a seat by Mindy's bed and reached for her daughter to offer her the formula.

It was a gesture she had made repeatedly in her thirty-two years. It was a mother's gesture. But in the months to come, there would be many people calling it something other— something, in fact, terribly different.

THE FORMULA

1

The modern, cement complex of Kaiser Hospital in San
Rafael, Marin County, was one of thirteen Kaiser hospitals in
the northern California region. It sat—pink and squat—in the
low, rounded hills of the section of San Rafael called Terra
Linda. Only two years old, it consisted of three interlocking
buildings: the General Services Building, the Medical Office
Building, and the hospital itself. With a patient membership of
about 80,000 and a bed capacity of 92, this facility was among
the smaller medical centers in the region. Its staff of 74 doctors
included 9 pediatricians.

It was a pleasant place to work, particularly for those on the
staff who had known the old dim and crowded San Rafael
offices. The center was well-designed and maintained. The
pediatricians' offices, on the third floor of the Medical Office
Building, were small but adequately furnished, each with
natural light supplied by a decent-size window. Initials *A*
through *D* had been parceled out to the four clusters in the
pediatric section. Dr. Sara Shimoda, along with Drs. Evelyn
Callas and Richard Viehweg, were assigned to Pediatrics B.

While Priscilla Phillips fed her daughter, thirty-six-year-old
Sara Shimoda sat alone in her office. A beautiful woman with
porcelain skin and dark, expressive eyes set in an oval face, she
wore about her a cloak of stillness and reserve that had always
prompted others to reach out to her. As a doctor she carried an
extra burden of cultural history that insisted that women
remain in the background, and this tended to make her
hesitant and occasionally distrustful of her sure instincts and
first-class intelligence.

Today Sara was to present the case of Mindy Phillips at the
weekly department meeting due to start at eight forty-five.
She did not look forward to it. She hated speaking in meetings,
even among friends. But this was not the primary reason for
her apprehension. This morning, her fears were professional

rather than personal because she was to present the case of Mindy Phillips. And except for its uncanny resemblance to that of Tia Phillips, everything about this child's case was unusual.

For one thing, Sara knew she had a particularly close relationship with Mindy's mother. It had always been hard to explain what attraction Priscilla Phillips held for Sara, but she was aware that it was more than their superficial resemblances in age or life-style. They had met at the American Association of University Women (AAUW)—Priscilla had been vice-president in charge of membership at the time Sara joined—but they did not approach that group, or anything else, in the same way. Sara knew well her tendency to sit quietly on the edges of things. In the months after their first meeting, she saw Priscilla volunteering her time, holding office, always at the forefront with ideas for activities or special projects. While Sara guarded her feelings, Priscilla hugged, kissed, cried, laughed, and even argued—all in public. It had to be their differences that attracted each to the other.

Certainly their early backgrounds differed dramatically. Sara had been born in the farm belt of central California and had grown to adolescence there. An undergraduate career at the University of California in Berkeley, and medical school at UCSF followed.

In 1971, by then comfortably married to a teacher of the handicapped named Tom Post, Sara joined the staff at Kaiser. In the seven years that followed, she dealt with many parents, but none affected her in quite the same way as did the Phillips family.

Priscilla had left an indelible impression on Sara at that introductory meeting of the AAUW. As she passed around her first pictures of the little Korean orphan she planned to adopt, she was so openly excited that Sara felt herself pulled into the event, too.

Later, of course, Tia had drawn Sara in. Tia, who resembled Sara's own daughter in both age and appearance, was a beautiful and loving child.

When Tia was under her care, Sara had broken down more than a few times. The period after the laparotomy had been the worst, when she could offer no more hope, when comforting words rang false: she had known Tia was probably going to die.

By then friends and colleagues on the staff were warning

Sara about her involvement with the family, insisting that Priscilla Phillips was like a leech, and that Sara must guard herself lest she be sucked dry. She found this perception of Priscilla puzzling: it was not how she saw her. Certainly Priscilla was demanding and intense, but Sara could do nothing but admire the woman for her devotion to Tia. At times she had to force Priscilla to go home. Priscilla always tried so hard, helping uncomplainingly with everything. She had always been right there when Tia needed her—as she was now for Mindy.

Sara had been increasingly troubled about Mindy. Her symptoms made no medical sense at all. As Sara crossed the hall to the Pediatric Conference Room the staff used for their weekly meeting, Mindy's plastic-covered chart in her hand, she wondered how her colleagues would react to her admission of failure.

Sara's case presentation, the first item on the agenda, was brief. In the small, plain room, she did not have to raise her soft voice. She began with the patient's history.

"Mindy Phillips is a thirteen-month-old Korean child with congenital cytomegalovirus and intermittent cyanosis. She has been hospitalized several times during the last month with chronic diarrhea. So far we can find no cause for the cyanosis. EKG and cardiac exams are normal, and Dr. Tarnoff from Cardiology believes that her cyanotic condition is due to a peripheral vascular disorder.

"In spite of Mindy's treatment with IV fluids and Cho-free formula plus polycose, she continues to have intermittent bouts of voluminous watery stools. In this she bears a quite striking resemblance to her sister, Tia, who at a similar age developed an intractable form of watery diarrhea with peculiar electrolyte abnormalities, including high serum sodium levels.

"As you will remember, after months of hospitalizations and repeated work-ups, tests, and procedures that yielded no real clue to her illness, Tia eventually died one year ago.

"I needn't remind you that although both children were adopted and of Korean extraction, they are not related to each other. I consider this a critically important point because it rules out the hereditary factor."

Sara looked around the conference table at the other pediatricians and paused.

"Are there any comments?" she asked.

2

Dr. Evelyn Callas sat squarely, leaning forward against a hand cupped under her firm chin as she listened to Sara's presentation. Her apparent relaxation was just a pose. She was a bustling, vigorous woman who thrived on work. At forty-eight, she had been in practice as a pediatrician for over twenty years and on the staff of Kaiser for nineteen, and had just been appointed Chief of Pediatrics. Sometimes it was hard for her to believe that she had climbed that high.

Evelyn Ridenauer boasted descent from rough country stock. Reared in rural Sonoma County, north of San Francisco, she had attended the fifteen-student, one-room Ridenauer School taught by a single teacher, her mother. Her father, a small farmer all his life, was head of the school board. Her family had always specialized in overcoming difficulties. In 1853, her great-grandfather had taken up a land site in Sonoma County that Evelyn remembered and often described as rather scenic but totally useless. He had added to his problems by sympathizing with the Unionists in a Confederate county, but the Ridenauers survived, and if they hadn't prospered, at least they had endured.

She had to manage without much money. But the Ridenauers did provide their only daughter with a modicum of ambition, an inheritance of extraordinary energy, and a considerable portion of intelligence. After an undergraduate career at nearby Santa Rosa Junior College, followed by a year at USC, Evelyn decided to apply to Southern Cal's medical school. It was 1951, and the Korean war veterans were descending in droves upon every medical school. There was a quota for women at USC and for this Evelyn considered herself lucky. Otherwise, she sometimes thought, they would not have taken any women. As it was, out of their class of seventy they accepted four women. Evelyn Ridenauer was one.

In the next four years she completed medical school—graduating near the top of her class—married one of those Korean veterans and produced a son. She had always known

6

she wanted to be a pediatrician, preferring to deal with acutely ill patients she could see, treat, and send home well, rather than with the chronically ill. And she had taken a realistic, practical point of view: pediatrics was one of the few specialties where her sex would be an advantage.

So following a year's rotating internship at Harbor General in Torrance, she completed a two-year residency in pediatrics at Children's Hospital in Los Angeles, the same hospital where Sara Shimoda was to train ten years later. And then she and her husband Jim, a pediatrician by that time too, moved back north to Marin County.

In twenty years she had altered somewhat. Her figure was now decidedly narrower at the top than at the bottom. Her clear-rimmed glasses were bifocal and thick enough to magnify her brown eyes; her short brown hair was going gray. Sometimes she waxed a little too enthusiastic and startled people. And she could be sarcastic and a little overbearing and formal when she was ill-at-ease.

As the staff began discussing Mindy's case, Evelyn realized that the possibility of deliberate poisoning would at least have to be explored. It was a highly unpleasant conclusion. No pediatrician was trained to look for it. Accidental poisoning was not so uncommon, occasionally occurring even in hospital settings. Sometimes salt would inadvertently be mixed into a formula in place of sugar. But deliberately? Repeatedly and before their very eyes? Unthinkable. Or nearly so. But Evelyn knew that Sara was finally considering it. So were they all. It might not be the answer, but it required examination despite Sara's understandable reluctance.

"You might contact Boyd Stephens—he's the San Francisco coroner," Evelyn heard Rainer Arnhold suggest to Sara.

"Yes, he's an expert on toxicology," Dick Stein agreed. "We need to have some sort of proof before we can act. He may be able to help."

"Oh, and this week's *Journal of the American Medical Association* has an article about mothers poisoning their children in hospitals, apparently out of some sort of misguided desire to be centers of attention themselves," Rainer went on. "I believe the syndrome has been called Munchausen Syndrome by Proxy. I'll give you my copy."

"Thank you," Sara said.

The meeting continued, but Evelyn Callas only half listened

to Dr. Arnhold's presentation of a patient with respiratory problems and Dr. Carte's report on minimal brain dysfunction in children. She had been struck by a thought that suggested a solution to the puzzle of Mindy's condition.

When at ten o'clock the meeting was finally adjourned, Evelyn flew after the departing white coat of Sara Shimoda and cornered her in her office.

"Sara, I've got it! I know what it is," she said.

"What?"

"What's being given to Mindy. I know what it is. It's got to be a sodium cathartic—it's got to be Epsom salts. Now what's in Epsom salts?"

Neither of them knew.

"Let's see your *Goodman and Gilman*. Do you have it here?" Evelyn persisted.

Sara did. She lifted the heavy pharmacology book and handed it to Evelyn, who hunched over it, leafing through the pages, her brown eyes intent.

"Sodium magnesium sulfates," she read. "Now how can we test for the presence of those? Can we test for sulfates? See if we can get the magnesium—I know we can get the magnesium!"

But because they both had patients to see and were late already, they did not have time to pursue Evelyn's idea. And, as Evelyn found out later, it would soon cease to matter.

3

Priscilla Phillips sat comfortably in the low, vinyl-upholstered, orange chair the hospital provided, her legs and feet trim in hose and low-heeled shoes, and looked down at her daughter. Mindy lay back in Priscilla's lap, sucking eagerly on her bottle; she had definitely improved. Sara had indicated that she might possibly discharge Mindy today and Priscilla had whooped in excitement at the news.

"It will be a double celebration," she'd said to Sara. "Today's my thirty-second birthday."

"Let's keep our fingers crossed then," Sara said.

Priscilla studied Mindy as she held her. Priscilla tried to avoid comparing her children, but sometimes this was inevitable. She saw none of Tia's beauty or charm in Mindy, who had a broad nose, slightly flattened against her high cheekbones, much yellower skin, and a wider face. Now even the bangs which Priscilla had proudly cultivated—thicker than Tia's had ever grown—had been shaved off with a razor so an IV could be placed in a scalp vein. This mutilation had been accomplished, Priscilla had complained to Steve, by a doctor without children of her own. Apparently it had never occurred to Dr. Janet Specht how a mother would view the results. Priscilla thought the uneven shave made Mindy ugly and destroyed her best feature, and for no reason. Dr. Specht could have used a different vein for the IV.

And Priscilla found Mindy less gratifying a child than her sister had been. Mindy did not accept things the way Tia had. She was a fighter—noisy and hard to please when she was irritated, which was often. She screamed at night, sometimes for hours. Still, Mindy had been with them only three and a half months—she was not legally adopted yet—and her previous experiences in a Korean orphanage and a Korean foster home hardly amounted to a stable home environment. Priscilla was a trained social worker, and she knew how hard it was for children to adjust to new family situations.

The doctors didn't really know what was wrong. They knew she had gastroenteritis, but they couldn't find a cause. Perhaps it was because Mindy was Korean, Priscilla had often said. It was a point she and Sara had discussed. After all, Priscilla had been told by the adoption agency to expect diarrhea at first. That was a standard warning issued to all adoptive parents of Asian children. Or maybe it was just a bad attack of flu, she had suggested. They had all come down with it in the days before Mindy's hospitalization. Priscilla and Steve, Erik and Jason. The whole family.

Priscilla moved awkwardly on the uncomfortable chair. She had learned a great deal with Tia's illness. She knew all about IVs and NGs, about electrolyte values and blood tests, about reducing substances and special formulas and dehydration.

She had always insisted on total involvement, repeatedly informing the medical staff that nothing bothered her more than to be left out of things. Once an ugly scene over Tia's care had developed at the Kaiser hospital in San Francisco. That had been in July, when the new year's group of interns joined the staff, fresh from medical school. Some of the new doctors reacted defensively to her questions at first, but she had explained that she only wanted to help, and certainly she was proficient. In fact, they ultimately allowed her to take Tia home with an open tube in place that led directly to her heart. Priscilla believed herself to be the only parent they had ever trusted to handle this procedure without supervision.

And she knew she had earned the respect of most of the nurses on the ward. Some had become real friends. In the beginning, Debby Roof, one of the pediatric nurses, couldn't stand Priscilla—thought she was high-handed and bossy—but Priscilla had won her over with her constant devotion to Tia.

Priscilla bent over Mindy's wriggling, slight figure and without a trace of false gentleness competently adjusted her bottle. When Mindy was finished, Priscilla swung her over a shoulder and began a brisk patting. So far Mindy had been on oral feedings and a naso-gastric tube had not been necessary, but the bottle alone could not provide enough fluid. Priscilla knew that Mindy needed the IV for rehydration, and that when her peripheral veins—which they preferred to use for the IV—had been depleted, Sara and the other doctors had been forced to try two other sites for cut-downs, to get down to the larger, deeper veins in Mindy's ankles. There they had found one vein completely missing and the other unusable. That is why the surgeons—and it had taken two of them—had worked so hard to place the line in Mindy's inner elbow. Shrieking in panic, she had been held down, her screams ringing through the ward. After this there was only one other vein available in the other arm. In an emergency they could try the jugular. At that point, Priscilla understood that they might run out of time.

4

An hour and a half later, Steve Phillips sat on the floor by Mindy's bedside with his sons, Erik and Jason. Priscilla thought it was important, and so did he, for the whole family to spend as much time together as possible, even if it had to be at the hospital. Mindy, after all, had not been with them very long, and she needed to feel that she belonged.

His family, it seemed to him, was just about perfect—but for the death of Tia. His two sons were blond and sturdy: Erik had just turned eight and was a smart kid—he took after his mother in that, Steve acknowledged—and Jason was five, sweet and serious. They were a happy and loving family, a solid family, despite the arguments they sometimes had.

Mindy was out of her crib and playing with the boys on the floor. She was full of piss and vinegar today, Steve thought. Things were definitely on the upswing this morning. Steve had given her the bottle of Cho-free himself, and she had practically inhaled it. The nurse had been in and noticed it, smiling. It appeared they might even be allowed to take Mindy home. Damn, he hoped so.

Neither he nor Pris did much to hide their emotions. That was why Debby Roof had suggested that they meet with Dr. Shimoda. To let it out, talk about the pressures, hang it all out there to dry—that was how he looked at it. They had met at the hospital last Sunday. Afterward he had stayed for almost twenty minutes, confiding to Debby that Mindy's illness was putting a strain on their marriage. It was worse than the pressures on Erik and Jason, though that was the topic they had mainly discussed in the meeting with Sara. Talking had been a relief, he thought, eyeing Mindy as she crawled toward him, trailing her tubing. He smiled down at her and helped her to stand against him.

Priscilla always wanted to talk everything through. Partly it was her social worker's training, partly just her personality, but when things turned rough for him, Steve retreated to the garage, puttered around morosely, and immersed himself in TV. Sometimes when he talked he felt he might explode, and he was too big a man for that.

He couldn't have held a position in juvenile hall as a group counselor very long without that basic insight. If he exploded around those kids, he could do irreparable damage. It was the same at San Quentin, where he had worked for a year as a correctional officer in '69 and '70. Day after day he had walked into that yard unarmed. When he thought about it, all he had between himself and oblivion at the hands of some space-case

with a hand-sharpened spoon was a brass whistle. So he didn't
explode. Not physically.

He thought it was all right to yell. He was big enough at 6
feet and 215 pounds, with a big bull neck disappearing into
wide shoulders, to intimidate a lot of people. And he knew that
if you have a nice South Carolina drawl and talk in pictures so
sharp and real that the guy you're facing really sees what's in
store for him should he put one foot outside the line you've set
up for him, that sucker listens. That's what he'd learned.
Maybe it *was* intimidation, but if they didn't cross Steve
Phillips, he damn well wasn't going to cross them. And that
was the bottom line, he felt. Or at least it was as good a way as
any to put himself across. Because underneath was something
a lot softer than he cared to admit.

5

At six P.M. that same Wednesday evening, Sara finished the
last of her progress notes on Mindy's chart. Her head in her
hand, she sat slumped at the nurses' station on the fifth floor of
the hospital, Five West, the pediatric ward.

Sara could see that Mindy had suffered through a bad
afternoon just by reading her chart. Suddenly at four o'clock,
after more than twelve hours of no stool, the diarrhea had
started again. Within two hours the baby had put out 274 cubic
centimeters of liquid stool in a total of six different stooling
episodes, and she was fussy and irritable. Her output far
exceeded her intake and this was a potentially dangerous
situation, especially in view of her poor veins. It might become
impossible to rehydrate her fast enough.

For the second time, Sara restlessly checked the four pages
of notes she had written in the chart. First she had summarized the patient's course since her admission on February
sixteenth, listing the intake and output for each day. Then she
had made another note.

This patient is not a typical case of gastroenteritis and is
falling into the category of chronic diarrhea. Her course

seems to follow one compatible with secretory diarrhea, i.e., not necessarily affected by p.o. intake. I have checked her several times for evidence of osmotic diarrhea secondary to carbohydrate malabsorption by checking stool Ph and reducing substances. This patient has had greater than 6–7 Ph and negative reducing substances and I will continue checking the stool Ph—and reducing substances—daily. She is not receiving enough calories yet to allow for weight gain. Patient's weight = 6.5 kg × 75–100 cal/kg = 500–650 cal per day. Patient just had another 270 gm stool output after a 12-hour period of *no* dietary change today and patient has been on Cho-free + 5% polycose × 36 hrs.

It was beginning to sink in. No matter what they put into this child, the state of her gastrointestinal tract did not, as it should, reflect her diet. This was not a case of gastroenteritis. Whether it was a case of secretory diarrhea, or something different—and more ominous—was now the question, Sara realized.

She still planned more tests for Mindy, although the workup was essentially complete. The normal blood tests indicated no immunodeficiencies that might cause diarrhea, but Sara needed to check with an endocrinologist the possibility that Mindy might be suffering from an unusual case of Bartter's Syndrome. There were some other possibilities, too—rare, but not impossible—to rule out. They were all things she had once investigated with Tia. She noted down her plan to increase Mindy's diet to allow for weight gain, her decision to try some rice cereal, and her plan to keep the IV running for as long as the cut-down appeared clean. She had decided to treat Mindy for the parasite giardia, despite the negative stool sample, because sometimes that parasite could be elusive. She had hesitated over it but finally concluded that it wouldn't hurt to treat her.

Sara lifted herself to her feet and stretched, one hand bracing her back, her dark eyes closed against the fluorescent glare. She had one more note to add, and she made it, finally. Once written on the copybook-style lined paper they issued for the progress notes, it did not look so dramatic.

Consider that some type of toxin may be responsible. Urine sent for heavy metal analysis.

The heavy metal test for mercury, lead, and arsenic had been run once before, on February sixteenth, and it had been negative. Janet Specht had ordered that test. Perhaps the result would be different this time.

There, it was done. And tomorrow was her day off. By Monday she would have some more answers, one way or another. And on Monday she would talk to the San Francisco coroner. It could all wait until then.

6

By the early hours of Friday, February twenty-fourth, Mindy had deteriorated sharply. She lay pale and flaccid in Priscilla's lap, her eyes black and dull. Since ten-thirty Thursday night, Mindy's stooling had been explosive, and she had been vomiting.

Priscilla had arrived the previous morning, Sara's day off, to learn of the new order for rice cereal. Mindy was only to have three teaspoons, to be increased gradually if she tolerated it well, but this represented a major advance, and Priscilla had danced around the ward, beaming. It was the very first time in her hospitalization that Mindy had been allowed solid food.

"This is my red-letter day!" Priscilla exulted to the nurse. "Debby and Maria are taking me out to lunch for my birthday, and now Mindy's on solid food. I can't believe it!"

At noon, Priscilla fed Mindy her noon meal. She was hungry and had a good appetite. But when Priscilla returned to room 503 following the birthday lunch in nearby San Anselmo with the two nurses, Debby and Maria Sterling, she was horrified. Dr. Arnhold, the pediatrician on the ward that day, had changed Mindy's entire intake protocol. Instead of the rice cereal, Mindy now had a naso-gastric tube for feeding. And Priscilla knew that meant she had been taken to the Treatment Room across the hall and held down while the tube had been threaded through her nose into her stomach. They had not waited for Priscilla. In addition, Priscilla was told, they had started up two new medications which—along with her Cho-free formula—would be given through the NG tube. These were to be quinacrine—a treatment for giardia—and cholesty-ramine, which might help to control Mindy's diarrhea. As both these treatments had been tried with Tia, they were not unfamiliar to Priscilla.

But they had not waited for her, and they had not told her in advance about the changes. To Priscilla this was monstrous, unforgivable, and she was in tears. Dr. Arnhold explained that Mindy's resumed stooling had precipitated the decision to insert the NG tube. Sara and Dr. Applebaum agreed with the change in treatment.

Priscilla knew that if Mike Applebaum was involved, the problem had escalated. Dr. Applebaum was the expert in pediatric gastroenterology from Kaiser-San Francisco. He had been the consultant in Tia's care, treating her himself many times during her hospitalizations in San Francisco. And if he was being consulted, it meant that far from improving, Mindy's condition was worsening, that once again they needed a specialist to help them.

Unhesitatingly, Priscilla called Sara at home.

"Sara, why didn't you tell me before they put the NG down? You know how I feel about their doing things and not letting me know. And especially when she's never had an NG, when she'd be so scared . . ." She was still crying, but through her tears her voice was high and strong.

"Because I thought it would upset you," Sara said. "I thought it would remind you of Tia."

"It did remind me of Tia. My God, what's going on?"

Sara hesitated. "I'll come in and talk to you about it, Priscilla. Just wait there for me." And so, on her afternoon off, Sara returned to the hospital.

"Mindy's not keeping enough down to grow on," Sara explained quietly. "She weighs the same today as she did when she came from Korea four months ago. She's not thriving. If we can't get her straightened out pretty quickly, she's going to need—well . . . she's going to need hyperalimentation . . . just like Tia."

"Oh, Sara, no! Don't tell me that!"

"Well, we may not need to. But her veins are so small, and—it's just that I want you to be prepared—"

"Will she have to go to San Francisco? I don't believe this. Oh, Sara, please—"

"I don't know. We might be able to handle it here."

"What about the central venous catheter? Will she need that? I know her veins are so bad. Oh, Sara!"

"Please, Priscilla. I don't know. I just don't know yet. There's no use getting so upset now. The CMV might be making her more susceptible. It's possible that what Mindy has is just a viral thing, but because she's behind in her development . . ." she stopped and hesitated. "Well, it could all be tied in with the CMV; it could all be relevant."

"I still think it's the flu. It's got to be that," Priscilla said. Sara did not answer.

Mindy continued stooling, fussing, and crying throughout the afternoon. The Cho-free formula was being dripped, drop by measured drop, into her NG tube. The IV continued in the cut-down, miraculously still holding in her right arm. Priscilla stayed with her, held her. Occasionally she took a break, wandering out to the little kitchen down the hall to grab a Diet Pepsi from the stock she was able to keep in the refrigerator there or stopping at the nurses' station for a chat. Then she returned and kept watch over her daughter.

At seven that evening, the nurse came in to give Mindy her medication. Priscilla watched the woman carefully because already that afternoon she had had to stop the same nurse from administering medication before it was due. Both the NG tube and the IV line were hooked up to separate pumps that precisely regulated the flow of formula and IV solution. Mindy was a mass of lines and tubing. The quinacrine that Sara had ordered to treat giardia was to be injected directly into the NG tube through one of the many joints in the tubing. But the tubing for both the IV and the NG were identical. And the nurse injected the medication in the wrong one.

For a moment Priscilla stood frozen as she watched the yellowish quinacrine entering the vein at the site of Mindy's cut-down. Then she screamed.

"It's the wrong one! It's the wrong one!" And as the nurse hurriedly cut off the flow of medication, Priscilla ran hysterically into the hall of the ward after Dr. Arnhold, shrieking his name.

Priscilla watched as an Unusual Incident form was filled out. Approximately two cubic centimeters of quinacrine had entered Mindy's vein instead of her gastrointestinal tract. This kind of thing happened in hospitals. Priscilla had seen it several times before, and that was one reason why she so carefully checked all of the procedures. She knew medical personnel were fallible. But that didn't help her deal with this mistake despite Dr. Arnhold's assurance that it was unlikely to cause a problem.

And there was a problem. Mindy had become confused and hysterical. She screamed and struggled and twisted until Priscilla thought her arms would burst with the effort of holding her. Priscilla talked to her and bounced her to no effect. Mindy suddenly started tearing at the dressing over the cut-down in her elbow in an attempt to rip the needle out of her vein. And then she began to pull at the NG tube, fighting it, trying to tear it out.

Finally Priscilla called out for help. Dr. Arnhold was summoned. Priscilla knew him well. He had been the pediatrician for Erik and Jason before he had left the country on a long sabbatical and she had changed to Sara.

"Priscilla, if she doesn't stop doing that, we're going to have to tie her down. You know that cut-down is too precious to lose, and her stomach is in no shape to deal with bottle feedings, so we need the NG drip, too. We can't have her pulling that out."

Priscilla reacted instantly. "My God, Dr. Arnhold! First you half kill her with the quinacrine in the IV, and now, when she gets upset about it, you want to tie her down?" The tears were tracking unnoticed down her face.

"Well—" began Arnhold.

"I'll stay with her!" Priscilla interrupted, her voice echoing throughout the ward. "Let me stay with her! I'll see that she doesn't pull out the lines!"

"Well, if you think you can, all right," Arnhold relented. So she had stayed.

Now it was midnight and Mindy was throwing up and stooling and deteriorating noticeably. Finally the nurse phoned the doctor on call. Mindy was ordered NPO. *Nil per os*. The medical shorthand for nothing by mouth. Even all the medications, for the time being, would be held. The nurse clamped off the NG tube, leaving it in place. NPO was a standard medical procedure for a patient suffering from diarrhea. Tia had once gone for weeks NPO. In Mindy's case, sometimes it seemed to work to make her NPO, sometimes it didn't.

This time it was successful. The rest of the night passed

without incident. At 6:45 A.M. that Friday morning, just as the
day nurses came on shift, Priscilla watched the nurse draw
Mindy's blood to check her electrolytes. This, too, had become
regular procedure. Still, Mindy screamed as the needle
entered the vein. The night nurse went off duty, and Priscilla
fell into Debby Roof's arms as she came on the ward to start
her shift. Priscilla had not talked to Debby since the birthday
lunch the day before. She told Debby all about the wrong
medication and the change in Mindy's treatment. How she had
fought to keep Arnhold from tying Mindy down. About
Mindy's deterioration.

"This is just like it was with Tia," she sobbed. "It's happening
again, and I can't control it, or stop it. And Sara's worried now.
I can tell!"

"But Mindy's better, Priscilla," Debby protested. "See, she
hasn't had any stool since she was made NPO. It'll be all right."

At eight-thirty, Mindy's NG tube was unclamped and the
formula drip resumed. She was given another dose of cholesty-
ramine through the tube. It might help prevent the diarrhea.

Priscilla, as she customarily did after spending a night at the
hospital in her clothes, went home for breakfast and to change.

"I'll be back later," she promised Debby.

7

At five-thirty that Friday afternoon, Dr. Sara Shimoda
planned to meet with Drs. Arnhold, Callas, and Estol Carte.
She was on the point of leaving for the weekend with her
husband and daughter to visit her parents near Fresno.
Arnhold would be on call that night, with Carte and Callas to
share hospital duties over the weekend. Sara needed to talk to
them.

Mindy's deterioration remained uppermost in her mind.
She was also concerned about the results of the test for sodium
that had been run on Mindy's stool sample collected on
Wednesday, the same day Sara had presented Mindy's case at
the staff meeting.

Like most doctors, Sara almost never ordered stool sodium

tests. Serum sodium tests were valuable, and often essential, diagnostic tools. But stool sodiums were rarely significant because a test of the amount of sodium in a patient's stool simply reveals what the person has eaten. If a patient has consumed a high-sodium meal of ham and potato chips, the excess sodium in his gastrointestinal tract will be thrown off in the urine and the stool. So the level of sodium in a person's excretions will vary quite a bit depending on his day's menu. In a normal, healthy child, a stool sodium might range between 20 and 90 milliequivalents per liter, with 20 or 30 as a good average. When a child is suffering from diarrhea, the level of sodium concentrated in the stool can go higher. Every doctor knew this, and knew a stool test would reveal this. So there was usually no point in testing stool sodium. Most doctors, no matter how long they had practiced, never had occasion to order the test.

But because Mindy's illness was beginning to look suspicious, because it might somehow be related to her intake, Sara had ordered a stool sodium test. And the results were indeed significant.

Sara had already calculated Mindy's known sodium intake. In the period preceding the time the stool sample had been collected on Wednesday, Mindy had received 14 milliequivalents of sodium: 10 by IV and 4 by Cho-free formula. There should have been an equal amount coming out.

But the lab test result was astonishing. On the sample collected Wednesday afternoon, Mindy's stool sodium level had reached an incredible 251 milliequivalents. This was totally unexplainable.

Nothing in medical school had prepared Sara for this. As late as this afternoon, before she had received these results, she'd still been trying to find a medical cause for Mindy's condition. She had telephoned Dr. Applebaum at Kaiser-San Francisco and asked him again about secretory diarrhea. He had not ruled it out. And as long as a diagnosis was still possible, Sara could put off thinking about the other cause, the nonmedical one, the one she preferred not to face.

She remembered the afternoon meeting with Priscilla and Debby Roof on the ward. Debby's concern was apparent. Mindy was stooling heavily, and was lethargic, just like Tia.

"It's not like with Tia, is it, Dr. Shimoda?" the nurse had asked. "After all, Tia had all those high serum sodiums."

Priscilla had nodded and smiled. "That's right," she agreed.

And Sara had said nothing, had not contradicted her. Because by this time, something was entering her consciousness, and it was certainly nothing she could say to soothe Priscilla. She was starting to know it in a place in her heart: whatever was happening to Mindy had happened to Tia, too.

She took out a copy of the current issue of the *JAMA* that Dr. Arnhold had given her after Wednesday's staff meeting. She had read and reread the editorial he had pointed out.

It commented on a British article about Munchausen Syndrome by Proxy, a variation on Munchausen Syndrome itself. Sara knew about Munchausen Syndrome. They all did. There were always jokes floating around every hospital about famous cases they had had of this person or that who came in with massively scarred bodies from procedures they had fooled doctors into performing on them.

People with Munchausen Syndrome craved the type of warm care and attention they felt they could receive only in a hospital setting. They would do anything, make up any symptom, to remain hospitalized. They would submit to—and welcome—any hospital procedure. They might rub feces into open wounds to cause infection, or pour blood into urine specimens to throw off a diagnosis. When their deceptions were discovered, they often left in a huff to try another hospital. Some hospitals even published lists of these people to look out for. They were sad psychological messes in Sara's opinion.

But Munchausen Syndrome by Proxy was a little different. Apparently patients suffering from this caused their own children to undergo unnecessary hospital procedures by giving false histories and tampering with test results. One of the two children mentioned in the *JAMA* article had died after having been repeatedly dosed with salt. The two mothers involved had both appeared to be loving and concerned, and only after their roles in the children's illnesses had been discovered did their psychopathic traits become obvious. The mother of the baby who died had attempted suicide afterward. The other mother's mental stability was also questioned when it turned out that she had tampered with her own specimens on an earlier occasion.

It was almost incredible that any mother would deliberately and repeatedly poison her child. Yet this fit with a case cited in a *Clinical Pediatrics* article that Evelyn had read, and if the mother were really mentally ill . . . Sara shook her head. It was too much to think about right now.

Sara replaced the journal on her desk and rose. She was suddenly struck by a tiredness so overwhelming that it frightened her. She welcomed the weekend, away, out of reach of all this.

8

It was the kind of morning characteristic of the Bay Area in February, overcast and foggy. A thick dew had settled on the grass outside Evelyn's house, and a mist had dampened the windshield of her car. It was impossible to predict how the day would turn out. The fog might clear by mid-morning, permitting thin, filtered sunlight to touch the dull pink of the hospital walls, or the fog might turn to heavy cloud and deep, mushy rain. Evelyn hugged her coat to her as she made her way up from the doctors' parking lot to the side entrance of the hospital where the Emergency Room was located.

She was already tired. She had hardly slept. Beside her last night, her husband had lain dreamless. Mindy was not his problem—but hers.

She had realized something would have to be done yesterday afternoon, after she had met with Sara and Rainer Arnhold and Estol Carte and heard about the results of Mindy's stool sodium tests.

They had decided that Mindy's intake and output would have to be carefully monitored. Sara planned to repeat the tests when she came back, and they had agreed this was necessary. They had discussed poisoning. Evelyn continued to believe that a sodium cathartic was responsible for Mindy's condition. Probably Epsom salts. They still had to research a method of testing for sulfates. Would a stool sample reveal magnesium? she wondered. Maybe Boyd Stephens would know. Sara planned to call him on Monday.

After the meeting, Evelyn had hurried back to her office and looked up the stool sodium values for cholera, the only illness she could think of that might produce anything close to the 251 milliequivalents per liter of sodium at which Mindy's stool sample had been measured. Not that Mindy could possibly *have* cholera, she realized. There was no possibility of that. It was simply a basis for comparison of sodium levels. There were no higher sodium levels in an illness than those that cholera could produce.

She could not believe the values she found. She rushed out of her office to find someone, anyone, she could tell. Jim Levine, another pediatrician, was still in his office at the other end of the hall. She jumped at him with her news.

"Jim. Jim!"

"What? My God, Evelyn! What's wrong?"

"It's Mindy Phillips. She's had a stool sodium of two hundred fifty-one; and you know what?" Her words tumbled over each other.

"What?"

"That's *twice* the level of the worst case of cholera I could find recorded."

"Good God!"

"Exactly, Jim. Exactly," Evelyn said.

Later she realized something else. Mindy's stool sodium was higher than the concentration of sodium in her blood. And Evelyn knew of no way that this could happen. Not naturally.

If they couldn't control the diarrhea and if they lost the use of her veins for the IV, Mindy would die. It was as clear-cut as that.

Sara was away. Dr. Stein, who had been the Chief of Pediatrics until just a few weeks ago and was now the Assistant Physician-in-Chief, was away. The Physician-in-Chief himself was away. Evelyn knew what she had to do, and if Carte, who was in charge of the ward today and thus officially Mindy's doctor, would not agree with her plan, she had decided to override him. She had the ultimate responsibility for the care of the patients on the ward. She didn't want to exercise her authority, but if she had to, she would.

Evelyn had maintained to her colleagues, laughing because she was a little embarrassed at her new position, that her appointment to Chief of Pediatrics meant that she was now merely some strange combination of secretary, agenda maker, and mother hen. But in fact, she realized there were added responsibilities of being what was essentially the first among equals.

And now she had certainly been plunged straight into the crucible. She had a sudden insight that what she did these next few days would either temper her or completely burn her out.

When Evelyn arrived at the ward, it was quiet, the doors to the rooms on Five West shut tight. Even room 503 was closed and darkened. Mrs. Phillips might be in there, she might not, Evelyn thought as she crossed to the nurses' station. It didn't matter. Evelyn nodded at the young, dark-haired nurse on duty, Christine King. She was not a regular pediatrics nurse, but a floater, assigned where she was needed, but Evelyn had seen her around.

Evelyn checked Mindy's most recent lab sheets and then pulled her chart. The nurse's progress notes confirmed what she knew in her heart she'd find.

After a few moments, Evelyn replaced the chart. She made some quick calculations on the back of a progress note. Mindy, she thought bluntly, was going down the tubes. In the past 24 hours, she'd lost 1,000 cubic centimeters of watery stool. This amounted to almost 15 percent of her body weight. Without the IV she would be dead. Evelyn was sure that the 7:00 A.M. sodium samples to be run on Mindy's blood, urine, and stool would confirm the deterioration. But she would not wait for the results. All she had to do was look at the lab results on the 1 o'clock samples. The concentration of sodium in Mindy's urine had been measured at 252 milliequivalents. And the stool was 159 milliequivalents. There was no doubt that both were much too high.

Evelyn pressed a long-fingered hand against her graying hair and looked up. Down the hall she saw the meager figure of Dr. Estol Carte approaching her. Herculean Pirate, as she liked to call him to herself.

Evelyn was an Agatha Christie fan, and it was an obvious comparison once you saw it, she thought. Estol, with his balding, egg-shaped head and his *moustaches*, all set on a precise five-foot-three frame, was detective Hercule Poirot to the life.

As she drew him aside, she could not know how apt a description it was.

"Estol," she said with a calm she didn't feel, "I've got to talk with you."

9

Priscilla had not intended to spend the night. She and Steve had decided earlier to take the boys to a promised dinner at McDonald's, despite the fact that Mindy needed to be tied down while Priscilla was gone to prevent her from pulling out the NG. Priscilla did not like to alter plans, especially not when her children were expecting some special activity. In any case, she intended to be gone only a short time, and she thought that Mindy seemed stable when they all left for dinner. But later that evening, Mindy's condition began to deteriorate. Priscilla phoned Steve to tell him she wouldn't be coming home. She still hoped that Mindy would improve by morning. She wanted Steve to bring the boys up in the afternoon to visit their sister, as they had arranged, and she never liked them to see Mindy when she was really sick. It frightened them. She had started this policy during Tia's illness. And sometimes with Tia, days had gone by before she was well enough for the boys to visit.

Shortly before nine, Dr. Carte entered Mindy's room. He was not Priscilla's favorite doctor. She thought he was weird, and so did most of the nurses, as far as she could tell.

Dr. Carte glanced at Mindy in her walker and at her chart that he held in his hand.

"She seems to be doing okay," he remarked.

"Yes, she's better," said Priscilla. "But it was a pretty rocky night."

With a nod, Carte left the room. Through the window in the door, Priscilla could see him at the nurses' station working with Mindy's chart. At that moment, Nurse King walked in. She had to refill Mindy's metriset with formula every two hours. Priscilla had never met her, and she and the nurse introduced themselves and talked for a moment, first about Mindy's condition, then about Tia.

"You know I lost another child a year ago," Priscilla confided.

"Yes, I heard," Christine King answered. "It must have been

just terrible. I have a child of my own; he's just a baby, too. I just can't conceive of losing Michael. How did you cope?"

"I don't know. Sometimes I really don't know how I lived through the last year. My friends helped—and my minister. And I had my boys. And then Mindy—I was so excited to hear about her, I just about burst."

"When did you get her?"

"In November. It was just nine months after Tia died—she was born the same week Tia died. Like a new life to replace the one we had lost. We had a new baby—it felt like it could have been our own," Priscilla said.

"What a strange coincidence."

"Oh, there have been a lot of those. Debby Roof and I talked about it, too. You know Mindy was admitted here a year to the day after Tia died—it was horrible." Tears came to her eyes and she brushed at them.

"I'm so sorry. I'm sure she'll be better soon."

"Yes," agreed Priscilla, turning to pick up Mindy.

Shortly after eleven, Christine King returned to Mindy's room looking puzzled. Priscilla glanced up as the door opened. Mindy was back in her bed.

"Do you know the recipe for Mindy's formula?" the nurse asked.

"Sure. Why? There's plenty of formula already mixed."

"Yeah, well it's gone now. We need some more and I can't find the recipe written down anywhere. I called the nursing supervisor and she didn't know either. It's supposed to be written in the cardex, but it isn't there."

Priscilla rattled off the recipe for the Cho-free formula plus the polycose that Mindy was receiving. When Sara had recently changed the percentage of polycose to be added, Priscilla and Debby had figured out the new recipe together—it was the kind of thing Priscilla liked to help with on the ward.

In a few minutes, Christine was back with the newly mixed formula and some fresh NG tubing.

"Why new tubing?" Priscilla wanted to know.

"Oh, Dr. Carte told me to," Christine answered. "Apparently he's testing the formula for sodium levels and to be on the safe side, he told me to change the tubing, too."

Priscilla shrugged. It did not seem important, she would later claim. But of course later, when Priscilla was to go over the events of that Saturday, February twenty-fifth, again and again, trying to reconstruct everything that had happened, every word, every nuance of expression and action, then it would seem terribly important, and its significance clear.

When Dr. Carte next entered the room, at about 11:30 that same morning, he wore a strange, set expression on his small face. Priscilla noticed it immediately.

"I need to talk to you, Mrs. Phillips. Please come out in the hall." He gestured her through the door ahead of him, and then held out a hand to indicate that he wanted her to walk down toward the end of the ward, away from the nurses' station so that no one could hear them.

Puzzled, for they were not given to privacy around the hospital, Priscilla followed.

Without preamble, Carte said tightly, "I'm moving Mindy to the Intensive Care Unit."

"What?" Priscilla went dead white. "Why?"

"Because we've just gotten back a blood test result on her and she's got a sodium level of a hundred sixty. That's in the danger area."

Priscilla's eyes filled and her voice, when it came, was high and loud. "But that's not so high! Tia had sodium levels much higher than that and you never put her in ICU!"

"Yes, well, we feel Mindy will be better off there. You know her sodium level shouldn't be above one-forty-five. She'll be better off there," he repeated.

The tears were spilling now, and Priscilla made no effort either to hide or control them. "But Sara promised! She promised there would be no changes this weekend. There have been so many already. And my husband's supposed to bring my sons to visit Mindy this afternoon—we've been planning this for days now. And Mindy's better; you saw her this morning! How can you say she needs to be in ICU?"

"I'm sorry. But it's a medical decision."

"But why? I don't understand why!"

"I've told you. High serum sodiums can be dangerous. They can lead to convulsions."

"I don't believe this! I don't understand it!" She was sobbing. "I'm going to call my husband." And she walked off—half running—down the hall to Mindy's room and the telephone. In a few minutes she was back.

"My husband's coming. But I still don't understand. Couldn't the test be wrong? Couldn't you repeat the test? I'm sure the test is wrong. Mindy's better. It's clear she's better."

"No, I think the test is accurate," said Carte.

"Well, maybe I can't accept the fact that I have a really sick child, but she doesn't look that bad. And she's never had high serum sodium before!"

"I don't believe that's true, Mrs. Phillips."

"It is true! You can check back! It is true!"

Carte leafed back through Mindy's chart. "Yes, well, you're right. Although her stool sodiums have been high, her blood sodiums have been all right until now. But now they're not."

"But, please! ICU is an adult unit. They don't know about children there. I know I won't be able to stay with her as much. She needs me to be with her. She's not even used to this country yet! She hasn't even been here five months. And so much has gone wrong with the medicines in the wrong tube and everything. And Sara said there would be no more changes this weekend. She promised me!"

Carte shook his head. "It's better for her," he said again.

"I want to talk to Dr. Callas."

"Why don't we wait till your husband gets here?" said Carte. "We can arrange a meeting then."

"All right." She thrust a hand distractedly at the tears running steadily off her chin, then turned and ran back in the direction of room 503 and the haven of her daughter.

She did not see Carte go to the little desk where the doctors wrote out their orders. His hand slightly shaky, he filled out the order for Mindy Phillips.

Sodium output appears far greater than intake. Maintain IV and transfer to ICU.

He checked his watch and added the time. 11:36 A.M. Then he headed for the elevator.

In Mindy's room, Priscilla, huddled in the steel and vinyl chair, sobbed until even the nurse outside heard her and came in.

"Can I do anything for you, Mrs. Phillips?" Christine asked from the door.

"Don't they see? It's so unfair. Mindy's so difficult to please. She'll be so scared! All the things they'll do! She needs me so much. What will it do to her? What will it do to me!" Priscilla cried.

"I'm sure it will be better for your little girl or they wouldn't do it."

Priscilla shook her head.

"Oh, I wish one of your friends was here," Christine added helplessly. She hoped Mr. Phillips was on his way.

10

Steve wandered about their three-bedroom stucco and frame house with an eye toward straightening it. Pris would be madder than hell if she saw it like this, he thought. She was an unbelievable stickler about neatness and they'd had some whoppers over that issue in their day. She could never accept the fact that when he came home from work, he just wanted to relax in front of the TV with his feet up; Pris always wanted him to help her clean up.

He eyed the living room furniture, much of it recently purchased. The short sculptured yellow and green carpet badly needed vacuuming, he decided. It made sense to do that last. He picked his way through some of the Fisher-Price toy people Jason had abandoned on the floor and pushed a solid forefinger into the soil containing the huge philodendron that they kept by the glass doors leading out to the small strip of backyard. They had planted it in a huge concrete urn they had carted into the living room from outside. Now the plant had crawled and plaited itself so high they had draped it over the ceiling beam. It was a great conversation piece.

He filled the green plastic watering can and circled the living room moistening the plants; most were baked dry. Then Steve headed for the bedroom, stopping for a moment to straighten one of Priscilla's diplomas on the wall in the little anteroom of their bedroom. She had practically a whole wall of framed honor society documents from Winthrop College, and her master's of Social Work from Berkeley. He was proud of that lady—she had one fine head on her shoulders, and a memory like a damn computer. His army discharge hung there, too, and his diploma from Sonoma State College. Hell, he was pretty damn proud of that one, too, he thought. He had sent his high school counselor a copy of it, and a copy of every time he made the Dean's list. That sucker had said he wasn't college material, and Steve had never forgotten or forgiven that.

He made the dark oak, Spanish-style double bed. He wandered back through the little hall, past Mindy's bedroom with its specially chosen wallpaper—big cats, elephants, and donkeys made out of daisies.

They had had a hell of a time hanging that paper over the old brown-stained walls, Steve remembered. After picking out all this special decor for Tia, they had never changed it for Mindy. Some of it, like the green, yellow, white, and rust tweed sculptured shag carpet, was practically brand-new. They had added it while Tia was still in the hospital.

He moved back into the living room, passing the boys' room. They were curled up in the mahogany-paneled family room watching TV, but he didn't stop to straighten in there. It was hopeless keeping up with those two. He settled for a minute on the sofa, his big body comfortably splayed, his head curved back against the wall. He studied the raisin tray painting they had found at Northgate Mall.

He remembered the day they had bought it, finally ending up with two of the paintings; they had liked them so much. They had spent more than they meant to, but something about those paintings was irresistible. The artist had explained how she had painted the nature scenes—one of yellow and orange flowers against a fence, another of a yellow flower vase—directly onto slats of wood that had once been racks for drying raisins. The result was unusual. Instead of a flat surface, there were small gaps between the slats and the painted image was broken up and distorted by those spaces. It was like a natural scene that somehow wasn't natural.

To him that was a good symbol for all of Marin County. He had never really wanted to live there; it was a place that counted its Porsches and BMWs. But they had moved there when Priscilla had landed her job with the county's Social Services department in 1969, working their way up through a series of apartments and a town house until they had been able to afford this house three years ago.

He supposed Marin County was reasonably decent if you were going to settle in California. It was undeniably scenic. Terra Linda stretched and ambled through mounds of hills and planned open space. In fact they had a hill right behind their house. And of course Priscilla liked being so close to San

Francisco, though that was not an attraction for Steve. He was your basic small-town boy. All the houses around them were identical, built by a developer named Eichler in the fifties. Everybody joked about the houses in Terra Linda all facing back in on themselves. There were no windows in the front of the house, and concrete walls and high planting blocked off any side view. It wasn't his style to live that way, nor was it Pris's for that matter. She was a joiner, always organizing some group activity—a church picnic, a nursery school dinner, a women's issues group. And they welcomed other people. They always liked friends in their home, and social activities arranged with other families. It wasn't their way to live all shut in on themselves. But if you wanted to live in Terra Linda— and it was a great place to bring up kids—you pretty much had to settle for an Eichler house.

Frankly, he wasn't all that fond of the people out here, either. They had some great friends, but in general, he'd take South Carolina any day, where a person was just who he said he was. Over here they all made themselves out to be nonprejudiced, but half the time they were talking out of two sides of their mouth. Hell, when they had first adopted Tia, some sucker at work had asked him if they were planning to get an eye job on her, to make her eyes round. It was unbelievable.

Steve picked himself up and went back into the family room. The Saturday morning cartoons scampered across the screen and he stayed to watch them. Priscilla hated TV and thought he watched too much of it. She was always after him to turn it off. But it was keeping the boys quiet, and since Mindy's hospitalization, he had pretty much had to take over with the boys, and with the house, too.

He had promised the boys a trip to the hospital to see Mindy—Priscilla had planned it days ago—and it was still enough of an adventure for them that they were trying to behave. He had also promised to take them fishing this afternoon with Skip Schaefer, one of his best friends. The Schaefers lived right around the corner; they had met when Nancy and Skip joined the baby-sitting co-op Priscilla had helped found in 1975. Nancy was a nurse in the intensive care nursery at Children's Hospital in San Francisco, and she'd taken care of Tia on Thursday mornings. They had always trusted her completely with Tia, even when Tia was sick.

Now he hated to think about baby-sitting. Since Mindy's CMV had been discovered and their baby-sitting co-op had voted to throw Mindy out, they'd had to start a new co-op. What a goddamned mess that had been! Pris had tried to reassure the other families that CMV was everywhere in the community. Ninety percent of the adult population had already been exposed to it, Sara had told them. But the other mothers were worried. There were pregnant women in the co-op and others who planned to become pregnant, and if a pregnant mother came down with CMV, it could attack the fetus. Apparently that's what had happened to Mindy. But Sara believed the risk of contagion was negligible. Priscilla had arranged for her to come speak to the co-op about it, but at the last minute she'd canceled—scared to speak in front of all those people was how Pris had seen it—and sent Dr. Arnhold instead. But even though Arnhold had told them they just needed to practice basic hygiene and wash their hands after changing Mindy's diaper, the co-op had still voted to expel Mindy.

Priscilla had fought like a hellcat. Steve grinned at the memory. She didn't want Mindy denied access to the community. But then suddenly it seemed like she had to battle everyone. The organization that Sara had referred them to, Aid to Infant Development, wouldn't take Mindy either because she was still contagious. Pris was in the middle of fighting them, too, or had been before Mindy's hospitalization, and she'd win. Steve smiled again. When Pris got off on one of those things, if you knew what was good for you, you'd best stay out of her way.

It was becoming increasingly apparent that Mindy's cytomegalovirus was going to cause considerable problems. After Sara told them about the CMV, he and Priscilla had faced a difficult decision. Friends started asking them if they were going to keep Mindy in light of the sacrifices raising her would force upon them all. It would be particularly hard for the boys, who had already lived through considerable hell due to Tia's illness and death. At that point Mindy had only been with them two months. Sara could give them no prediction regarding the future effects of Mindy's CMV, but she tended to downplay potential problems. Still they knew that Mindy might be retarded; certainly they could expect some learning problems.

In the end they had handled it the way the Phillips family always handled problems. They yelled and argued, fought and disagreed and looked at it from all sides until finally they arrived at a decision they could all live with. When she had told them about the CMV, Sara had reminded Priscilla that Mindy needed her more than ever, and that's what they all decided. They'd fight to enroll her in all the programs to which she was entitled, whatever sacrifice that involved.

Steve wanted to talk to Skip about his problems at work. He had a boy who was breaking every rule in the book. He had a difficult schedule, with ten-hour days that were killing him, and some counselor had been accused of raping one of the girls. It went before the grand jury and the Juvenile Justice Commission was down all over them. The pressure was incredible.

But there was one little thing that was beginning to worry him about Mindy, he realized. He knew, because of Tia, that when you start adding and subtracting IV fluids and electrolytes, you can cause more problems than you solve. And that's what Kaiser was doing now.

And that is why, when the phone rang and Priscilla was yelling and crying about them putting Mindy in ICU, his first thought was: What have they done now? Had they screwed up? Because, like Priscilla, he knew it wasn't normal procedure. No way.

11

Evelyn Callas had spent a very busy morning in the Emergency Room. It was an accepted statistic in pediatrics: children were always sickest in February. It had been particularly difficult to concentrate. For a moment she acknowledged a tiny feeling of relief that she had been stationed at the E.R. today and Estol on the ward. Otherwise she would have been the appropriate person to tell Mrs. Phillips. She frowned guiltily and turned back to her patient. Later Evelyn checked the clock. It would soon be noon. When she looked up again, Dr. Carte stood in the doorway.

"Estol, what happened?" He looked pasty and tired. "Here, sit down." He did, perching like an exhausted sparrow on the edge of the examination table.

"I told her and she's very upset. She's furious. She said Sara told her there would be no changes this weekend. She said something about how her kids were supposed to visit this afternoon. She kept asking me why. So I told her about the serum sodium that just came back from the lab. It's a hundred sixty, Evelyn."

"Really? Well, I'm not surprised. Have you got her moved out yet?"

"No, but the order's been written. They're working on it. Turns out there's a pregnant nurse working ICU today, and they'll have to transfer her out because of Mindy's CMV."

Outside the door of the Examining Room, Evelyn saw a nurse hovering with a buff-colored patient's folder in her hand.

"Estol, I've got to get back. It's a madhouse here this morning."

"Yeah, me, too. Oh, Mrs. Phillips wants to meet with us and her husband. Shall I set something up for this afternoon?"

"Yes. Let's do it at one-thirty. We can meet for lunch at one o'clock and discuss what we want to say. Tell her the Quiet Room across from ICU, and I'll meet you at the cafeteria at one." She pushed herself up and walked him to the door.

"Evelyn?"

"Hm?"

"On a hunch I took a sample of Mindy's formula down to the lab and had them run a sodium on it. I just got the results back. It's loaded. I'll tell you about it later."

"Yes, okay," she answered. Her mind did not focus on this information. She was already thinking about her next patient, and worrying about what to say to the Phillipses at one-thirty.

The proof of this particular pudding, and this was how she looked at it, lay with the patient. If Mindy Phillips recovered in ICU, that would be proof.

Later, when so many people asked Evelyn why it never had entered her mind to have the formula tested, she could only shrug. It just had never occurred to her, to any of them, until it occurred to Estol Carte. She had thought only how to make the patient's body reveal the information, how a test on the stool would disclose the presence of a foreign substance. She was not a detective. She was a doctor.

12

Priscilla Phillips, her eyes still red from weeping, her broad, fleshy face sunken and bleached, watched as her husband and Christine King eased Mindy's portable hospital crib into the elevator.

Dr. Carte had told her to meet them at one-thirty in the Quiet Room, and it was her impression that they were going to discuss the move to ICU. But they were moving Mindy now. They weren't waiting to discuss it. They didn't care how she felt, or Steve, she realized. They didn't care how Mindy might react.

Mindy was thrashing and screaming, her little face bright red. As they entered the elevator, the IV suddenly broke apart, and at once the watery liquid began puddling on the floor. Christine bent over the IV site on Mindy's arm.

"It's infiltrating again," she said.

"Oh, I can't stand it—not again!" cried Priscilla. The needle had come out only a short time before, while Mindy was still in her room, and Priscilla had collapsed in tears while they tried to reinsert it in the cut-down. If they lost this site, only the vein in the other arm remained. And now the needle was out again.

Finally they arrived at the second floor. Christine still held the dripping IV while Steve maneuvered the crib out of the elevator and down the hall to the door of the Intensive Care Unit. Christine rang the bell, and one of the ICU nurses came to admit them. There were eight separate rooms in the unit that ringed the central nurses' station.

Steve and Priscilla helped push Mindy's crib into her room. Priscilla had not had much time to talk to Steve. When he had arrived following her frantic phone call, he had been furious.

"Damn it—can't you see it's just the same old Kaiser runaround, Pris?"

"Calm down, Steve—"

"Hell, no! I've had it up to here with these jerks! That's just the kind of crap they were pulling at the end with Tia."

34

"This has nothing to do with that."

"Maybe not, but it's all the same kind of power-hungry play. Goddamn hospital. I hate these places."

"The point is Mindy—what all this is going to do to her. They can't do this to a one-year-old—"

"Yeah, and—"

"She needs me," Priscilla interrupted heatedly. "I've got to make Carte and Callas understand."

"Well, good luck, lady! That Carte's a cold sonovabitch and Callas doesn't strike me as too much better."

Priscilla nodded. They didn't say much after that, as though consciously deciding that it was more important to focus their energies on the upcoming meeting.

The ICU Quiet Room was about eight feet square, with a small sink in one corner and room for a few chairs. Four chairs had been drawn up, two on one side of the room, two on the other, like the start of some elaborate game. Steve and Priscilla took chairs next to one another against the far wall. Dr. Callas and Dr. Carte came in, their faces expressionless. Priscilla noticed that Dr. Carte locked the door. For a moment no one spoke. Then Dr. Carte began.

Later, Priscilla could recall only the highlights. She remembered that she cried her way through the half-hour meeting. Dr. Carte never looked at her or at Steve. Formal and stiff, he told her first that they wanted to isolate Mindy because she was receiving sodium from somewhere. That it was important to change and monitor everything about Mindy's treatment— the formula, the equipment, the nursing staff, everything.

"But the same nurses work ICU as Pediatrics," Priscilla said at once.

"Everything will be much more rigidly controlled," Carte answered.

"But I still don't understand—"

"It's simple, Mrs. Phillips. Mindy is getting excess sodium from somewhere—" began Carte, looking at the floor.

"What are you saying?" Steve broke in.

"Steve—"

"No, Pris—I want to know. If you're saying what I think you're saying, someone's going through the wall!"

"Mr. Phillips—"

"I just want some answers, Dr. Carte."

"Mr. Phillips, we believe this excess sodium is what Mindy had all along," Dr. Callas said.

"No," Priscilla protested, her voice shaking. "Mindy just had the flu at first. We all had it. Now maybe it's from sodium, but not at first."

Dr. Callas shook her head but didn't answer.

"Well, what about visiting?" said Priscilla. "Can my sons visit Mindy? We've had this planned for so long. Sara said—"

"I'm afraid not, Mrs. Phillips," Dr. Callas said. "The visiting in ICU is very restricted. Children are not allowed. You and Mr. Phillips can visit five minutes an hour."

Priscilla started screaming then.

"She's a baby! You can't do that! She's had so many changes!"

"It probably won't be for long, only a couple of days," Dr. Callas said.

"Can you at least make the time cumulative?" Priscilla's voice was shaking uncontrollably. "Fifteen minutes every three hours?"

"No," Dr. Callas said.

13

It was like dealing with a couple of two-year-olds, Evelyn thought. You say the same thing, slowly, over and over again, patiently, calmly, and you let them scream and cry and drum their little heels on the floor until eventually they hear you, and stop. Or just stop out of exhaustion or a sense of futility.

It was the way Evelyn had designed the meeting, but it was still difficult to live through. At lunch she and Estol had discussed strategy over a sandwich in the cafeteria. They had already reached the decision to transfer Mindy, and that was not to change. So the purpose of this meeting was really two-fold: primarily, Evelyn felt, it should be a meeting for the parents to ventilate their feelings. She expected a mammoth explosion because that's what you always got with those two. She and Estol would just have to sit there and take it.

Secondly, Evelyn had decided that she wanted to provide the Phillipses with the minimum possible amount of basic information about why they were moving Mindy to ICU. And that was going to be the hard part. Because by now she knew a great deal more than she had this morning when she had made the decision to transfer Mindy.

Estol had been brilliant, really. He'd made a quantum leap she had never considered. He had looked at Mindy's intake and output of sodium and realized that the natural place to start was not the output but the intake. She was getting the sodium from somewhere, obviously, so why not start with the formula?

He had told her what he had done—taking a syringe full of Mindy's formula to the lab and ordering a sodium test. When he had returned for the results, the lab tech informed him that the formula contained 4,480 milliequivalents per liter of sodium.

"I told her that was in the direction I expected, but seemed awfully high," Carte had said at lunch. "And she called me back with a corrected figure of four hundred forty-eight. She'd forgotten to put in the decimal point. Still, of course, that was an unbelievable figure!"

"What's the expected sodium content of Cho-free?" Evelyn asked.

"Fifteen milliequivalents. I looked it up."

"So, what did you do next?"

"Well, I contacted the nursing supervisor and asked her to witness what I was going to do. Then back at the ward I took the whole bottle of Mindy's formula out of the ward refrigerator and brought it back to the lab. I told the technologist to label it, make sure no one threw it out, and keep it in the lab refrigerator."

"And then?"

"I returned to the ward. The nurse was already mixing new formula for Mindy, so I instructed her to change all the tubing, and keep the new stuff in the Medication Room—not to let it out of her sight. Then I thought I'd better get a control sample tested, so I took some of the newly mixed formula and ran that down to the lab. I haven't received the results back on that yet, but when I got down there, they handed me the slip on Mindy's most recent serum sodium. Since it was one hundred sixty, I figured I might as well use that as an excuse to move Mindy to ICU, as we'd discussed. And that's what I did."

"But what made you think to test the formula?" Evelyn was stunned at the simplicity of it.

"I don't know. I guess maybe it was on my mind somehow—

the fact that Mrs. Phillips was involved with that formula. You know, on Monday I heard Debby Roof on the phone to Mrs. Phillips, asking about mixing the formula. I thought Debby was talking to Sara. When I found out the nurses had to turn to the mother for what should be normal care in the hospital—I thought it outrageous. I told Debby, and wrote it in the orders, that no one but the nurses were to mix the formula. I didn't make any real connection then. But it must have been floating in the back of my head."

There was one other thing of paramount concern to Evelyn, especially in view of what Estol had discovered about the formula. It might occur to the Phillipses to check Mindy out of the hospital against medical advice. And to keep them from doing that, Evelyn realized she would have to be prepared to call security.

It did not occur to her that she and Estol might be the ones to need security. She expected anger from the parents, but later she was struck by the inappropriateness of their response. She saw Steve Phillips react way out of proportion to the situation. He seemed to burst into a towering rage.

She had always thought that Steve Phillips, at best, was a rather frightening sight. Not only was he mountainous, but he was naturally somewhat menacing, with brown eyes too small for his face, and very thin lips which narrowed and disappeared when he was angry, revealing yellow teeth. He had a short, meaty nose, and several small white scars around his brow and chin. And she couldn't help herself: his strong southern accent made her wince.

And Steve was furious. When he screamed that threat about someone going through a wall, Evelyn had to swallow against a sudden chunk of fear hardening in her throat.

And why were the Phillipses so angry? she wondered. Why weren't they more concerned? Why weren't they worried that she and Estol thought Mindy's health to be so jeopardized that they were insisting on the Intensive Care Unit? Wasn't this how normal parents would react?

And why did it seem to matter so much that the boys couldn't visit their sister? Instead of being scared, the parents fought. That was what was so strange. They argued, claiming that 160 was not so high, that it didn't justify the ICU.

And then Steve Phillips had talked about enemies. He said that with his job and his wife's, they were sure to have made lots of enemies over the years. It wasn't a normal dialogue, Evelyn thought. The small room began to ring with the sound of raised voices. It was hard to tell what Mrs. Phillips thought, what anybody actually believed. All they were getting was pure, shimmering rage.

But Evelyn knew what really mattered to Mrs. Phillips. It was the part about the limited visiting. And that just added to Evelyn's suspicions. Mrs. Phillips hadn't really been all that upset until then, she thought. And in ICU, the woman's every move would be supervised. She would never be alone with Mindy.

Evelyn's hands shook as she unlocked the door of the Quiet Room to let the four of them out. The irony of the room's name suddenly struck her. Never had that room, she was certain, been less quiet than it had been for the last thirty minutes.

Still, the meeting had accomplished what Evelyn had hoped. The Phillipses had harangued and screamed and cried, but they had not signed Mindy out against medical advice, and the situation had not escalated.

14

Steve Phillips knew an accusation when he heard one. And he had heard one here. All that pussyfooting around about "someone" doing "something" with that sodium, and changing all Mindy's routines. It was horse manure, he thought.

"Look, Pris, don't you see what they're saying?" he said again in the van on their way home from the hospital.

"Steve, you're crazy." She looked at him in disbelief. He felt himself go red.

"Pris, you idiot. You're so goddamn naive sometimes! They're saying you put something into Mindy."

"But they didn't say that. They said there was more sodium going into her than they could account for. They're worried about the high sodium, that's all."

"Right, Pris. They're not saying it up front, but that's what they mean. They practically accused you right out! Goddamn those idiots; they've got their head up their behinds!"

"Steve, I don't think they're saying anyone gave something to Mindy. How could they be saying that? Who would do that?" said Priscilla.

"That's just what I was trying to get at in there. If someone did it, we gotta think who it might be. Because we know it wasn't you and we know it wasn't me. So maybe it was someone I sent up to C.Y.A. sometime, or someone you refused benefits to. I've gotta get a list of Kaiser employees out of those suckers, see if maybe there's someone on there I recognize. You know how these kids are always threatening to do me in or come after my family. Well, maybe one of them did."

"Oh, Steve!" She spoke through her hands.

"Well, you got a better idea?" He pulled the camper off Woodbine Drive in a vicious left turn into their driveway.

"No, but I still think you're wrong." She was crying again. "I wonder how Mindy is doing."

"You want me to cancel the fishing?"

"No, no. The boys are counting on it. You'd better go pick them up." She pushed herself off the high step of the van, landing heavily, and started for the front door.

"Okay. See you later."

She didn't answer. He watched her sturdy duck-footed walk as she passed under the bottle brush that sheltered the walk. She usually walked everywhere fast and head high, but she suddenly looked old and worn out.

Steve backed the camper out of the drive and headed for the neighbor where he had hastily dumped the boys after Pris had called him. Then he'd stop over at Skip's and go out for some fishing along Point San Pedro Road. He wasn't ready to tell Skip about it because he needed to pull his thoughts together.

He had no doubt the doctors were saying that someone had put something into Mindy, and that pretty damn soon they were going to be saying it was Priscilla. He was sure they were laying the railroad tracks right to her door. So he was going to have to work and head them off because he knew damn well that Pris hadn't given anything to Mindy. They were probably trying to hide something, he thought. But Kaiser was a pretty damn big operation to be taking on as an adversary. There was just one vague glimmer of hope, and Steve clung to it now. Maybe when Sara came back, she'd straighten it all out. Maybe it was just one giant mistake.

15

Priscilla stood in the shower for a long time. She had lurched into the bathroom in time to throw up into the toilet. But now she couldn't stop crying. She had been crying all afternoon in her bed, immobilized.

Lifting her swollen face to the jets of water, she let it all pour down her. A river of tears, she thought. They could not do this to her. They could not. The hot orange rug reflected back at her, mocking her with its cheerfulness. The water turned cold finally, and she shut it off.

She dressed in her room, choosing at random a dark corduroy dress to go over slip, nylons, and fresh underwear. She pulled a comb through her wet hair and fluffed at it with her fingers, wondering vaguely if she should set it. In the mirror her face was a ruin, her eyes red and sunken in their puffy lids. Her eyes seemed to weigh her whole face down.

She had decided to see Carte again to find out what he meant. She could not live like this, not knowing, shut out.

She couldn't see Mindy again till four o'clock, when they would allow her five minutes, like some prisoner in jail. So at four, she was at the door to the ICU, ringing the bell to be admitted.

She couldn't believe what she saw. The naso-gastric tube was gone. There was no IV. Priscilla looked over at the nurse who had come on shift while Priscilla had been at home. It was ridiculous, she thought. It was Lesley McCarcy, the same nurse who had been on Pediatrics with her the night before.

"So much for the change of staff Carte mentioned," she muttered to herself. "Where are Mindy's NG and IV?" Priscilla asked aloud.

The nurse shrugged. "She pulled the NG out right after I got here, about an hour ago. And the IV kept infiltrating, so Dr. Carte ordered Pedialyte. She's taking it really well. She's been just fine since she's been here, Mrs. Phillips," she added reassuringly.

"I knew it! I knew she'd do something like that if I wasn't

with her. She's been trying to pull out the tube since she got it. But I don't understand these changes. Do you know where I can find Dr. Carte?"

"Well, you could try the pediatric ward. I believe he's on duty up there today."

"Yes, I know."

Priscilla finally tracked down Dr. Carte, who agreed to meet her again in the Quiet Room.

So, for the second time in that room, and for the third time that day, Priscilla and Dr. Carte confronted one another.

"Dr. Carte, I've just been in to see Mindy. She has no IV and no NG. If she's so sick, why doesn't she need these? I don't understand."

"Well, she pulled out the NG and the IV kept infiltrating. There's only one site left for a cut-down and I don't want to use it if I don't have to. Her diarrhea is improved so I started her on Pedialyte. That's just an oral solution of what's in the IV—"

"I know. What I don't understand is if she's so sick that she needs to be in ICU, why doesn't she need an IV? I mean, why keep her in ICU?"

"She's doing all right on the Pedialyte, Mrs. Phillips. So far. I've already explained to you why the ICU is necessary. I really don't have anything to add."

He did not tell Priscilla, nor did she find out until much later, that although he'd ordered only a small amount of the solution be given to Mindy, the nurse, seeing how eagerly Mindy had taken it, how thirsty she seemed to be, had let her have the whole bottle of Pedialyte. He did not tell Priscilla how dangerous that could be. If a child with a high serum sodium level is rehydrated too quickly, it can cause the brain to swell with fluid. And when that happens, there is no place for the brain to expand, encased as it is in the hard shell of the skull. So brain damage can result, as can convulsions and even death. But they had been lucky with Mindy: she had tolerated the large amount of fluid well.

It was Priscilla who now brought up the topic she really wanted to explore. What had Carte really been driving at in the earlier meeting? And this time, he confronted the issue more squarely.

Mindy's sodium level, he said, indicated that she was receiving an external source of sodium that was causing her diarrhea, and it was the sort of thing you could get over the counter at any drugstore.

"What do you mean?" Priscilla asked.

"Something with a laxative effect, that all of us are familiar with," he answered.

"I'm not familiar with that," she said. "There are no laxatives in our house."

"Well, it's common knowledge. You can buy it anywhere."

"I don't know anything about that," she said again. And Carte did not answer her and did not look at her.

"It's obvious to me that I can sit here and tell you over and over again, till I'm blue in the face, that I don't know what you're talking about," she burst out. "But you're obviously not going to believe me."

And again, he looked away and didn't answer.

Later, Priscilla swore she made the next suggestion. Carte would swear it was his own.

"The Child Protective Services has to be called."

They would both agree, however, that Priscilla then said, "I've worked there and I know the procedure. You shouldn't just call the social worker on duty. Call Annie Jameson. She's the head. I've got her home number in my car. I'll get it for you."

Startled, Carte replied, "Yes. All right."

Afterward, Priscilla claimed that at this point in the conversation, she demanded that there be a criminal investigation. Carte was to deny that she said it. Instead—and she always denied this in her turn—his recollection was that she made a very damaging admission.

"That makes me a prime suspect," he swore that she said.

Priscilla half ran to her car in the parking lot behind the Medical Office Building. She found and opened her briefcase, dug in it briefly till she came upon Annie's number. Then she hurried back to Carte and handed him the number she had written down.

"Thank you," he said. Then he turned and without another word walked away from her. She stood, rigid and alone, and watched until he turned the corner and was gone. Later, returning home—and as though in preparation for coping with what was to come—she began a journal.

16

The Emergency Room had emptied out by five-thirty that afternoon. There were no more pediatric patients to be seen in the outpatient clinic. Evelyn could go home.

She had never spent a harder day. She hadn't had that kind of pressure since joining Kaiser. Most of her work here—for all the pediatricians—was outpatient clinic work, just like a private pediatrician's practice. The only difference was that with Kaiser she had the advantage of constant consultation, any time she wanted it. It made the job less lonely, the atmosphere more relaxed, and the pressures easier to bear.

The drawback, Evelyn reflected, was that when something as nerve-wracking as this situation hit you, you weren't prepared. You weren't used to living on the emotional edge. And you weren't twenty-five years old, either. You were Chief of Pediatrics, dealing with parents who had hair-trigger emotions, and a very sick little girl with terrible veins and a bad case of dehydration. You were dealing with a potentially serious crisis.

Estol Carte had just left her office. He had spent a worse day than she had, but he had stayed on top of it in a way that would never cease to impress Evelyn.

He had sat by her desk and told her that the control sample on Mindy's new formula contained precisely the right amount of sodium. So it appeared that the source of the sodium overload in Mindy's original formula was not contaminated factory stock. And then he had described his most recent meeting with Priscilla Phillips. Apparently Mrs. Phillips had denied all knowledge of laxatives or cathartic salts.

"I told her I'd have to call the Child Protective Services, and she said I should call the head of it. She went down to her car and brought me back the number!" he'd told Evelyn, shaking his head.

"What did you do?"

"I called her. Also the San Rafael police. They're meeting me here later."

"God, it never occurred to me to do that, Estol. We're going to have to write up a child abuse report."

"I know."

"I'll do it. I'll work on it tonight. Have you been up to see Mindy?" said Evelyn.

"Yes, she's doing fine. I ordered oral Cho-free for her. She hasn't had either the IV or NG in all afternoon."

"What about serum electrolytes?"

"I'll leave an order for them to be drawn in the morning. That'll give her body a chance to equilibrate whatever's still in there. But I'm sure the sodium will be down."

"Well, I'll check first thing when I come on the ward in the morning," said Evelyn. "I can't believe we've got another whole day of this to go through." She felt a sudden sense of comradeship—they could be two shipwrecked survivors on a lifeboat. She hoped they wouldn't sink in the next storm.

Estol left, and Evelyn went back upstairs to collect her things. She shrugged out of her stiffly starched white doctor's coat and into her warm one. She gathered up a handful of copies of the child abuse forms that Kaiser supplied in quadruplicate and stuffed them into her bulging bag, then walked back through the hospital to the parking lot. The fog had returned, she thought briefly, or perhaps it had never lifted at all.

17

Later Priscilla would not be able to remember how she arrived home that Saturday afternoon. She did notice that the camper was not there, so Steve and the boys had not returned yet. This was a good thing, for she did not want to be distracted now. She had to telephone Annie Jameson and warn her that Carte was going to call.

Annie Jameson was the head of the Child Protective Services in Marin County, a branch of Health and Human Services, and Priscilla knew her quite well. They had worked together on and off for the past ten years. Annie had been Priscilla's manager when Priscilla had returned to work on a month-to-month basis in January 1975, and she had supervised Priscilla's work as an on-call social worker in the Child Protective Service's program when it started up in the fall of that same year. Annie's grandniece was the same age as Erik, so that gave them something to talk about, and Annie had met Steve and the boys, but Priscilla considered the short, dumpy, sixtyish woman a professional rather than a social friend.

Annie's line was busy, but after repeated attempts, Priscilla finally got through.

"You're not going to believe this, Annie," she began.

"I already know. The doctor just called. I'm on my way to meet him now. It will take awhile. I understand he's already called the police—you know that's the procedure."

"I know, Annie. Oh, Annie—I can't believe this is happening to me. It's totally unreal!" She broke into tears.

"Priscilla, I'm sure it's a misunderstanding. We'll straighten it all out in no time, I'm sure. The policeman and I will come over after we meet the doctor at Kaiser. Now don't be upset—"

"Oh, Annie, I've been crying all day! I don't know if I can bear it!"

"Priscilla, please don't worry. Take some aspirin. Try to calm down. I've got to go now. But I'll see you soon."

"Yes, all right." Priscilla hung up the phone, found some aspirin, and waited for Steve to come home.

He was furious.

"Why the hell did you go up there, Pris!"

"Because I had to know. And you were right. They think I did it. Carte said it was something you could buy in the drugstore, and he implied I did it. I don't even know what he's talking about. I gave him Annie Jameson's number, and she's meeting them over there—Carte and the police."

"I'm going to call that sonovabitch right now and get a list of the employees out of him," Steve exploded. "There's gotta be somebody we know working over there. Somebody with a grudge, Pris."

Priscilla heard Steve's end of the phone conversation. She watched his face redden. Finally he hung up.

"Well?" she asked.

"He doesn't think it's necessary," Steve minced in apparent imitation of the doctor. "Well, I'll get it out of him, or some damn administrator up there, you can bet on that!"

Somehow they got the boys to bed. Mechanically, Priscilla

tidied the house, picking up clothes and toys, polishing the kitchen counters, waiting for the doorbell.

The visit was worse than Priscilla expected; she spent most of it in tears. From the beginning it was obvious that both Annie and the young, officious police officer she had brought with her, believed that a finger was being pointed straight at Priscilla. And not just because of Mindy.

"I understand you had another child who died," the officer said. "We're going to have to investigate that, too."

For a while, Priscilla sat wordless, the tears streaming in fine runnels down her face. Steve was yelling about their enemies and a list of Kaiser employees and kept saying that the boys were fine, that they'd be sick if Priscilla was going around poisoning the children. That she was the best mother anyone could have. That she had worked against child abuse for years, that they both had fine reputations in the community. He was shouting.

"But what about Mindy? What will happen to Mindy?" Priscilla finally broke in over Steve.

"I don't know. Maybe a foster home, Priscilla, just for a little while," Annie said.

"Oh, no!" Priscilla was shrieking. "Annie, you know I lost one child and now they want to take another! You can't do this to me!"

"Well, I don't know, Priscilla. Why don't we talk to the doctor tomorrow. I'll set something up. Maybe we can work something out."

"Annie, you've got to do something about the visiting. They're only letting me visit five minutes an hour. They won't even let it accumulate. She's not used to being alone like that."

"All right, Priscilla. I'll see what I can do. Why don't you and Steve plan to come by the hospital tomorrow about noon? I'm sure we can work this out. Please don't worry."

Priscilla sat motionless on the orange sofa as they rose and then left. She did not even move when she heard Steve slam the front door after them. She felt rooted, helpless. Because, for once, she didn't know what to do.

18

Annie was there to meet them as promised. Steve felt as though he'd been treading water in a deep pond for an hour. His big, burly body was floppy with no sleep and worry and uncertainty.

That morning he had called Jim Hutchison.

"Someone's trying to poison Mindy," he said. There had been a pause before the minister replied.

"What?"

And Steve had repeated it, explaining what had happened. "We need you up at Kaiser, Jim. Can you come?" It was for Priscilla, really, that he was asking, he knew. Priscilla had leaned so hard on Jim when Tia had died.

"Yes, of course, Steve." The heavy Irish voice had been reassuring. "I'm just getting ready for the service, but I'll be up as soon as it's over. By one o'clock certainly. Don't worry," Jim had said.

So they expected him in time for the meeting that Annie Jameson had arranged with Dr. Callas in the ICU Quiet Room.

At noon, Steve and Priscilla drove to the hospital to visit Mindy. Steve did not go in. He couldn't bear some nurse standing over him, watching every move. He looked through the glass door as Priscilla moved to Mindy's bed. He knew Pris was crying.

"How is she?" he asked when Priscilla returned five minutes later.

"She looks okay. They're giving her cereal and bottles. She hasn't had any diarrhea."

So it *was* something in the bottle of formula, Steve thought. Maybe the damned doctors had done something right for once. But who? How had it happened? In a way, Steve didn't want her to be better because now they'd surely be coming after Priscilla. Well, they weren't going to do it. Not if he had anything to say about it.

And now here with Annie Jameson was Dr. Callas, her face set in accusation. Steve almost flinched. Jim Hutchison wasn't here. He had called at the last minute and said he couldn't make it till later, that they should go on without him.

The Quiet Room seemed smaller still, Steve thought, as though a black cloud of threat and danger had entered, seeping under the single door, filling the room. Steve could almost feel it hanging there, ready to shroud them all.

Priscilla was crying before they went into that little room, and she cried on and off throughout the meeting. Annie said they were there to talk about the visiting. It felt good to Steve to have some support. And Annie was effective. She was an older woman with a calm voice and an air of reason.

"I don't see why the visiting can't accumulate," she said to Dr. Callas. "It is so inconvenient for the Phillipses to arrange their lives so that they can be here five minutes each hour."

"That's right," Priscilla broke in. "It's too exhausting. Either I have to sit outside the door for the other fifty-five minutes and watch the clock, or go home, try to live a normal life, and then rush back."

"What I suggest—" began Miss Jameson.

"It's totally ridiculous—"

"Steve—"

"I just wanted to—" he began again.

"Let her finish!"

"Okay. Sorry," he muttered.

"Why not fifteen minutes every three hours? That's what I propose."

Dr. Callas hesitated. "All right, Miss Jameson," she finally said.

"Now tell me more about these sodium levels," Miss Jameson said.

They were trying to tie it in with Tia, Steve realized as he listened to Dr. Callas, and that didn't make sense. Now they were claiming that Mindy was getting sodium from outside. But when Tia's sodium levels had been elevated, the doctors had always explained that this was a physiological response; Tia was experiencing too much output of fluid too quickly, causing an increased level of sodium in the blood.

So what was going on? he wondered. Had they screwed up in Tia's case? Was this thing with Mindy just an excuse for Tia? Pris kept saying they'd never tie Tia into this, that Tia was a whole different thing. But Steve wasn't so sure.

At the end of the meeting, Priscilla and Annie wanted to

look in again on Mindy, and as they crossed the hall to the ICU, Steve turned to Dr. Callas.

"Something I don't understand here. Are you saying it has to be an additional sodium source and not a natural process? Tia always had high sodiums and you explained it away as a physical reaction to diarrhea. Couldn't Mindy and Tia have the same thing?"

Dr. Callas stopped and looked at him squarely.

"Yes," she replied. "The two cases are exactly the same."

But what she meant and what he understood were entirely different, and this conversation, much later, was to come back to haunt him.

19

All through the meeting, Evelyn struggled to stay detached. She was outnumbered. It would be easy to give in. It would stop the tears and the shouting and the hysteria.

But over and over, Evelyn kept reminding herself, we know the chemistry, we know what we know, and we know no matter how loudly they scream and holler, that child was poisoned. Remember your data, Evelyn; keep your head.

Last night, at midnight, the nurse had recorded a perfectly formed brown stool. The 9:15 A.M. electrolyte readings reported back from the lab had shown a sodium of 138 milliequivalents per liter, a potassium of 5.3, a chloride of 106, and a carbon dioxide of 26. All were completely normal. And Mindy's appetite had returned. There was no getting around the evidence of the patient's own body. It was irrefutable proof.

It had taken Evelyn three tries and lots of scratch paper last night before she had been satisfied with the child abuse form she had filled out. This report was going to the San Rafael police, and to the Marin County Child Protective Services. It involved a family with a certain standing in the community. Both parents were county employees. Evelyn knew she had to be careful with this report. She wanted to be certain that she accused no one, yet she had to make sure that Mindy would be protected. She was proud of the finished product, which ended with the sentence, "The illness is consistent with the addition of a saline cathartic to the child's intake by some person." No one could ignore that report.

But they might not know exactly how to deal with it. It was clear that Miss Jameson, for one, was confused about the implications of what had occurred. After the Quiet Room meeting with the Phillipses, Evelyn had conferred with the social worker alone.

Didn't Dr. Callas think that Mindy might go home with a public health nurse in attendance? Miss Jameson had asked.

"No, it's not safe," Evelyn answered.

"Well, couldn't Mindy go home with them on some sort of basis? Mrs. Phillips has offered to have someone move in with them to keep an eye on Mindy. The most upsetting thing for her is to have Mindy taken away from her, especially after the loss of Tia," Miss Jameson persisted.

Evelyn looked at her in disbelief. "Look, I know you're trying to help, but I have to disabuse you of the notion that Mindy can go home with Mrs. Phillips on any basis. Don't you understand, she's already killed one child and has tried to kill another!"

"What do you mean? What other child?"

"Tia! At this point I'm sure Tia didn't die a natural death, either!"

"My goodness! That's really difficult to take in. I can't believe it! What evidence do you have? I'm just sure she couldn't have done that—that you'll find you're mistaken," Miss Jameson said numbly.

"Frankly, I think that's unlikely. When we start looking through Tia's chart—knowing what we do about Mindy—I think we'll find medical evidence. Now we know what to look for. It is so easy to introduce a substance into a child with a naso-gastric tube in place, you know. Just mix it with a little water and inject it into the tube. With a bottle, of course, it's even easier. And there have been some articles recently about mothers—perfectly ordinary-seeming mothers, incidentally—doing this sort of thing to their children. We were just never suspicious enough, unfortunately."

"Well, this is a delicate situation as you know. Mrs. Phillips is a county employee who has worked in the Child Protective Services. I don't want to malign her or slander her or jeopardize her position without proof," Miss Jameson said.

"You saw Mindy. She's the proof!"

"She's also the problem here."

"Exactly," Evelyn said.

"Obviously her needs come first. She must be protected. I don't necessarily agree with your conclusion about Mrs. Phillips, but you're rendering a professional opinion, and I will go by it. Mindy will not be released to the Phillipses."

"Thank God!"

So that was one fewer battle that had to be fought, Evelyn thought. But something else was gnawing at her now. Yesterday she had finally admitted to herself the significance that all this had on Tia's death. But how was she going to tell Sara?

That afternoon, Evelyn started telephoning Sara's house every half hour. She wanted to make certain she reached her before anyone else. She was worried about what the Phillipses might do to Sara, verbally or possibly even physically. And she was concerned about how Sara might take the news.

She tried, distractedly, to plan for her trip tomorrow to Sacramento. She had been working for months on another child abuse matter, an assembly bill that would enable doctors to take photographs of suspected cases of child abuse without parental consent.

Now she was supposed to go to the capital, sit in on the Criminal Justice Committee, and possibly testify about the bill. The timing was ironic, she thought. If nothing else, it would be a relief to get out of the hospital and away from the Phillipses.

But she still had today to get through. That afternoon, she had finally reached the Physician-in-Chief. He didn't want to hear about it when she told him what was happening. He made it plain that it was too abhorrent to think about. As though that closed the matter. She sensed that administrative support would be minimal.

Finally, at ten that evening, Sara answered the phone.

"Mindy's in ICU but she's all right. Stay there, I'm coming over to tell you about it," Evelyn said, just as she had practiced it all afternoon.

Evelyn drove slowly west along North San Pedro Road, past the huge pink sprawl of the San Rafael Civic Center with its vivid turquoise roofs, through central San Rafael.

Sara lived in a little cul-de-sac in a two-story block house that lay up alone against a wooded hillside by a stand of pine trees. It was very quiet and hidden. You wouldn't know it was there if you weren't looking for it, Evelyn thought randomly.

She focused her mind on Sara, who like her house, was difficult to find. Sara revealed so little of herself. Evelyn realized suddenly that she was not even sure how Sara would react tonight, exactly how shattering this all would be to her. But she knew it would be grim because Sara had trusted Priscilla Phillips and because, when it came down to it, the responsibility for the health of Tia and Mindy belonged quite properly to the primary physician. And that had been Sara.

Sara met her at the door. She looked so slender and frail and tired. Evelyn put her arms around her.

"Mindy's formula was contaminated with sodium," she said. "But now she's okay. Sara, the nightmare is over." There was a pause.

"No," said Sara, stiff and still in her arms. "No," she said again. "The nightmare is just beginning."

Then she hesitated, breathed in deeply, and added, "Evelyn, Tia need not have died."

And because it was exactly what she had realized, Evelyn could think of nothing to say.

THE FAMILY

1

In 1966, Winthrop College in Rock Hill, South Carolina, was still a women's college. It was not a stately, tree-lined campus of the type that characterized many colleges in the area, but that didn't matter to Steve. The important characteristic was statistical. There were five thousand women on campus.

Hell, it was going to be paradise, Steve thought. After Don, his friend from high school, had gotten him a blind date for the Valentine's Day dance, the two of them had taken off in Steve's '60 Nash Rambler for the hundred-mile drive from Williamston to Rock Hill without a moment's hesitation. Don had arranged it perfectly, even picking up reduced rates at the Andrew Jackson Hotel in Rock Hill for the night.

The Lettermen were playing in person at the Winthrop dance, and if the date didn't work out, Steve was certain he could find someone else out of those five thousand he could relate to, especially with the romantic three-part harmony those guys put out when they sang. There was no way this weekend could fail.

He was supposed to pick Priscilla up at her dorm—the same dorm where Don's date lived, so he and Don went down there together. One after another the girls in their pastel ball gowns wafted down the staircase. They looked like fluffs of delicious cotton candy, Steve decided, and after each one he and Don traded notes.

"That's the one," Steve announced suddenly. "Man, just look at her. I'm going to marry that one!"

"You sucker, I think that's actually your date, cuz there's my Sandra pointing at her and waving. See her?"

Steve was bowled over. Priscilla was perfect—neat and shiny with a nice figure and big brown eyes.

"Where do you go to school?" Priscilla asked him, as they danced around amid the crepe-paper decor of the gym.

"Oh, I just finished out at Anderson Junior College—it's a Baptist college."

"The one near Greenville?"

"That's it," said Steve. "My folks live in Williamston right down the road. I wanted to go to a university and play some football, but my knee got torn up and that was the end of that career!" He laughed.

"So what are you going to do now?"

"I don't know. My dad's in the furniture business in Greenville, but I don't think I want to go into that. Maybe some other business. I'm still looking," said Steve. He didn't mention that he was planning on looking after a stint in the U.S. Army. Some girls were funny about the army these days, he had discovered, now that the service meant Vietnam.

"What about you?" he asked her. "You going to settle down with a house full of kids and just look beautiful?" he flirted.

She looked serious. "Well, I do want children. But I want a career, too. I'm going to be a social worker. I'd like to work with children—I've been at a Y camp for years and was a counselor, and I really like kids. I'll finish here next spring by doing four years in three, and I'm going to summer school this summer in Greensboro—that's where I live. And then I want to go to either Berkeley or Columbia or Chicago for graduate school."

Steve looked at her admiringly. "Hey, you sure do have it all planned out. Don't your folks mind you going so far from home to school?"

Priscilla shrugged. "My father died when I was eleven, and my mother approves. She's the adventuresome sort herself—went and taught school in Puerto Rico after she got out of college—that's where she met my father. She knows I've got my mind set, anyway. She's always laughing about how I always get what I want when I make up my mind."

They danced several more dances, then Steve went for glasses of punch. The conversation was easy. Steve told Priscilla about growing up in Williamston, about the fishing and swimming and golf. Golf was big in Williamston. He told her about his family. Every Wednesday at twelve o'clock, the town closed down and his father always spent that afternoon with him, sometimes on the golf course, sometimes just talking or doing nothing. Steve's older sister Betty had married and moved out in 1957—she was ten years older than Steve—so it had been like growing up an only child. My miracle baby, his mother had always called him. Steve never lacked for anything.

"I was probably a little spoiled," he confided to Priscilla. "But my dad wasn't getting too much intimacy from my mother; she's been sick with one thing and another for years, so him and me are close. My sister, too. What about you?"

Priscilla had an older sister she told him. But they had their differences. Louise had her nose in a book all the time, and couldn't decide what to do with her life, though she was two years older than Priscilla. Steve could tell this irritated Priscilla.

"She's so smart," Priscilla said. "But she was always laying around the house and never did well in school. She started college and dropped out, then went to school for a while to be a dental technician and dropped out of that. Her laziness used to drive my stepfather crazy. They couldn't stand each other, but I got along with him very well because I was always out and about and busy. He bought me a sewing machine when I asked him, and a car as soon as I got my license, and he used to take me and my friends out waterskiing, buy us all lunch."

"It sounds pretty good," Steve said.

"Yeah, but Chester and my mother didn't get along after they got married," she went on. "They had been college sweethearts, and they met again right after my father was killed down in Florida in a construction accident. They dated for a long time while he was trying to get a divorce from his first wife, but then when they got married, nothing was any good anymore—he used up her money for his things, and they fought. They separated in '63. She didn't need Chester. She's always been independent."

"Wasn't it awful hard after your father died?" Steve asked. He was charmed with this girl who laid it out as though they had been friends for a long time.

"Oh, yes. My parents hadn't been together for a while—they had been having problems. He was on this job in Fort Lauderdale, and my mother had taken a job with the Methodist Children's Home in Winston-Salem as a housemother, and we were living in the home, too, not in a separate apartment with her, but with the orphans. It was September and we were supposed to get together with my father for the first time in months at Christmas. He was going to stop drinking and go to AA, that was the arrangement, because things got bad when he was drunk—I know a couple of times he even hit my mother. But then he died instead. And there wasn't even a funeral I could go to. Then Chester came into our lives and talked my mother into moving to Greensboro. So we've lived in North Carolina ever since. We had moved around so much before, following my father's construction jobs; it was nice to finally stay somewhere for a while."

"I've only lived three places in my whole life—counting the dorm—and they're all within a few miles of each other. But I don't feel like I've missed anything. I'd like to live around here all my life," Steve said.

"I wouldn't. I can't stand small-town life," said Priscilla. "I'm getting out and staying out."

Man, this little lady was something else, Steve thought. She had so much get-up-and-go it took your breath away. She said she was involved in a model U.N. program—Steve had heard of it but never knew anybody actually doing it—and was on the school newspaper and in some honor societies. Steve had pulled down more Ds in his college career than he cared to remember, and he had spent an extra semester at college to bring his grades up to a more respectable position. Hell, he had to admit he hadn't gone to college for the academic part—he had never been much of a student. He liked to party and date. But he had had a run-in with the school administration his second year at Anderson that had taught him something about responsibility and injustice. A panty raid and an argument with a proctor about getting up for church had resulted in Steve's expulsion from the dorm. But he had stuck it out at college anyway—the other students had all supported him, so had his father—and he'd learned something valuable about what he labeled the "big people's world": You could get screwed, glued, and tattooed there as well as anyplace.

So now he was taking things more seriously. He had enlisted and basic training was due to start in a few weeks. But meantime he had a cute little date, and he was going to try all his moves with her.

He got nowhere. He took Priscilla out of the crowded gym and parked by a little lake where he tried everything he knew. But it was as though she had been briefed on every single move. He asked her to write her last name down. Eichholtz. It was some helluva name to spell. It was German for oak wood, she told him.

Hell, he was going to have to stay with this lady.

2

Travis Air Force Base was about forty-five minutes east of Berkeley on the way to Sacramento, and Priscilla was nervous that her tan suit would not survive the drive unwrinkled. When she got out of the car, she smoothed it down, then checked her makeup in the hand mirror from her purse.

Steve had been stationed in Okinawa—with a tour of duty in Vietnam—for sixteen months; Priscilla had not seen him in a year. Priscilla smiled at the memory of their reunion at last year's Valentine's Day dance at Winthrop, exactly a year after she had met Steve.

Her roommate and suite mates had been in on the secret, as had the housemother, but they had kept the surprise, and when she had walked downstairs the night of the dance to find Steve there, she had practically died. He was supposed to be overseas. They had fallen into each others' arms, laughing and crying, hugging and dancing around each other like a couple of crazy puppies. She had been so worried about him, but he looked fine. Maybe it was just the uniform, but he acted more like a man that weekend, too. Not that he didn't try some more of those childish moves on her, Priscilla remembered.

"I'm just trying to keep in practice," he kidded her.

"Forget it, boy! None of that. You know I'm saving it for marriage. The army couldn't have addled your brains that much!"

He'd cocked his head and put on a little-boy look of disappointment, but he didn't really push her on it—he knew how she felt.

Priscilla wasn't quite the same small-town puritan she had been a year ago, however. Seven months in Berkeley had left their mark. Her last year at Winthrop had been packed with commitments. She had held the presidency of both the statewide Sociological Association of South Carolina College Students and Alpha Kappa Delta—the national honor society for sociology students. She had worked on the Winthrop newspaper and involved herself with a program for helping mentally retarded children. In her spare time she had studied,

well aware that in order to qualify for the financial aid she
needed to attend graduate school, her grades had to be top-
notch.

Berkeley admitted her on a full HEW scholarship covering
all her fees plus a stipend of $200 a month the first year of
graduate school and $220 the second. Last May, following
graduation from Winthrop—completed in the three years she
had scheduled for it—she and two friends had driven across
the country.

She had found herself a studio apartment in Berkeley, at the
outer radius of what she calculated to be a walkable distance to
the campus, for $75 a month. Days of looking had left her feet
sore, and although she hated the place when she first saw it,
she took it eventually out of desperation. At the time she
hadn't noticed its lack of heat. She did see the hippie children
playing on the block, and their disheveled appearance shocked
her. But soon she was accustomed to them, adjusting to
Berkeley's casual approach to childrearing.

Next Priscilla had pursued a job, finding work as a sales clerk
at the PX on Treasure Island under the Bay Bridge. But once
she started school in September the commute became impossible, so she accepted part-time work at Capwell's Department
Store in El Cerrito working nights. She also joined and
became secretary of the Associated Students of the School of
Social Welfare, and along with her classes, she started her field
placement work at a research project in Richmond working
with disturbed children twice a week.

She started dating. She had always intended to flap her
wings, and she'd informed Steve of this in advance. He was in
the army, she said. This was a perfect time to test what they
had.

She genuinely liked Steve. He attracted her physically.
More, they shared an interest in children and strong family life
and a commitment to openness in a relationship. As an
adolescent, Priscilla had become deeply involved in church
activities; for a time she expected to work as a missionary for
the Methodist Church. Steve had been strongly affected by his
family minister, and both Steve and Priscilla still attended
church. Then, too, Steve was romantic, and Priscilla found
that appealing. On one of their first dates, Steve had learned it
was Priscilla's birthday and had brought her some candy and
taken her to see a movie. Afterward he had driven them to a

park complete with pond and ducks; they had walked around holding hands, pretending they were in a movie of their own.

But Priscilla wasn't sure she approved of Steve Phillips. His enlistment at a time when most of her friends were hunting deferments was an embarrassment. He certainly didn't fit her picture of an ideal mate. He wasn't educated and in fact expressed no interest in becoming so. To Priscilla, education was paramount: the only way to get ahead. Her mother was educated; her friends were all college students. Greensboro boasted several colleges, both black and white, and its population was principally middle- and upper-middle class. Priscilla accepted but one road and its first stop was a college education that prepared you for an appropriate career. But Steve didn't think that way. Then, too, it worried Priscilla that Steve didn't seem to have any goals, no plans beyond the army. More problematical still, he preferred life in a small town.

So Priscilla was hesitant to pursue the relationship. She had set her sights high and she just wasn't certain that Steve could be a part of the life she saw for herself. She planned to find out at Berkeley.

Adjustment to the college did not prove difficult, because although Priscilla found herself in the midst of political upheaval on campus, she refused to be distracted. She wanted an education; she couldn't be bothered with confrontation. Socially she was drawn to the more conservative students. In fact, she did not go out frequently, but she did date a couple of engineering students. One was from India. Priscilla was intrigued for a while, partly because he made no advances for a long time, but suddenly he made pass after pass and she dropped him. Then she began seeing another engineering student, but he demanded immediate sex. Although her sexual standards had changed to conform to the Berkeley students' more relaxed attitudes, she was still a virgin. So that relationship was abandoned. She and Steve continued to correspond regularly, until he announced he was coming home on leave.

The occasion was not joyful: Steve had been notified that his mother had cancer and was probably dying. But Steve and Priscilla intended to spend a week together before he returned to South Carolina. She wondered how it would feel to be with him again. She had planned a lot of things for them to do.

"Pris!" He was flying across the grass to meet her, arms

wide, an enormous grin splitting his wide face. They hugged and patted each other, both talking at once.

"I wasn't sure you'd be here," he said, his eyes moist.

"Of course I'd be here, you big dummy!" she said. "Where do you think I'd be?"

"Out having a big ole time with one of your Indian friends," he answered.

"Oh, that's over. You know I wrote you that's over."

"Yeah, but I wasn't sure I believed you, Pris."

Priscilla leaned against him and drew him down for a long kiss. "Now do you believe me?" She offered a coquettish smile.

"Wow! You know it, lady!"

They spent the day touring San Francisco. Priscilla showed him Fisherman's Wharf, and they snapped photographs of each other and laughed and kissed.

"It's like we've never been apart," Steve said. "I was so nervous about this, but it's just beautiful."

"I know," said Priscilla. "I feel like that, too."

That night, Priscilla brought Steve home to her new apartment on Sacramento Street she had recently rented with a Japanese-American friend from graduate school.

They had a spare couch in the living room, but Steve didn't sleep there. Priscilla took him to her room and to her bed.

Sometime later, and before they were married the following June, they discussed their plans for children.

"Let's have lots of kids," Steve said.

"Well, maybe two of our own. And then we could adopt more. Okay?" Priscilla answered.

"Okay. Sounds pretty damn good to me."

3

It was awfully late for Erik and Jason to be up, Steve thought for the tenth time. He wasn't so sure that they should even have brought the boys to the airport, but Pris was set that the whole family should greet Tia when she landed.

They had left hours ago for the San Jose Airport—way too early. He and Priscilla had fought endlessly about what time to leave, what route to take. Would 101 be faster or 17? What should the boys wear? Would it be cold at nine-thirty on a November night? Would Tia even be on the flight from Los Angeles? Technically they should have flown to L.A. to meet the plane from Korea, but by chance a social worker on the Korean flight was continuing on to the Bay Area from Los Angeles and had agreed to bring Tia with her—if she could make the connecting flight.

It was a big if. They had no description of the social worker who would be carrying Tia except that she was blond. To make matters worse, the boys were falling apart from excitement and fatigue. Five-year-old Erik was streaking about the deserted airport, and Jason, just three, was clinging to Steve's leg, weary-eyed and whiny.

Steve shifted in his chair and a big weight of anxiety resting heavily in his stomach moved along with him. Had they done the right thing with this adoption? he wondered. Would he love this child as much as he did his own? How would he really feel about a Korean child in their family? How would the boys react?

He got up and half-ran after Erik, who was just disappearing from sight at the far end of the terminal. That boy was a handful sometimes, Steve thought. They had nicknamed him Bam-Bam after the destructive little kid in *The Flintstones*. He'd been rambunctious from the beginning, deciding to sail into life on his own timetable almost a month early—February 6, 1970. They had taken LaMaze classes and were prepared for natural childbirth, but the delivery was hard, and they had to pull Erik out with forceps. He had the ugliest forceps marks Steve had ever seen, and his skin was yellow, but to Steve he was beautiful. The jaundice had worsened, though, and they had taken Erik back to the hospital after a few days at home for a complete blood transfusion.

Erik recovered but life around him was never easy; he found all kinds of trouble. He had his skull X-rayed twice already—once after he had been thrown to the floor in the truck—stitches a couple of times, both a sprained and a fractured foot and numerous treatments for his lazy eye. Jason had pulled down his share of problems, too, Steve realized. A year ago he had practically drowned at Crazy Horse campground and Steve had gone down on hands and knees to give him mouth-to-mouth resuscitation.

The seven and a half years since their marriage had not rolled smoothly. First Steve's mother had died; then a year later they discovered his father had cancer, too, and in July 1969, he had followed his wife to the grave. It had torn Steve apart.

The next year had worn particularly hard. The problems resulted from a combination of factors, Steve knew. Priscilla was in early pregnancy with Erik and was experiencing severe morning sickness and back pain. After Steve took a job as a guard at San Quentin, everything slid solidly downhill. Steve had been casting around for a career. Correctional work appealed to him, as did the thought of an army career, but Priscilla was against the service. He tried part-time work as a commodities broker and attended school at a junior college while Priscilla finished her last year of graduate school, but he hadn't hit on anything he wanted to do. Priscilla pressed him to return to school full time, but her pregnancy put an end to that possibility because the Marin County Department of Social Services mandated a leave seven months into pregnancy.

The pressures of San Quentin almost brought their marriage to a halt. Steve could look at that now with a measure of objectivity, but at that time he had lived daily with controlled fear. The inmates were as scared as he was; it didn't take long to figure that out. In that place, fear was the governing factor. The Chicanos and the whites played off against each other, with the blacks holding the balance of power, and everybody looked sideways at everybody else. He had had to deal with them on their own level, and he had been good at defusing the situation when it threatened to get hot.

At home, though, he hadn't been as successful. He and Priscilla spent the year screaming at each other. She wanted him to assume control of his life while he could hardly control what was happening at work. And he knew he relied on her for a lot; the army had made him peculiarly dependent, and with his parents both gone, he'd leaned hard on her.

They'd had some real high-level hassles, he remembered. One time Priscilla had been worried enough about the possible effects of all this emotional stress on the baby she was carrying that she'd even gone down to Kaiser to talk to a psychologist about it.

But one day he had been talking to a friend at work who had put it all in perspective for Steve.

"Do you love her?" he asked.

"Yes."

"Then get your head out of your ass and do something about it!"

Steve had gone home, and he and Priscilla had sat on the couch and talked and cried, and from that point on they'd both known they were working toward building something instead of fighting each other every damn step of the way.

Things had picked up from that point, Steve thought as he grabbed at and caught Erik's waving shirttail. He latched onto the boy's hand and walked him firmly back down to the gate where Tia's plane was due to land.

He had left San Quentin on schedule the summer of 1970, to attend school full time at Sonoma State. Priscilla had really encouraged him, insisting that he was smart, that he just had to learn how to study. He had started out on probation because of his poor record, but he had done well, and after a year and a half of intensive study he had earned a B.A. in Sociology. By then Priscilla was working full time in the Homefinders unit at Marin County's Health and Human Services, and she was pregnant again.

The second pregnancy had been difficult from the beginning, and by the end Priscilla's high blood pressure and signs of toxemia landed her in the hospital for several weeks of complete bed rest. The doctor finally induced delivery three weeks early. Steve began working for the state Department of Vocational Rehabilitation in Oakland doing disability evaluations. It wasn't what he wanted—he hoped to work at Marin County juvenile hall, but jobs were tight and he took what he could. But his main satisfaction was his family. He wasn't embarrassed at how important his boys were to him. He always cared for them as much as Priscilla. To him, childcare was a fifty-fifty proposition—he and Pris had no argument there. He couldn't understand families where the women did all the work in the home and the father sat with his feet propped up and a beer in his hand. Steve even participated at Erik's nursery school. His kids were an extension of himself, he felt, and he owed it to them to give them what they needed. And that came down to changing their diapers and fixing them meals—doing whatever was necessary.

Then in 1974, a job opened up in juvenile hall and Steve grabbed it. He had been there a year and a half now, and found it incredibly exciting. He was working in an open program for young boys—there were no locks on the doors—and he was really making some progress toward rehabilitating these kids.

He could see the effect. He was good at counseling. The kids trusted him and he felt he was particularly strong at evaluating whether he was dealing with retardation, or a learning disability, or delinquency, or a neurological problem, or a problem with diet.

Steve's home life was stable, too. Later he would look back at this period as one of his happiest. They had started talking about adoption right after Priscilla's hysterectomy in January of last year. She had never fully recovered from childbirth with Jason, never stopped bleeding; it had turned her into a wreck, so she had needed the surgery. There had been a few complications but she'd come out of there a new woman, Steve had bragged to everyone, smirking.

They decided to try for a Vietnamese baby. For one thing, there had been tremendous coverage on TV about the mixed-race children of American GIs whom nobody wanted, and also it was increasingly difficult to adopt white American infants. It turned out they had both been considering a Vietnamese child but neither one had said anything to the other. Priscilla thought he wouldn't accept a racially mixed child, she told him—but he didn't care at all. "A child is a child," he said.

So Priscilla wrote letters to various agencies, and after she was released from the hospital, she attended a meeting of prospective parents at Catholic Social Service in San Francisco. Then they sent in an application asking for a girl any age up to Erik's age. It was important not to get one older than Erik, Priscilla said, to avoid giving the oldest child's place to a newcomer in the family. After the home study—including interviews and physicals—was completed, the social worker sent their application to Vietnam to be matched with a child. That was in the fall of 1974. Then they waited.

In January of 1975, Priscilla returned to work, and in April the Vietnamese babylift into Travis Air Force Base began. Priscilla volunteered to help process the children as they landed, ferrying a number of them into San Francisco in the middle of the night. She met the director of the New York agency there and asked whether all the children had been assigned to adoptive parents. Ninety-five percent of them had, it turned out, and soon they learned they weren't going to get one of the others.

They had been terribly disappointed, but then their social worker asked them if they'd be interested in a Korean child, and of course they were. Just a couple of months later—in July

1975—they had received a preliminary report on a Korean child. Surprisingly it was an infant.

Pris was so goddamned excited; Steve would never forget her reaction. She had called him at work, screaming and crying that the social worker had a two-month-old baby girl for them and that they needed to drive to the city, see her picture and the report on her, and decide whether they wanted to keep her.

Priscilla couldn't wait another minute. She took the afternoon off—Steve was just finishing for the day—so they could both go over there at once. They had wanted that little girl immediately. No question about that, Steve remembered. The social worker handed them some forms to fill out, immigration questionnaires, papers to be notarized, other forms for the bank to process. They completed all the paperwork the next day—Pris rushing them around like there was no tomorrow. They even had to be fingerprinted at the sheriff's department at the Marin County Civic Center where Pris worked. She was talking a mile a minute about working out her schedule so she could get time off when the baby came.

The wait had been the hardest. Priscilla spent the time collecting new baby things and fixing up Tia's room—right next to theirs. She bought a baby book especially for adopted children—she was religious about that sort of thing: Erik and Jason's baby books were all filled in to the last detail. Then they were given an arrival date, but it was canceled and the waiting began again.

Steve peered up into the overcast night and thought he saw the red and green wing lights flashing not too far above. He watched as the plane circled and landed. The plane sported a big painted smile and Steve grinned back suddenly in response.

Beside him the boys wriggled and punched at one another. Priscilla's face tightened as she searched the incoming passengers. Steve felt his heart jerking in his chest.

"There!" said Priscilla suddenly. She pointed.

"No, that child is too old," said Steve, studying the child she had indicated.

"You're right. There's a blond lady—but I don't see a baby. Where's the baby?"

"Which one?"

"That one! The blond lady—the one with the orange comforter over her arm. See, she's looking around."

Priscilla rushed up to her, and in a minute was unwrapping the comforter the woman carried.

"Oh, Steve, look! She's so tiny. She's so beautiful."

They crowded around, and Steve looked down at the tiny pale face of the six-month-old child. He felt the breath leave him in a rush. It was just like when Erik and Jason had been born. It took your damned breath away. She looked up at him with big black eyes and he thought he would cry. Priscilla was already crying, and laughing, the baby jiggling in her arms.

Together they brought Tia to the airport nursery and changed her. She had a terrible rash.

"I think it's more than a diaper rash," Priscilla said. "Look, she even has blisters on her elbow—and there's a couple on her thumb."

"What have we got to feed her?" asked Steve. The blond woman had given them a bottle and some formula in a Korean can but they couldn't read the directions.

"Oh, I bought some baby formula. Dr. Shimoda told me what to get. Don't worry, she'll be all right. Won't you, little Tia?" She bent over, smiling into the little face and received an answering smile.

"Look, Steve, she smiled at me! Oh, look, Jason—see how tiny she is, Erik?"

Steve watched as his family closed around Tia. His eyes were full and he raised a hand to them. His family was complete.

4

"Dearly beloved, baptism is the outward and visible sign of an inward and spiritual grace, through which grace we become partakers of life eternal and heirs to God's righteousness. Those receiving the sacrament are thereby marked as Christian Disciples and initiated into Christ's holy Church.

"Our Lord has expressly given to the little children a place among the people of God, which privilege must not be denied them. Remember how Jesus said, 'Let the children come to me. Do not forbid them, for to such belong the kingdom of God.'

"Beloved, do you in presenting this child for baptism confess your faith in our Lord and Savior Jesus Christ?"

"We do."

"Do you accept as your duty and privilege to live before this child lives that become the Gospel, to exercise all godly care that she be brought up in the Christian faith, that she learn to give attendance upon the private and the public worship of God, that she be taught the Holy Scriptures?"

"We do."

"Will you endeavor to keep this child under the ministry and guidance of the Church until she by the power of God shall accept for herself the gift of salvation and be confirmed as a full and responsible member of Christ's holy Church?"

"We will."

"What name shall be given to this child?"

"Tia Michelle Phillips."

"Tia Michelle Phillips, I baptize you in the name of the Father, the Son, and of the Holy Spirit." Reverend Jim Hutchison dipped his finger into the holy water and made the mark of the cross on the baby's forehead, and she looked up at him peacefully.

Then the thirty-seven-year-old minister with the map-of-Ireland face and the vivid blue, wide-set eyes, returned the baby to Priscilla's arms, turned toward the congregation, and commended Tia to its care. The ninety-minute Methodist service ended with the Benediction, and at once the congregation separated into little clumps to talk and drink coffee. One large clump surrounded the Phillips family to congratulate them and see the baby.

Many of the parishioners came up to Jim as he walked about outside the church during the little social time he had established after Sunday worship.

"Lovely service, Jim."

"Thank you, Marj. How are the kids? Are the girls watching the little ones?" He gestured across the way at the room where day care was provided for the children of the congregation who were too young to attend the service.

"Yes," she answered. They chatted for a minute. Marj Dunlavy was one of Jim's favorite parishioners—she knew everyone and was comfortable and a little motherly, and Jim liked that. Women had always tended to see him as a little lost boy, and he supposed he had always been looking for a mother. He had lost his when he was only five years old, back when his father and eight older brothers and sisters still lived in Bray, near Dublin.

The Hutchisons had moved shortly after her death to Hillsborough, in County Down, Northern Ireland, where his father took up the produce business in nearby Belfast. His father was a rigid man with a rigid set of beliefs and an iron hand, and he hadn't had much time for mothering Jim.

Jim moved from group to group, smiling, greeting, hearing the latest gossip. What different sorts of people these Marin County people were from the kind he had grown up with, he thought. Not that his family hadn't achieved wealth and standing. But growing up in Ireland was a different type of experience because being Irish was different. It was because he was a proper Irish lad, with a typical Celtic wanderlust and spirit of adventure, and because nothing held him closely to home that at the age of fifteen he had done a properly Irish thing and run away.

He had gone to Liverpool, crossing at night on a terrible old ship, he remembered; a week later it had sunk. He often used that story when he counseled runaways. "If you're going to run away, don't put it off for a week!" he'd joke gently.

He had met another runaway on the ship, who had taken Jim with him to some friends he knew in Liverpool, and they had stayed awhile and then gone down to London and become regular Edwardian teddy boys, living in Chelsea and bumming about. In those days one could sleep all night in Hyde Park and nobody would notice. But he had managed to live in that fashion for quite some time, an outsider. And during all that time, he never gave a thought to religion.

Then one day in 1957, after nearly five years spent aimlessly on the London streets, a woman came up to him as he stood at the window of Selfridge's Department Store and took him home with her. Jim never knew why she did it. Ethel Allingham was a devout Baptist, though, and somehow she decided to save this nineteen-year-old scruffy Irish boy. She kept him with her for the next four years—a mother to him, never forcing her religious beliefs on him, but quietly introducing him to a field he found that interested him. He became a nurse.

Jim made his way to the little group surrounding the Phillipses. His pearl-gray robe and black stole with its white pennant-and-cross insignia of the Methodist Church flowed loose behind him. The robe was particularly beautiful, more decorative than most, but Jim found no harm in that. It was not the outer trappings that made the man, of course, but lovely things had their place in life. He enjoyed his own extensive collection of Waterford crystal and the Royal Doulton figurines that he displayed at the parsonage—many pieces in the collections were gifts from friends or members of the congregation. People had always liked to bring him things; they knew the pleasure he took in their gifts.

When he had arrived at Aldersgate in 1972, there had been a membership of perhaps thirty families. It was a church in trouble, the bishop had told him, and because Jim had successfully increased church membership in other parishes—a green-thumb pastor he liked to think of it—they'd sent him here to Terra Linda from a congregation in central California. He had spent some money to put in a new sound system, and was working to have a sanctuary—which he thought was very important—and in the past three years he had been able to raise the membership to over three hundred. Now he and the board were trying to conclude an arrangement with Kaiser Hospital, to finance the construction of a new church up on the hill in exchange for the deed to the building the church was currently using. Then they could have their sanctuary and a new church as well.

Jim stopped by the Phillipses.

"Oh, Jim, can we take a picture of you with Tia—for her baby book?" asked Priscilla.

"Of course, Priscilla." He posed, smiling. "How is she doing, then?" he asked.

"Oh, fine. She's had a continuous bout of ear infections, just like Jason had when he was young, and then an abscess on her thigh. But everything's all cleared up—the doctor gave her a clean bill of health on Friday," said Priscilla.

"She does seem such a serene child, doesn't she?"

"She is." Priscilla laughed. "Such a difference from the boys! She's just a little lady."

"And do the boys like her? How are they adjusting to a little sister?" Jim worried about this sometimes because he thought the Phillips boys were terribly rough, and that Priscilla and Steve encouraged this. In fact when Priscilla had asked him to write a preadoption reference to Catholic Social Service, he had hesitated to recommend the family for placement of a little girl. After some soul-searching, he had finally written in the reference that he didn't feel the family was ready for a baby girl—that the boys were still very wild—but that perhaps later things would be calmer around the home. It was the only time he had ever written a negative reference, but it had not been strongly negative, and apparently the adoption agency had decided that the home life was satisfactory because the adoption had gone forward.

"Oh, the boys just love Tia. She's only been here six weeks, but she is a real member of the family already," Priscilla said.

"I'm glad, Priscilla." He patted the little child, smiled at Steve, and moved on. Tia was a pretty girl, he thought, very fragile looking with pale skin and those enormous dark eyes. Priscilla had confided in Jim one of the first times he had stopped to see the baby that she believed Tia might be part Caucasian.

"Maybe that's why her mother abandoned her," she had said. "You know, in Korea, mixed-blood babies are just the worst kind of outcasts. I figured it out, and it would just work mathematically: Tia's mother might have been the daughter of an American GI stationed in Korea during the war. And that would make Tia one-quarter American!"

Perhaps it was true, Jim thought. The idea seemed to please Priscilla. Steve would probably like the possibility that Tia had white blood. Secretly Jim had always been a bit surprised that Steve had agreed to this adoption. He was basically a redneck, Jim thought, with all the accompanying racial prejudices. But Priscilla had been so strong about wanting a little girl, and Steve would come around to whatever she wanted. That seemed to be the pattern in the family.

Those two had an immature sort of relationship—Jim had noticed it the very first time he had met the Phillipses, back in July of 1972, when he had first been assigned to Aldersgate. The Phillipses were already church members, and one of the first things Jim had done upon becoming the new pastor was to visit with the members in their homes. Priscilla and Steve were living on Los Gamos Road in a three-bedroom town house then. Priscilla had seemed much the brighter of the two, the more dominant, Jim remembered. On the other hand, Steve appeared more religious. Both had already been quite active in the church. Priscilla served on the Social Concerns Committee and was a member of the executive board of the United Methodist Women. Steve talked about joining the church board of trustees, which he had later done.

But what Jim most particularly noticed about Steve and

Priscilla was their constant competition for his attention. Steve would say something and Priscilla would jump right into the conversation and argue against him. It sometimes seemed that Steve compensated for her dominance with his wild talking. If something crossed his path, he was always going to blow it up or blast it. Then Priscilla would come in and try to draw attention back to herself. Often she'd tell a story about Erik's or Jason's latest fearless exploit or horrible accident. It seemed as though something was continually happening to her boys— and she'd always let the church know. Either she'd stand during the service to report the incident or she'd call in and ask for prayers or concern. When anything was called in, it was announced from the pulpit or called around to the congregation.

And of course Jim was especially interested in the accidents or medical problems of his parishioners because of his own medical background, which was quite extensive. He had trained in London and Liverpool, working for several years on the neurological unit at the Edinburgh Royal Infirmary after earning his R.N. By then he had had his conversion.

Jim eased himself back through the crowd in front of the low rectangular Eichler-built church and entered the building. It was not an attractive church. Originally it had been a recreation center, and it still resembled one, with the two long sides of the rectangular building constructed entirely of sliding glass, and nearly all the rest of the exterior done out in drab gray cinder block. The interior floor was a honeycomb of speckled gray-on-white linoleum squares found in many institutional buildings. The seats were the cheap metal sort— there were no pews. The altar was the nicest part. There were brass candlesticks and vases of flowers, and both his own chair and the one for the lay reader were lovely polished mahogany. But the large wooden cross on the wall could not disguise the cinder block behind it.

Off to the left of the altar was his own office. There were files spread out on his desk, and several tapes from last month's services—which he kept for the shut-ins who could not attend—piled loosely on one corner. He took off his robe and stole and carefully hung them up.

He had some counseling to do later—a young couple whose marriage was in trouble. He had had firsthand experience with that problem, as his own marriage had ended seven years before in annulment. The Church of England, of course, did not recognize divorce, so an annulment was necessary. But he strongly believed that his painful experience had made him a better minister and a better counselor. As he said, it was like the cross becoming the resurrection: you utilize the very thing that is painful and difficult. He had majored in Pastoral Psychology at the Pacific School of Religion in Berkeley, and he enjoyed counseling. He felt it was an essential part of his purpose.

Right now he had Christmas to think about, only four days away. The church would be crowded, the children jittery with excitement as they gathered for the service. He smiled at the image. In a few years little Tia would be among them. He liked to think of the children he baptized taking their places in the Christian community, being confirmed, and then finally becoming members themselves someday. He doubted he would be around even to confirm Tia, as it was unusual for a Methodist minister to remain above five years with any one congregation. Still, he had started her on her way in her Christian life. She would be all right.

5

Evelyn Callas finished her examination of the ten-month-old Asian infant. Gross examination revealed a normally developing, well-nourished female child. Her rectal temperature of 99.6 was normal. Evelyn turned to the mother.

"Now, Mrs. Phillips, Dr. Shimoda called me a few minutes ago and gave me a brief history on Tia. Can you tell me what prompted you to bring her into E.R. tonight?"

"Well, she's been sick really ever since we got her from Korea four months ago. She's had recurrent otitis media and urinary tract infections, and a persistent rash. Once she had an abscess on her thigh. She's been on antibiotics practically the whole time, and she had some diarrhea from that. She has a urinary tract infection right now, and Sara has been treating her with different types of antibiotics—Ampicillin and Gantrisin and Furadantin. And she also still has an ear infection."

"And what happened today?"

"Oh, I brought her into the clinic for her regular follow-up appointment. I had told Sara the last time we saw her about

Tia's violent vomiting and diarrhea. Then today I told her that Tia's been vomiting the whole week. Yesterday she had some fever, and she's been real cranky—not like herself all this past week. Today she refused her lunch and dinner and she wouldn't take her bottle. And then at five o'clock she started crying loudly, and when I went in to her she stopped crying all of a sudden and then kind of stared into space."

"Did she roll her eyes up? Did she change her position at all?"

"No. She didn't jerk or anything. She just looked blank. But then about a half an hour later she did it again."

"What happened?"

"Well, she just stopped crying all of a sudden, like before, and looked off into space."

"Was she pale or flushed?"

"Kind of flushed. The first time she was pale."

"And then what happened?" asked Evelyn.

"Well, she seemed pretty much okay until about nine-thirty tonight. Tia has a jump chair and I'd put it in the kitchen and she was holding her bottle, and suddenly she fell back and dropped the bottle. I picked her up and she seemed all right. But then she did it again. So I immediately called Sara—Dr. Shimoda—at home, and she said it sounds like a seizure and to bring her in."

"How long did this last staring episode last?"

"Oh, about a minute—maybe half a minute."

"Did she jerk or roll up her eyes? Did she seem to be holding her breath?"

"No. It was exactly like before—sort of staring into space. But her arms did fall away from her sides when she dropped her bottle."

Evelyn made some notes in the baby's chart. Then she glanced back through the outpatient history, quickly scanning the past entries. This child had a very thick chart considering she had only been a patient since November, she thought. Here it was the second of March, and Tia had already been into the clinic—Evelyn counted quickly—twenty-five times. Persistent low-grade infections—mostly ears and urinary tract—both of which could prove difficult to cure. Well, maybe they could sneak in a bilateral myringotomy while she was here to drain some of the fluid that was causing the otitis media. They'd have to admit her for the seizure activity, she decided. Sara wanted her admitted and Evelyn agreed. The baby would need both an ENT and neurology consult.

"Mrs. Phillips, I think we'd better admit Tia for observation," Evelyn said.

"Yes. Sara indicated that you'd probably want to do that."

"We'll have the pediatric neurologist, Dr. Leider, check on the seizure activity. He roves around the different Kaiser facilities and is here on Thursdays. And we'll have a specialist from Ear, Nose, and Throat talk with you. He may want to recommend a myringotomy and PE tubes, a very minor surgical procedure where tiny plastic tubes are inserted through the eardrums to drain off the fluid back there and keep the canals open so infections won't keep developing. It's nothing to worry about at all. We'll try to get all this straightened out at one time and it shouldn't take too long."

"Will I be able to stay with her?"

"We do encourage the parents to stay with the children as much as possible. And if there's room up there on the ward, you can sleep over. I think we're pretty crowded up there tonight. But we do like to encourage the parents to help with as much care as they feel comfortable with. It seems to make it much easier on the kids."

"Yes, I know. I'm a social worker, and I know about what happens to institutionalized children. You do think Tia will be all right?"

"I certainly hope so. There's no reason to be alarmed yet, Mrs. Phillips. Tia really looks quite well. Now, you'll need to take this to the admissions office. Then we'll get Tia squared away in a bed on the pediatrics ward."

Evelyn quickly arranged for the admission of Tia Phillips. She seemed a sweet child, she thought. Possible encephalitis of course. Leider would want to do a lumbar puncture. And the mother was a sensible sort. She had given a very clear history. It made everything much easier when the parents were clear on what had happened and could describe it accurately. In Pediatrics, especially, you had to rely so much on what the parents told you. It certainly helped if they knew what they were talking about, and this mother seemed sharp.

Evelyn could go home now. She was on call the rest of the night but she didn't have to stay at the hospital: they would phone her if they needed her.

Before she left, she took the elevator upstairs for a final check on Tia Phillips. Because the ward was so crowded, the nurses had put her crib in the hall, but they'd find her a room tomorrow. Evelyn could see that her patient was awake and taking her bottle, so she didn't go over. The parents were there with her—Mrs. Phillips and a big bulky man with her who must be the father. Evelyn waved at the nurse and then stepped back into the elevator. The baby's case did not seem serious, Evelyn thought. It was likely that Tia Phillips's hospital stay would be a short one.

6

Priscilla smoothed Tia's thin black hair one more time and arranged her new pink and white party dress for the picture. Then she took some of the toys Tia had received for her birthday—the shape sorter and the Fisher-Price floating family and some others—and placed them around Tia's feet.

"Smile, Tia!" And she did, grinning her open-mouthed little smile as the picture was snapped. Priscilla considered this a major occasion, and she had invited Tia's social worker from Catholic Social Service, all the other patients on the ward, the doctors and the nurses, and of course Steve and Erik and Jason and her own mother. Tia was having a good day, showing off for everybody, smiling and waving and saying hi, Priscilla noted proudly. Everybody commented on what a cute child Tia was, how normal she acted. "It's a real tribute to you, Priscilla," somebody said. And that was true, she felt, because in spite of everything, Tia *was* a normal child; she was a happy child, even after two straight months of hospitalizations—first in Kaiser-San Rafael, then here in Kaiser-San Francisco, then back to San Rafael, now here again.

Dr. Applebaum came up to Priscilla, smiling widely under his large black mustache. She liked Mike. He was young and cheerful and very smart, and he explained things to her.

"Oh, Dr. Applebaum, doesn't she look cute?"

"She sure does. One year old today! How's the party been going?"

"Just fine. There's her cake over there. Have you had a piece yet?"

"No, but I'll make it over there in a minute."

"I sure wish Tia could have a little taste—it's *her* birthday, after all!" said Priscilla wistfully. It was impossible, of course, she knew that. Tia hadn't had anything by mouth since the middle of April and it was already May seventh.

"She'll just have to save it all up for her second birthday!" Dr. Applebaum said, smiling at her. "We'll get her on solids one of these days, Mrs. Phillips, you'll see."

"Well, I sure hope so, Dr. Applebaum. Sometimes I think she'll never eat again, never get out of the hospital." Tears welled up and threatened to spill. "You know in the beginning it all just seemed like nothing—like just a matter of a few days. And she hasn't been home since."

"Yes, but at the beginning Dr. Shimoda thought she was dealing with a neurological problem, and with persistent urinary tract and ear infections, as I remember."

"That's right. How I wish it were that simple," said Priscilla, her hand brushing at the tears, remembering. Tia's first bad stooling and vomiting episode hadn't begun till March seventh, five days after Tia's admission by Dr. Callas.

Since her arrival from Korea, Tia's stools had normally been loose, but nothing like on that occasion. The fluid had just poured out of her. She had been so lethargic that Priscilla felt as though she were holding a rag doll. Sara diagnosed viral gastroenteritis. She ordered a set of serum electrolytes, and the results came back high in sodium.

"That's a direct result of the diarrhea," Sara explained. "Water is drawing sodium out of the cells as it passes through the digestive tract, causing the concentration of sodium in the cells to rise. Diarrhea typically causes electrolyte imbalances," she said. "We have to be very careful about replacing not only all the fluid Tia is losing in her diarrhea, but also the proper amounts of each electrolyte—the sodium, potassium, and chloride—because diarrhea and vomiting can lead to dehydration; that can cause severe problems in children."

The next day they started the first IV on Tia. She was losing too much fluid through the diarrhea to be replaced orally. At that time Priscilla began to keep notes on Tia's treatment—something she was subsequently to regret. By then Priscilla was familiar with the medical terminology, and she was given access to Tia's chart whenever she wanted. She had a vague idea after awhile—and she always maintained that Debby Roof and some of the other nurses had suggested it—of writing up Tia's story for a magazine. In any case, she didn't want to forget all the treatment. By then there had been a considerable amount.

Her own life was in a shambles. Gradually she realized that she was simply going to have to reorganize things, that Tia was not coming home. She would have to make the time to be with Tia. She was working three-quarters time now, but the hours were flexible. Sometimes she cheated a little when reporting her hours. It was the only way she could manage. On March twelfth—ten days after Tia's admission—Priscilla wrote in her journal:

> Friday—Neutramagen [sic], rice cereal in P.M., to be discharged on Saturday. Then late P.M. diarrhea and vomiting again, screaming, cramping, fever of 102.2, Dr. Arnhold on, did blood culture, etc.

Saturday brought deterioration, not discharge. Priscilla noted:

> Fever of 103.4, discharge delayed until Sunday. Seemed better, then early P.M. vomiting began, then severe diarrhea—by 5:00 P.M. had put out over 1,000 cc stool plus continued vomiting. Dr. Carte started IV. Weight down to 6.6 kg, lethargic, pale.

On Sunday:

> Called Sara at home re my concerns—she's to talk to Dr. M. Applebaum in S.F. on Monday.

Sara consulted Dr. Applebaum on March fifteenth. He agreed with Sara that the most probable cause of Tia's diarrhea was irritation of the intestinal lining.

"Continue the IV," he recommended. "Try a little more sugar in the solution and increase the rate. Her nutritional status is marginal. I know you've checked for reducing substances, but better do it again. If she's not absorbing even simple sugars, that could be the problem. We may have to go to peripheral hyperalimentation."

"What's that?" Priscilla asked.

"Well, the only way we can give Tia's bowel enough time to heal is to prevent it from working. So we don't feed it. Now obviously the body needs food and fluid and that's the purpose of the IV. But the problem with maintaining a child on IV over long periods of time is that the sugar in the standard IV solution does not provide protein. And you need protein to build tissues. Now there are solutions that exist which do provide not only sugar but amino acids—or protein—and fats. And when we talk about hyperalimentation, we mean providing enough nutrition by vein—in predigested solution form— for a child to grow on. Tia needs that. Peripheral simply means by way of the peripheral veins—the ones that run around the outside, or periphery, of the body. Basically, they're the ones you can see. And the advantage of all this is that we can bypass the digestive tract entirely by using the IV, and that gives the bowel time to rest from its normal digestive function and repair itself."

"I see," said Priscilla. Hyperalimentation was then initiated. Sometimes they permitted Tia a little diluted formula, too, because they were having trouble locating peripheral veins, and she was very hungry. But every time they fed her, it seemed her diarrhea started again.

Then on March twenty-second, twenty days after her admission, Tia had her first cut-down, in her right ankle. But within a few days the site became infected and the cut-down had to be removed. Sara ordered penicillin and a new cut-down in the other leg, and after another consultation with Dr. Applebaum, made another decision.

"We're going to make Tia NPO for ten days," Sara said.

"My God, that seems so long! Why?" asked Priscilla.

"The problem may be that her bowel still hasn't had enough time to heal. If she improves we can give her feedings through an NG, drop by drop."

"Why not a bottle?"

"Because with a bottle you get what we call a bolus—or bulk—landing all at one time in the stomach, and it appears that Tia's digestive tract can't handle that. So we'll keep her going on the NG and IV."

"I understand," Priscilla said.

Dr. Applebaum returned for another consultation. He told Priscilla that there were further tests to be done. But none showed anything, and Tia still remained sick.

On March thirtieth, Sara found a blood clot at the site of Tia's second cut-down, mandating its removal. Only one site remained. They tried a scalp vein, but the needle infiltrated, pushing through the wall of the vein and pouring the fluid into the space outside the vein where it was ineffective.

"We're going to transfer her to San Francisco," Sara told

Priscilla on April first. "Her situation has become a little precarious and she needs a full-time house staff. We can't provide that here. She will go in an ambulance—you can ride with her. It will be all right. Now don't cry—"

But Priscilla burst into tears. Later she wrote in her journal:

Thursday—NPO—hyperal. Intralipids. Left leg began showing signs of vein irritation—Dr. Arnhold decided cut-down must come out. Sara over in P.M. (day off), ordered move to city because only one vein in hand left— Ambulance to city 4 P.M.—Dr. Diamond started IV. Very upsetting move.

In San Francisco, Tia improved almost immediately. But for Priscilla it was a difficult time. She didn't know anyone but Dr. Applebaum, and he wasn't around much. The San Francisco pediatric ward was entirely different—much noisier and busier than she was used to. It was the first time Tia had been treated by interns and residents. Everything was done differently; even the machines were unfamiliar. The hospital was old and big and unfriendly. It needed paint. Parking was impossible. The hospital was thirty miles from Terra Linda, and Priscilla could not dash home as she was used to. The pace at Kaiser-San Francisco was so accelerated that no one stopped to talk with Priscilla. She was miserable. But after a week's stay in San Francisco, Tia was much improved.

On Wednesday, April seventh, Priscilla jotted down in her notebook:

NG feedings—full strength Vivonex and proper amount—I was upset and requested move to San Rafael—agreed to return her on 4/8.

But after the transfer, the diarrhea resumed almost immediately. Two years later many people looked at this information and wondered about it. It would seem damning that Priscilla's unhappiness in San Francisco coincided with Tia's improvement and that her transfer back to familiar territory was followed immediately by recurring symptoms. Tia had a bad episode on April tenth in which she lost two and a half pounds, plunging her weight to thirteen and a half pounds. Her IV infiltrated again. Her acetone level soared.

"What does that mean?" Priscilla asked Sara.

"It means she's not getting enough nutrition—even with the hyperalimentation."

"You mean she's starving?"

Sara hesitated. "Yes," she said.

"Oh God." Priscilla reached for Tia. "Please, God. Why are you doing this to her?"

"We'll find it, Priscilla," Sara said, putting a hand on Tia's head.

On Easter Sunday Tia reached a low point. Priscilla wanted to attend church. Since Tia's hospitalization she had not been once. She arranged with Steve to sit with Tia while she took the boys and her mother, who was staying with them, to Aldersgate. After the service, half the congregation crowded around to ask after Tia. Following the service, Priscilla, her mother, and the boys walked up the hill with a basket of toys.

"How is she?" she asked Steve.

"Dr. Arnhold says she's a little better. He got all excited because she cried some real tears. It means she's not too dehydrated," he explained to Priscilla's mother. "She's still malnourished, though."

Priscilla nodded. Tia lay very still in her bed, just following them with her eyes. She didn't lift a hand to the toys the boys put on her bed.

"Here, Tia. Why don't you try to sit up? See the toys we brought? Here's an Easter basket." She tried to help Tia to sit but Tia slumped back as soon as Priscilla let go.

Priscilla and Steve exchanged glances. Marietta bent over the crib and took Tia's limp hands. Tia smiled faintly at her grandmother.

The next day, Priscilla talked about Tia's deterioration with Sara. Sara had been away on a week's vacation and Dr. Arnhold had been covering. When she saw Sara coming onto the ward, Priscilla rushed up to her, crying.

"Oh, Sara—it's been so bad. The IV's infiltrated again. She's so lethargic, and this morning she's cramping and screaming."

"Take it easy, Priscilla. I'm going to talk to Dr. Applebaum again. Give me a chance to examine her and check her chart."

At noon, Sara returned to the ward and found Priscilla.

"We're going to transfer Tia back to San Francisco," she said. "She will need to be there at least three weeks. Dr. Applebaum wants to try central venous hyperalimentation. That's the same as peripheral alimentation except that a catheter is inserted surgically into a central vein that leads directly to the heart."

"Oh, Sara—"

"I know it sounds scary, but though it's a little delicate, it's really quite a minor procedure. And then we won't have to worry any more about cut-downs getting infected or IV's infiltrating. We'll always have a vein directly accessible and open."

"Well, why didn't we do it before?"

"Because it carries some risks. For one thing it has to be carefully monitored all the time. There is always the danger of infection, and because you're dealing with a vein leading directly to the heart, that's more of a problem when infection occurs. And that's why it has to be done in the city. We simply don't have the staff here to watch Tia as closely as she has to be watched. The point is that her nutrition is so marginal now, it's become essential to get those calories in and circulating. And her peripheral veins are just too depleted. So we don't have a choice anymore. I know how much you hate it over there, but we're just going to have to do it."

Priscilla wrote:

Monday. Sara back. IV infiltrated so started Pedialyte in NG tube slowly. Violent cramping, screaming, so sedatives given—slept—then at noon Sara told me about transfer to city—3 weeks at least—central venous line, hyperalimentation, etc. Plans to be firmed up this P.M. as to exact time of transfer. At 4:00 P.M. diarrhea started again so Sara started IV and stopped NG feeding. Lost 10% of body weight—down to 5.84 kg and looked horrible—very upset—Sara came over later in P.M. (11:00) to check her out.

Tia was transferred and scheduled for surgical placement of the central venous line the next day. After the surgery, Tia was returned, semiconscious, to her room. She had dressings on her neck and also on her chest covering the site where the plastic line emerged from her heart. Priscilla picked Tia up and lay back in the recliner holding the baby, dressed only in a diaper, on her lap.

When he next saw her, Dr. Applebaum asked Priscilla what had happened. He had never heard of an eleven-month-old baby pulling out a central venous catheter. There were those who, in light of later events, never believed what she reported.

"I don't know," she said. "I was asleep and so was Tia, and the next thing I knew, she was dangling the tube from her hand, and I could see that the bandage they had taped over the chest wound was pulled loose. I didn't realize at first that she had pulled the whole thing out. The nurses came in and applied pressure. Then the next thing I knew they were saying they were going to have to go through the whole surgery again! I was really kind of embarrassed that it happened while I was holding her!"

On that day, Priscilla left her journal blank.

Two days later, the catheter was replaced. This time they stitched the external portion of the tube to Tia's chest so it couldn't pull loose. Priscilla and the nurses kept Tia fully dressed from then on, with the end of the central venous line threading out through the bottom of her playsuit.

A week after the reinsertion of the central catheter, she began stooling again. Subsequently Dr. Applebaum was to reconsider the opinion he expressed to Priscilla at the time.

"I think this resumption of stooling is confirmation that what Tia has is secretory diarrhea," he said. "Because it's not affected by oral intake. Tia hasn't had any oral intake—nothing has gone through her digestive tract except in tiny drops. I don't think this can be a result of an inflammation of the lining of the small intestine. So at least we're starting to be able to rule things out."

"What exactly is secretory diarrhea?" Priscilla asked.

"It's an illness caused by the secretion of a hormone that increases intestinal motility. We'll be able to test for some of these hormones—some of them are just being discovered and written about now. But first I want to get Tia's nutritional status back to where it belongs."

They were still trying to do that, Priscilla knew. She crossed over to Tia's crib to take off her party dress.

"Your next birthday, you can leave your dress on all day," she said to Tia, working at the buttons of the dress. "And have as much cake and ice cream as you like."

Tia smiled.

7

"Look, mister, you can't camp here. This is all part of Stanford University, and there's no camping allowed anywhere on campus."

Steve pounded a big hand on the steering wheel of the van.

"Damn it, man, I've got a sick little girl in your hospital and my two little sons in the van here and we've come from San Rafael to be with my daughter while she has some surgery. I've been circling around this place for hours! Where the hell can we go?"

The guard shrugged. "Sorry, mister. No camping allowed."

"Well, what about parking? You allow parking here? Or is that off limits, too?"

"You can park. But there're limits. Most of the spaces are for two hours. And you gotta pay. This is a busy hospital, buddy. You allow free parking around here and all the students and visitors and everybody else takes advantage. Then you never have parking for the families."

"Yeah, yeah. Let me through, all right?" Steve pulled the camper into the lot and parked in one of the spaces. He'd deal with the camping problem later, he thought. Right now he had two bored kids to deal with and Pris up there on the pediatric ward with Tia. First things first.

God, he hoped this trip would prove worthwhile, Steve thought as he made his way up the long drive to Stanford Hospital, the boys leaping and running in front of him, just dodging the high arcs of water put out by the sprinklers on the huge lawns.

They had planned to spend four days at Stanford. It was decided that Steve should take the boys to Marine World tomorrow to get them out of everybody's hair while Priscilla stayed with Tia. It gave the whole trip a purpose for the boys, other than just for Tia's surgery. The boys needed some special attention. They hadn't been getting much from Mama, Steve thought. Not since Tia had been hospitalized in March. God, it was hard for him to believe she had been hospitalized four straight months now—half of her life in America. And Pris had been pretty much of a stranger. Their sex life was going down the tubes. Hell, they were both exhausted all the time, even when they did get together.

Steve collared the boys and located the escalator leading up to the pediatric ward. He found Priscilla and she showed the boys the cheery, toy-filled playroom in the center of the ward. The ward was well-designed, with a little outdoor patio, a section with soda machines, and a waiting room with a TV. Erik and Jason would have enough to keep them busy for a while.

"How's Tia doing?" Steve asked.

"Oh, it's a big mess. You know how Sara said we could bring her here ourselves instead of by ambulance only if we agreed not to stop anywhere, so her treatment wouldn't be interrupted or anything?"

"Yeah. So?"

"Well, no one even came in to see her—not for two hours. And they haven't given her anything to eat. And now a doctor finally arrived and looked at her chart and said her case was too complicated and that she shouldn't be in the ward but in a private room. So after all that they're going to move her, and she still hasn't had anything to eat."

"Damn, Pris—you know how these hospitals are. After all your experience, you know how these places operate."

"I know, but this is supposed to be such a great hospital. I expected better," said Priscilla.

Eventually Tia was settled in the ICU baby nursery next to the nurses' station. The nurses could look through a window and keep an eye on Tia and the other child in the room, a drowning victim in a coma. Steve was immediately drawn to Stanford's unique setup for their IV equipment. The IV bags were suspended from the ceiling and attached with little mots and chains. If a solution had to be added to the bag, down it came on its little chain. Otherwise it was out of everybody's way. Neater than hell, he thought. They had hooked Tia up to a pump that forced the formula through her naso-gastric tube. Steve sat and watched it for quite some time. They didn't have anything near as fancy at Kaiser, he thought.

That night they spent in the camper dodging the campus guards. It had been Priscilla's idea to bring the camper down. She did not want to leave Tia alone in a strange hospital, and the long drive to San Rafael ruled out any possibility of commuting. They had thought it would be practical to camp at

Stanford, but it hadn't occurred to either of them that there would be no place to camp. Tomorrow they were going to have to get some kind of parking permit. They'd figure out something, Steve decided.

The next morning they were introduced to Dr. Philip Sunshine. He was a noted pediatric gastroenterologist, Dr. Applebaum had said, and he was to perform Tia's small bowel biopsy.

But Steve found him neither high-powered nor self-important. He was a man in his fifties, balding with a fringe of white hair and smiling brown eyes behind gold-rimmed glasses, and he seemed friendly and down-to-earth. He carefully explained the procedure for the biopsy.

"There's a little knife inside the capsule and a rubber dam that goes across the top," the doctor said. "And what we'll do is apply some suction and pull back on the outside end of the tube, and that pulls some tissue into the cap. Then the suction changes the position of the blade from locked to unlocked, and it cuts off a little bit of tissue."

"Won't that hurt her?" Steve asked.

"No, that part's not painful. The only part that's uncomfortable is passing the tube, but she'll be very sedated. What we do is take her down to X ray and see if we've got the tube in the right place. And then we cut the tissue. And if there's any trouble passing the tube through the stomach sphincter, we have a new drug we can use. But before that, we'll get your permission because it's still technically experimental, though it's nothing to worry about."

"Dr. Applebaum said you'd also check her vasoactive intestinal peptides and look for intestinal parasites," said Priscilla.

"Yes, we'll do a series of tests. We'll measure her immunoglobulins—her antibodies—and do a standard blood count and stool and urine cultures. As you know we're still operating on the theory of mucosal or inner lining damage in the bowel— that's the purpose of the biopsy. But there are other possible diagnoses. I'm sure Dr. Applebaum has explained that to you. And you know I have the greatest respect for Mike Applebaum. I worked with him at UC when he was doing his training. We tried to entice him here as chief resident, but he went and chose UC. You couldn't be in better hands than his. Meanwhile if you have any questions, Dr. Lamb will be here—

and he's a fine doctor, one of the best interns we've got here, so don't hesitate to ask."

"Okay. Thanks, Doctor," said Steve. Then he departed with the boys to explore Marine World-Africa U.S.A.—the large amusement park up the peninsula. Later that day, Dr. Sunshine and Priscilla talked again.

"The nurse says Tia is doing so well, she wants to change her status from intensive care to intermediate intensive care. That way a nurse will not have to remain with her all the time. I'll see you tomorrow morning for the biopsy. She really looks remarkably well considering all she's been through."

"Well, you haven't seen her at her worst, Dr. Sunshine," Priscilla said. "She really does get sick. She'll be well like this and then suddenly—she's very ill."

Dr. Sunshine shook his head. He thought she sounded almost—offended. "I hope the biopsy will tell us what is wrong then," he said. He did not tell her how puzzling he found the tone of her comment but he did not forget it. And two years later, when he had reason to remember her reaction, he began to believe that perhaps she had wanted to prove him wrong about Tia's status—that perhaps she was making a prophecy.

When they returned around dinnertime, Steve left the boys in the van and went up to the ward to look for Priscilla. He found her white-faced and teary in Tia's room.

"She's starting an episode," she said. "She was just fine up until a little while ago. She was playing in the playroom—she found a little toy—if you press the right button Disney heads pop up—and she played with that all afternoon. But then she started stooling at five-thirty and she's all gray and lethargic. Oh, Steve—"

"I know, Pris, I know." He went in to see Tia lying in her crib, her legs drawn up.

"Hey, little girl. Hey, Daddy's girl. Are you feeling bad? Come here to Daddy." He lifted her and placed her gently in his lap, cradling her. Her head fell back against his chest. He could feel the tears pull at the back of his eyes.

"Pris, what do you want me to do? I can stay with her if you want to be with the boys."

"No, I'll stay. You get something to eat and a place to park the van and then come tell me where you are. I'll come when she's better."

"All right." He kissed Tia and returned her to Priscilla. He was unable to return to the ward until after eleven, however, following several more confrontations with the guards and one conversation with the campus police about long-term parking.

Pris looked exhausted.

"How is she?" Steve asked.

"She's starting to improve. I think it's okay to leave, but it's been pretty bad. She began vomiting around nine—two episodes of real projectile vomiting. And then heavy stooling. She's been real listless. The resident just examined her and stopped all feedings—she's not to get formula or the breast milk, and they took a blood sample for electrolytes. I just hope she's all right for the biopsy tomorrow."

"She will be, Pris. Come on, let's go get some sleep. I finally found a place for the camper where they don't hassle you."

By the next morning, Tia was much improved. Her electrolyte readings had returned to normal, Dr. Lamb told them.

"Last night Tia had high blood sodium levels," he explained.

"Yes, we're used to that," Priscilla answered. "That's not unusual when she's having an episode."

Later that morning, Tia's scheduled biopsy was performed and progressed normally. They wouldn't know the results for a while, but as long as she was stable, Tia could leave tomorrow, Sunshine told them.

That afternoon, Steve and Priscilla drove into Palo Alto and found the Disney toy for Tia.

"Wait till you see her play with it," Priscilla said.

The next morning, Saturday, July tenth, Tia was discharged. They'd been told that Dr. Sunshine would decide whether Tia was to go to San Francisco or San Rafael. A decision to try more hyperalimentation or further surgery would necessitate hospitalization in San Francisco. Otherwise, Sara had told them, they could bring Tia back to San Rafael.

"Tia looks okay," Dr. Sunshine said. So they had carefully carried her downstairs—she was still hooked up to an IV that was running off a vein in her foot—and fastened her into her car seat in the van. Steve attached the IV bottle to the roof of the van for the hour-and-a-half ride back to Kaiser-San Rafael. Priscilla snapped a picture of Tia as she sat there sucking on her pacifier. Then they drove up the peninsula, through San Francisco and across the Golden Gate Bridge to San Rafael. They were just settling Tia on the ward when Sara hurried up to them.

"I'm sorry—I tried to get you before you left Stanford.
You're going to have to take her to San Francisco."

"Oh, God, no!" said Priscilla, bursting into tears.

"Look, Dr. Shimoda—we just drove all this way—and hell,
we drove right past the goddamned Kaiser in San Francisco!"
Steve yelled.

"I'm sorry—"

"Well it's so damned inconvenient. Now we've got the boys
and we've gotta figure out something to do with them, and it's
hotter than hell out there, and we've got the damned IV to
worry about—" began Steve.

"Yes, and we thought Tia's treatment was all straightened
out, that she could be here," Priscilla sobbed. "Why didn't you
tell us if you were changing the plan? You've gone back on
what you said, Sara."

"I'm sorry, but everybody seems to agree that it's better if
Tia is treated in San Francisco. We're not equipped to do
hyperalimentation by IV here, which is what she needs. And
she may require surgery. That's just the way it's going to have
to be," said Sara uncomfortably.

Priscilla buried her face in her hands, still sobbing.

"Damn all these goddamned institutions," Steve said.

8

Six days later, Priscilla bent over Tia and pushed a tiny
spoonful of rice cereal into her mouth. It was the first solid
food she had been allowed in months.

The week following Tia's return from Stanford had proved
difficult. They had not exactly arrived in style, furious that they
had to take Tia to San Francisco at all. And to Priscilla it had
seemed to be the crowning blow that the house staff should be
changing then, too, just as the doctors were talking about
revising Tia's treatment protocol. In the first few days, Priscilla
had confronted Dr. Lou Guill, the new resident, and Dr. Rich
Coolman, the incoming intern, because at first they both
seemed unwilling to keep Priscilla informed about Tia's
treatments. It seemed to Priscilla that Coolman, in particular,

reacted with defensive hostility. And the very first Monday following the trip to Stanford, Dr. Coolman exploded.

Priscilla was accustomed to having access to Tia's weight chart. At San Rafael it was kept by the bed and Priscilla could check it whenever she wanted. At San Francisco, however, she was refused access to this. She asked Dr. Coolman about the policy and also questioned why Tia was not on IV.

"We were told Tia was to receive hyperalimentation by IV— that was why she has to be here instead of San Rafael," Priscilla said. "If she doesn't need it, I want to take her back to San Rafael."

Dr. Coolman barked back angrily, apparently believing his authority was being questioned. Priscilla decided he felt threatened, so she asked Mike Applebaum to set up a meeting to discuss the situation. There she and Steve poured out their frustrations over Stanford and the lack of communication at San Francisco.

"Just keep us informed," Steve said. "Don't pull that mucky-muck big doctor routine." And the social worker who was there to facilitate their dilemma supported their position. Priscilla believed that things were already much improved. But despite their efforts, the San Francisco staff still hadn't succeeded in improving Tia's status.

Priscilla wedged another spoonful of rice cereal into Tia's mouth. Tia looked surprised and pleased.

"Did you forget how to chew?"

Tia smiled back at her. She put her hands up in front of her face for a moment, then threw them apart, laughing.

"Peekaboo," she said.

Priscilla smiled. "Can you do this, Tia?" She snapped her fingers.

Tia put her fingers together and rubbed them, grinning.

Priscilla rushed to the door of the room and looked out at the nurses' station.

"Look, Pat, come look at this!" she called. The nurses' aide, Pat Middleton, who had spent so much time with Tia during her hospitalizations at San Francisco, came in and watched the show, smiling.

"She's getting so big, Priscilla—and so smart."

"I know," said Priscilla. "I just wish they could figure out what's wrong. I want to take her home so badly."

"I know you do. What were the results over at Stanford?"

"They didn't find anything. A normal biopsy, and the gastrin level was normal, too. You know that gets raised with certain kinds of tumors. They were also supposed to do a vasoactive intestinal peptide, but something happened to the sample—it got lost or something. And then the upper G-I series Dr. Applebaum ordered a couple of days ago—after Tia's real bad episode on Monday—that was normal, too. So now Dr. Applebaum's talking about exploratory surgery. Oh, Pat—I really don't want that! She's so little for that!"

"I know, Priscilla. But the pediatric surgeon here is really good. Maybe they'll find something."

"Well, I keep hoping they won't have to do it. That's why I suggested to Dr. Applebaum that we try feeding Tia. You know I have these friends—the Hamiltons—and their little boy was having lots of diarrhea and a failure to thrive syndrome. And Dr. Applebaum was called in on that case and recommended food, and it worked wonders. I know Dr. Applebaum thought I was nuts suggesting it—he probably thought he'd just humor a crazy mother—but he said we might as well try, that nothing else seemed to be working. I mean it was a lot less drastic than surgery, I thought."

"Well, that's for sure!" Pat laughed.

"Oh, God! I just thought of something!"

"What?"

"She should be getting viokase!"

"What?"

"With the solid food! She should be getting viokase! How can we tell if this is going to work if we don't do it right? She can't digest anything without viokase! Where's Dr. Coolman or Dr. Guill? We've got to get someone to write the order."

"They're all at a party to welcome the new house staff. Maybe we shouldn't bother—"

"Of course we should bother them! Come on, come on—we've got to give it a chance to work."

And Priscilla persisted until a doctor was tracked down and the order for viokase written.

That night, Priscilla went home for dinner. "I think she's getting better," she told Steve. Later she sat down with Tia's baby book to bring it up-to-date. She had stopped keeping the daily journal of Tia's treatment after Tia's central venous catheter had come out in April; then she had briefly restarted the journal for a week in June before abandoning it once more. "It's too painful," she told Steve.

But she still tried to keep up with this book. She had already used up a whole page—the one called "Your Medical History," and she'd have to move on to a second page meant for later illnesses. But she found she couldn't fill it in anymore. In fact she hadn't written anything since March second, the day of Tia's hospitalization.

Steve glanced over at her from his place on the couch. "Are you filling in her medical stuff?"

"No. I think I'll wait till she comes home," Priscilla said. She leafed back through the pages of the baby book and finally found the page she'd filled in the day Tia had arrived. In the little box that was labeled, "A Few Words to You from Mother," she had written:

(11/5/75) My love for you existed long before I actually held you, but the first moment that you were handed to me, I was overjoyed. You were beautiful, perfect in every respect, more than I had dreamed and hoped for. After caring for you only a few hours, I felt that you had been mine forever. My feelings for you were indescribable. I only hope that I can be the Mommy that you need and deserve, that I can make up for the six months that you had no Mommy. You're mine, Tia, and I will give you all the love and care that you need!

Below that box was one labeled, "A Few Words to You from Father." It was blank.

"Steve, you've got to fill in this box for Tia's baby book," Priscilla said. "When she grows up, she'll want to know how you felt when we got her."

"I will, Pris," Steve said. "There's plenty of time."

9

Sara Shimoda leaned over the still figure of Tia Phillips, willing the ambulance to accelerate.

"Come on, Tia, come on," she muttered. "You can do it. Open those eyes." But Tia lay quiet. It was the sickest Sara had ever seen her. She was not responding to stimulation and was in the early stages of shock.

She had been doing so well, Sara thought. At least for Tia, she had been well. After the solid food had been offered to her over in San Francisco, she had begun to improve. Mike Applebaum had been amazed. He had gradually increased her feeding, giving her banana as well as rice cereal. And then Mike had put her on the milk-based 60/40 formula, which was a risk because she was probably allergic to milk. But she had continued to improve, her weight rising by half a pound, then a bit more, till she reached seventeen and a half pounds, the highest ever. Mike permitted Priscilla to take Tia home on passes. Finally he discharged Tia on July twenty-eighth. Priscilla had called Sara, brimming with the news.

"She's coming home! My God, can you believe it? After five months, she's coming home!" she had screamed. Sara had smiled into the squeals. Please God, let her stay awhile.

But at Tia's first posthospital check, Priscilla reported some problems.

"Three days ago she ran a fever of a hundred three and vomited and threw up three times," she said. "But it was gone in twelve hours."

Sara's examination revealed nothing other than the chronic diarrhea—but that had become normal for Tia. Tia seemed happy and at nearly fifteen months, almost ready to walk. Her weight had increased to eighteen pounds, four ounces. Priscilla reported her vocabulary at fifteen words.

"Let's advance the feedings and increase the time between them," Sara said. "Call me if there are any problems." She knew that eventually there would be. Because whatever Tia had, they weren't coming close to finding it. And Sara was at her wit's end. They had pretty much exhausted their diagnoses. It wasn't viral gastroenteritis. It wasn't an inability to digest sugar. It wasn't parasites. It wasn't an inflammation of the bowel lining. It didn't seem to be secretory in nature, but that could not yet be ruled out. She had ticked off the negatives.

The positives didn't tell much either. Tia's episodes did seem to be triggered—sometimes, at least—by infection, but there was nothing wrong with her immune system. They did seem to be affected—sometimes—by intake, but changing her intake yielded unpredictable results. They did produce—sometimes—electrolyte abnormalities, and in particular, hypernatremia. But the abnormalties and high sodium levels might be explained by the fluid loss itself. At best these symptoms occurred intermittently. Nothing was consistent. Nothing quite fit together. Sara knew that she—and now Mike Applebaum—were beginning to clutch at straws. Yes, Tia was at home. But nobody except Priscilla thought it would last.

Then this morning, Priscilla had called, hysterical.

"Sara, I called the E.R. like I was supposed to do when Tia got bad, and they've given me the runaround for half an hour now! I tried to explain that Tia was stooling and vomiting badly—that she was getting dehydrated and needed to be seen immediately, and the nurse there said she'd get in touch with a doctor and call me back. And then finally half an hour later she called back and said very offhandedly, that she understood my baby had the flu and that she was getting dehydrated. They don't understand anything about Tia—about how sick she gets. Sara, she's really bad!"

"Okay, Priscilla. Take her over immediately. I'll meet you there."

By the time Sara arrived at the E.R., Tia was in extremely bad shape. She was eleven percent dehydrated, Sara estimated, which was very dangerous. Her weight was down nearly two pounds—all fluid loss. Her skin was cold and doughy, and she was deeply lethargic and difficult to arouse. In addition, her right tympanic membrane was red, indicating an ear infection.

Sara moved quickly. She pushed fluids by IV and ordered penicillin. They had to replace those fluids at once or they could lose Tia from circulatory failure. Sara requested serum electrolytes and ordered a special nurse; Tia would need what amounted to ICU care in her room on the ward. When the electrolytes came back from the lab, the readings were badly awry. Tia's sodium was 180 milliequivalents, or 35 milliequivalents over high-normal. Her potassium was a very low 2.3 and her carbon dioxide reading was greatly elevated at 55. Only her chloride reading—at 102—was normal. Her BUN, which was a reflection of how well her kidneys were operating, was a somewhat elevated 26, but this was normal for a child with dehydration. Replacement fluids should correct the electrolyte imbalance.

Within an hour of Tia's admission, Priscilla reported that the child was clenching the fist of her right hand. She was quivering and curling her toes and feet. "And I think the ear infection came from an allergic reaction to having that cow's milk formula," Priscilla said, referring to the formula Mike Applebaum had ordered.

"Maybe. I'm going to do a lumbar puncture to check for infection in the brain," Sara said. But the spinal tap proved negative. So were blood and urine cultures. A repeat electrolyte test at 2:30 showed a decreasing but still elevated sodium of 166, a decreased potassium of 2.0, and a carbon dioxide reading that was still about 15 milliequivalents elevated at 43. The replacement fluid therapy was working, but slowly. An EKG showed abnormalities of the T and U waves consistent with the low potassium reading. These were potentially dangerous heart changes.

At 3 o'clock, Sara called Mike Applebaum. Tia remained very jittery. She had voided no urine despite the high rate of fluid replacement, and that was a bad sign. Mike suggested that Sara add potassium.

"I think the vomiting the mother reported probably explains the high sodium and low potassium," he said. "Try giving her some calcium for the jitteriness."

"I think we'd better transfer her over there, Mike. She still doesn't look good, and the doctor who will be on call here is not familiar with Tia's case. In fact we're going to have to develop a much clearer protocol for treating Tia. The E.R. here didn't know how to deal with her when Priscilla called, so Tia was in a lot worse shape than she needed to be when I got here."

"Okay, bring her over," Mike said.

The ambulance was nearing the Golden Gate Bridge. Priscilla was riding beside Sara. She appeared calm. She usually seemed to do well when Tia was at her sickest—as though emergencies brought out the best in her. Evelyn had pointed that out to Sara. Some people were like that. They always expected the worst, so that when it happened they were strangely prepared and almost at ease with it.

Sara touched the little face beneath her. Lately it had been increasingly difficult for Sara to deal with Priscilla. Tia's condition was more and more upsetting; her episodes were worsening. This one was truly life-threatening. It was hard enough for Sara to cope with her inability to cure Tia. But Priscilla wanted so much for herself—so much intimacy and sharing. For a moment Sara looked over at the attendant riding with her and thought of her husband. She had met Tom in just this way—he had been an ambulance attendant when she was in medical school. Theirs was a close relationship, the only one she permitted herself to relax into.

Sometimes it was hard for her to leave her family in the morning. They weren't going to have any more children; they had decided that after Elizabeth was born. Her career was of so much value to Sara and there was no additional time in her life to give to more children. She was straining even now with her job and her daughter. But what if something happened to Elizabeth? How did one bear it?

"Tia. Come on, Tia! Answer me, Tia." Sara bent and stroked the cold forehead.

Tia's eyes opened then.

"Hi," she said.

10

It was almost 10:00 P.M. on Sunday, October 17, when Evelyn received the phone call at home. Only 36 hours earlier she had examined Tia, who was about to be discharged. But now the child was apparently in trouble again.

Evelyn rushed to the hospital, arriving just as Mrs. Phillips drove in. They met at the elevator, and there Mrs. Phillips handed over her daughter.

Evelyn realized immediately that Tia was in very serious condition. If she didn't get a needle into the child within fifteen minutes, she'd lose her. Tia's peripheral vascular system was shutting down due to fluid loss from massive diarrhea and vomiting. She was in shock.

Evelyn worked quickly. Tia was totally limp and unresponsive on examination and her extremities were cold and blue from poor circulation. Her skin turgor was markedly decreased—another sign of dehydration. Her weight was down half a pound since yesterday, when she had been discharged from the hospital. Raising her eyes to heaven at her good fortune, Evelyn managed to get two IVs started and then ordered fluids pushed at the rate of 12,000 cubic centimeters per meter squared per day. Good God, she had never set a rate that high! she realized. But that was the rate Tia needed; her fluid loss was so critical.

At least Mrs. Phillips was calm, Evelyn thought. She was not shrieking or demanding emotional support for herself. Evelyn was scared she might lose Tia. But Mrs. Phillips said nothing: she just stood at the bottom of the bed and watched, silently letting Evelyn work.

By eleven forty-five, Tia was improving. Her color had returned—her toes were now pink instead of the dull blue of circulatory collapse. She was attentive. Evelyn ordered serum electrolytes.

The results came back from the lab after midnight. Tia was very irritable, and looking at the electrolyte levels, Evelyn could see why. She had a sodium level of 170—an excessively high level—and a low potassium. Where was she getting all this sodium? Did this kid have a salt mine in her body or something? Evelyn wondered. Tia continued to pour out stool at an amazing rate. Another sodium test at 2:00 A.M. came back a still high but decreasing 160. But the losses were massive—no other way to describe them, Evelyn realized. By 6:30 the next morning, Tia had passed more than a liter of stool and vomited another 55 cubic centimeters. Evelyn calculated the replacement. She had already pushed almost 40 ounces through the IV just to keep up! But Tia was coming out of it. By 7:00 A.M. she was stable and asleep.

Evelyn looked down at the pale little face. You made it, she thought. You're a tough little kid and you made it.

But would she make it through another one? These episodes were coming closer together now, and each was more severe. Evelyn remembered the one last month. Despite being made NPO, Tia suffered huge losses which continued for four days. The child had tested positive for viral meningitis that time, too, which was untreatable but fortunately not serious. And she had almost continuous hypernatremia—with that blasted sodium just hanging up there sky high, Evelyn recalled. Evelyn had finally ordered a sodium on Tia's stool—the first time she had ever requested such a test. She had felt they needed a total balance study to see if the expected levels of sodium and potassium in the stool would correlate with the blood electrolyte shifts. But the results had made no sense. Tia had had two stool samples collected and tested, one at midnight and the other an hour and a half later. The first had come back from the lab with a sodium reading of 166 and the second with a reading of 198. This extraordinarily high level was inexplicable—and particularly when a blood sodium level drawn at 2:00 A.M. came back with a reading of 171—lower than the stool! If all that sodium was still concentrated in the blood, how could so much be coming out in the stool? Evelyn had chewed on that. It didn't make sense, and it certainly didn't help her to decide how much sodium to replace through IV fluids. So she had just discarded the data as useless.

Later Sara had discussed these confusing stool sodiums with Mike Applebaum and reported her conversation to Evelyn.

"He said stool sodiums should be in the sixty-to-eighty-milliequivalent range," Sara said. "He felt the higher level implicated secretory diarrhea."

"What treatment did he suggest?"

"Cholestyramine for the diarrhea. Then he said to repeat abdominal and skull X rays to look for calcification to rule out a tumor. But the X rays were normal."

"You're just not getting anywhere, are you?" Evelyn said. Sara sighed.

"No."

By now Sara was calling on experts all over the country to help with a diagnosis. She had contacted Dr. Sunshine at Stanford at the end of September and told him of Tia's persistent problems. The specimen of vasoactive intestinal peptide (VIP), which was a secretion released by a pancreatic tumor, had unfortunately been lost by Stanford, Dr. Sunshine reminded her. Perhaps another VIP specimen could be collected. This suggestion jibed with that of another expert Sara telephoned, Dr. Larry Finberg of Montefiore Medical Center in New York.

Of course they were all exhausted by this case. There wasn't one of the pediatricians who hadn't treated Tia when she was in one of her life-threatening episodes, who hadn't experienced that frightening, pit-of-the-stomach knowledge that if they couldn't get the needle in and couldn't calculate exactly the replacement fluids and weren't awfully careful with this tiny fifteen- or sixteen- or seventeen-pound patient, she was going to die on them. Since her last hospitalization in August at Kaiser-San Francisco, she had been admitted to Kaiser-San Rafael on five separate occasions. It had reached the point now where it was almost more frightening for the staff when Tia was not hospitalized than when she was. When she was out there somewhere, she could come in at any moment in critical condition, and they had no control over it. At least when she was hospitalized, there was a semblance of control. And it seemed as though Tia was always in the worst shape when she was admitted from home, like tonight. It was just another one of those strange things about this case Evelyn was thinking as Sara came on the ward to relieve her.

"How is she?" Sara asked.

"Better. But it was a rough one," said Evelyn. Sara touched her shoulder and Evelyn smiled in return.

"Hang in there," Evelyn said.

11

Steve stood with his back to the wall in Kaiser-San Francisco's Waiting Room. It had been about an hour since they had wheeled Tia into surgery. There has to be some kind of word about her condition, he thought.

Sara was pessimistic. "I think it's unlikely we're going to find something," she'd said. "A laparotomy is basically exploratory surgery. But there's a possibility there's a tumor in there. We've had some slightly abnormal readings on Tia. Dr. Burnip feels that in particular Tia's VMA is elevated for a child. It's not very high at all, but there is a possibility that it is due to a tumor, probably of the adrenal. The surgeon is going to do a thorough search—I don't want you to be shocked by the length of Tia's scar—it will run from the base of her breast bone all the way to the pubic bone. If there's anything there, Dr. Mogen will find it."

But Pris was always the eternal optimist, Steve thought. She was sure they were going to find something, that Tia was going to get well. And she was, damn it, she had to. She was such a joy when she was feeling good. She had loved those two camping trips they had taken in early September—only a couple of months ago.

They had taken a chance, no doubt about it, bringing Tia on a camping trip. But they had decided it was no use living like they had, scared to do anything or go anywhere. They had always been campers until Tia had fallen sick. They had finally decided they were just going to resume. They wouldn't go too far; by now they knew the warning signals that preceded Tia's episodes. She would start to run a little fever or fuss or cramp up. They would have time to return.

But it hadn't happened. They had camped at Gualala with the Hansens over Labor Day and then at Blue Lake for the Admission Day holiday. Tia had been in her element up there, playing contentedly in the sand and driftwood where she sat for hours in the brand-new red tennis shoes Priscilla had bought her, laughing and talking to herself. She had loved the campfire—they had been hard put keeping her away from it, Steve remembered. She couldn't eat the cook-out food, of course, but she was allowed rice cereal and bananas.

At night they had put her up in the loft bed in the camper with the boys, but she just giggled and wouldn't go to sleep, so they had taken her down with them, and she had lain there on Steve's chest, pulling his chest hair. It hurt like hell, but she and Pris just thought it was the funniest damn thing they had ever seen, so he had played it out a little—pretended it hurt even worse than it did—just to hear Tia laugh.

It had felt like a family again, he thought. They needed so badly to live a normal life, not to sit waiting for the next awful thing to happen. But since then, Tia had been in and out of the hospital, and it looked like maybe she was getting worse. She had had one bad period right after they returned from camping, and another one in October.

A few weeks later, the doctors who had been treating Tia held a group meeting in San Francisco to discuss future treatment. They had decided on exploratory surgery.

"She's in no condition for surgery yet," Sara told Priscilla and Steve. "We want to run some preoperative tests on her."

Steve looked up. Priscilla was down the hall with Mercedes Murphy, the social worker from Catholic Social Service (CSS) who had worked with them on Tia's adoption. She had come to the hospital and taken them out to lunch. Everybody from CSS had been so nice to them.

Then Steve saw Sara. She had been attending the surgery. She looked right at him, held out her hands, palms up, and shook her head.

Tears scraped at the back of his eyes. Silently Sara came up to where they had waited.

"The surgeon wants to talk to you," she said.

"What happened?" Priscilla asked. She was dead white.

"Nothing. She found nothing." Sara's voice was tight. They went in to talk to the surgeon.

"How's Tia?" Steve asked her.

"She's fine. They're closing the incision right now, and then she'll go to recovery. I'm sorry, but we just didn't find anything. I removed one of Tia's adrenal glands because I thought I felt a tumor, but there was nothing. I'm sorry." And she turned and left.

Steve felt the tears sliding down his cheeks. He couldn't talk. Priscilla and Sara had their arms around each other. They were both in tears standing there in the hall.

"She examined everything. There was just nothing there," Sara wept.

"What can we do now, Sara? God, what can we do?"

"There's nothing, Priscilla. We can keep putting Band-Aids on, that's all. She's not going to be cured, Priscilla. Do you understand what I'm trying to tell you?"

Priscilla shook her head and didn't answer.

Suddenly, Sara wheeled and ran off down the hall.

"Pris?" Steve went to her and they stood, their arms around each other.

"It's just going to go on and on and on," Priscilla finally said. "I can't bear it."

"I know."

"Well, I know one thing. From now on we're going to feed her whatever the family's having and treat her normally. Because it doesn't matter what we do and she might as well have that," Priscilla said fiercely. "At least she's going to have that."

12

On Tuesday, February 1, 1977, water rationing began in Marin County. The drought was in its second year and the water shortage all over the Bay Area was critical. Priscilla bent over the bathtub in the orange-tiled bathroom and dipped the plastic watering can into it. She filled it just a little way so that it wouldn't be too heavy for Tia.

"Here, Tia, let's water the plants."

"My bath, Mommy? My bath?" Tia said, pointing at the tub and grinning.

"Yes, your bath, you silly! The plants need to use your bath."

"My bath," Tia pronounced as she went around to the plants, the spider, the two prayer plants, the giant philodendron, spilling a little water into each one. For twenty-one months, Tia was particularly well-coordinated. Priscilla had enrolled her in a kindergym class, and today, for the first time, Tia had mastered every single piece of equipment—even the ladder.

Lately Priscilla had noticed a developing streak of mischief in Tia. Priscilla had scratched her eye on Saturday, necessitating a trip to the Kaiser E.R. to have it checked and patched. Then yesterday she had returned for a check by an ophthalmologist and she had taken Tia with her. In the Waiting Room Tia had put on a little show, prancing about, throwing her blue furry coat on the floor, defiantly refusing Priscilla's demand to pick it up. And she kept trying to pull off Priscilla's eye patch, repeating over and over in mournful tones, "Mommy, owie."

Then at her regularly scheduled appointment with Dr. Applebaum, Tia had continued her antics, crawling all over the examining table in her diaper. She found a particularly dusty shelf and within minutes was covered with dust. Priscilla and Dr. Applebaum dissolved in laughter.

"She's been well a long time, Dr. Applebaum," Priscilla remarked after the examination. "Almost three weeks. And she's getting to be so mischievous—almost a little devil in some ways."

"Good for her!" Dr. Applebaum approved.

In those three weeks home, Tia had been reasonably healthy, despite a period of general ill-health in the Phillips household. Although she had come down with a cold and an ear infection, for once the infection had not triggered one of her bad episodes. She had also had some loose stools. But the rest of the family had been ill with flu as well. In addition, Priscilla had contracted a case of strep throat. It had not been a good week.

They were all feeling better, finally. Priscilla had suggested to Dr. Applebaum that it was a good sign that Tia hadn't started an episode after this latest ear infection.

"Maybe Tia's system is building up some antibodies," she told him.

"Well, perhaps she'll just grow out of this. It's certainly not impossible."

Steve was working the afternoon shift—three to eleven. That evening Priscilla fed the children dinner, and afterward she put Tia to bed. Around nine, Tia started crying, and Priscilla went to find she had vomited in the bed. She cleaned Tia up and changed the bedding; Tia went back to sleep without trouble.

Soon after, Steve came home. Once again they heard Tia crying and discovered she had vomited again.

"You change the bed," Priscilla said. "I'll get her fixed up. I think we'll have to keep her up a little while, just to make sure she's all right."

"Okay," Steve said. An hour later Tia fell asleep in his arms. "Do you think it's safe to go to bed?"

Priscilla nodded. Silently, Steve lifted Tia, carrying her through the little hall to her daisy-covered room. He put her down and covered her with a fresh blanket.

"We'd better keep checking on her," Priscilla said. She knew she would do the checking. Steve slept like the dead.

13

Steve woke to the sound of Priscilla screaming.

"Steve! Steve! My God! My God!"

His feet hit the floor before he could account for their movement. He shot a quick look at the clock. It was nearly four in the morning. In his underpants he ran to Tia's room.

Priscilla was standing next to Tia's crib, her hands over her face, her eyes pulled wide. Steve leaned over the bed. The whole bed was drenched with diarrhea and vomit. Tia in her nightclothes lay covered with it. All down one side of her body she was twitching. Her eyes were closed.

"Get something on her!" Priscilla's voice was wild. "I'm calling the E.R."

Steve stood for a second watching the twitching—he couldn't move. Then he picked Tia up, fumbling for a blanket to put over her. Her diarrhea came off on his bare chest. He felt his own vomit rise in his throat. He prayed something without words. Dr. Applebaum's voice came back to him, playing over in the dead space of his brain where he had put it, not wanting to hear it. "It's progressive, Mr. Phillips. If we don't find out what it is, eventually it will kill her." He had never told Pris. He had never told anyone.

Priscilla was back. "I got them. Dr. Viehweg is on call. He's going to call me back. Just hold her. I'm going to get dressed." She sounded almost under control now.

Steve stood holding Tia, feeling her shaking. He squeezed her against him to stop it but it just went on. The phone rang and Priscilla talked into it for a moment before hanging up.

"He's meeting me there," she said. "Thank God he's moved from the city—it won't take him so long to get there. Come on, put her in the car."

Still in his underwear, Steve ran into the cold February night and, bending, strapped Tia into her car seat. The boys— he had to find someone to stay with the boys, he thought suddenly.

"Call me! I'll find a sitter," he yelled through the closed window at Priscilla. He saw her nod as she jerked the car out of the driveway.

He went back into the house and stood shivering in the living room. All the lights were on. The smell of vomit and diarrhea was strong and he brushed at the patches of them on his chest. Suddenly everything in the room looked wrong to him—the crazy philodendron climbing across the roof beams as though it thought it was in the jungle somewhere; and the raisin tray pictures in orange and yellow with the big space between the slats so the flowers were all broken up and strange; and the photograph of Erik and Jason and Tia that Pris had had taken somewhere—all the kids in pink outfits. Who put little boys in pink denim outfits?

Everything stood out in the room so bright and ugly. So wrong. Steve stood in the center of the living room and shook and shook until he thought the house would fall down around him.

14

In the E.R. Priscilla stood and watched as Dr. Viehweg worked over Tia. The E.R. nurse had started Tia on oxygen immediately, and Viehweg had arrived a few minutes later. Tia was breathing harshly and she was blue and still twitching. She looked unconscious.

Dr. Viehweg pushed fluid through Tia's central venous line. "Get me a CBC and serum electrolytes *stat*," he said.

"What about blood gases?" the E.R. doctor said.

"No, we'll wait on that. This is the way she gets during one of her episodes," Dr. Viehweg said. Tia's blood was drawn for the blood count and electrolytes, and the results were telephoned back within minutes.

"Christ, her sodium's at one-ninety-seven! No wonder she's out," Dr. Viehweg said.

Priscilla stood closing and unclosing her hands. Tia had never looked like that. But in awhile the seizures stopped. Tia appeared calm.

"Is she better?" Priscilla asked Viehweg.

"She seems to be stabilizing. The fluids are helping."

"But she seems so out of it. Do you think that's okay?"

"Yes, Mrs. Phillips. She's been this way before."

Shortly before seven, Priscilla telephoned Steve. "Dr. Viehweg says she's stabilizing," she said. "Get the boys off to school and then come up. By then Sara will be here. She's on call today and Dr. Viehweg's getting ready to phone her."

"Will Tia be all right?"

"Well, she looks more out of it than usual. But they're treating it like the other episodes," Priscilla said.

"Okay. I'll be there as soon as I can." His voice sounded furry.

Priscilla went back to Tia. She was having another seizure. Suddenly she seemed much worse.

"Should we give her Valium for the seizures? What do you think?" asked the E.R. doctor.

"No, it might suppress her breathing, and her blood pressure's really down," Dr. Viehweg answered.

Priscilla watched as they started Tia on medication to raise her pressure. She was still unconscious.

"When will she wake up?" Priscilla asked. No one answered.

15

Sara stopped and put a hand to Tia's forehead. It was cold and clammy. Tia did not move or respond in any way. Her breathing came slowly and with difficulty. Then suddenly she convulsed all up one side of her body. Sara had expected to see Tia in the midst of a bad episode, but this was a whole other thing. When she had arrived at the E.R. just minutes ago, at not quite eight o'clock, Dr. Viehweg's expression and the white pastiness of Priscilla's face had told her that.

Tia's serum sodium was tremendously elevated. Despite the fluids pouring into her, she was dehydrated. And she couldn't breathe. Sara ordered Valium and Phenobarbital to control the seizures.

"We'll need blood gases *stat* and I want her bagged. Get an inhalation therapist down here," Sara said. Quickly the blood was drawn for the blood gases.

The inhalation therapist arrived and fitted the mask over Tia's still face. She sat beside the baby and began to squeeze the bag to assist Tia's breathing. In a moment the blood gases came back from the lab. Tia's oxygenation was adequate but her ventilation was impaired. God, what was happening? Sara thought. She ordered an immediate chest X ray. Then she walked over to Priscilla. Priscilla came out from where she had been huddling in the corner, her arms extended as if to greet or plead with Sara.

"What's the matter with her? Why is she convulsing like this? Why does she need that bag?" Priscilla said, the tears beginning to track her white cheeks.

Sara forced a calm response. "Priscilla, Tia's in very bad shape. This is the worst she's ever been. I don't know yet why she's having a seizure but it may be due to the high level of sodium. The Valium and Phenobarbital should control the seizures. At this point we're more concerned with her breathing. If an inadequate amount of oxygen is getting to her brain, that can cause convulsions, brain damage, coma. That's what the blood gases measure: the amounts of oxygen and carbon dioxide in her blood. It tells us whether she needs to be helped to breathe."

"And that's what that bag's for?"

"Yes. The blood gases show that the pO_2—the index of the concentration of oxygen in her blood—is okay. But the pCO_2—which measures the content of carbon dioxide in the blood—is elevated. That's why we're helping her breathe. The chest X ray may show us why she's having this problem."

Steve came in then, and Priscilla threw herself into his arms. "I'm so scared, Steve! I'm so scared!" she cried.

Sara swallowed against her own fear. She walked over to where Tia lay and looked down at her. The ventilator bag covered her nose and mouth—her face had disappeared. Where are you, Tia? Come back, she thought. But the X ray didn't look promising.

It showed a right-side infiltrate in the lung. Tia had inhaled some of her own vomit and that was causing the respiratory failure. And Tia's breathing was worsening. Her respirations were decreasing and another blood gas analysis showed that the carbon dioxide was building up. The mask and bag weren't sufficient.

"Call Anesthesiology," Sara said.

At nine A.M. the bag was replaced by an endotracheal tube. But Sara realized that Tia needed a mechanical respirator, and Kaiser-San Rafael wasn't equipped with a pediatric machine. She would have to go to San Francisco.

Sara went out to tell Priscilla and Steve, who were waiting outside. They clung to each other as she told them the news.

"We'll move her as soon as she's stable and as soon as we can get the special ambulance over here from San Francisco. I'll go with her," Sara said. They didn't ask her how bad it was. They looked at each other and didn't ask. So she didn't say anything more.

16

They had moved a child out of room 369 so that Tia could have her own room back, somebody told Priscilla. It felt like home, coming back to San Francisco, she realized. How different this hospital seemed now. It wasn't like San Rafael, where they had chosen to throw Tia out last Christmas—that was the way Priscilla perceived what had happened. Tia's condition put too much strain on the staff, Dr. Stein had said during the Christmas Eve meeting. Their hospital wasn't designed to care for a child as seriously ill as Tia. Priscilla saw that as just an excuse. She believed they had handled Tia fine. It was too much trouble for them; that was the inference she drew. Steve had raged at Stein.

"You want us to take her to San Francisco? What if she's in shock? You know how she gets!"

"Well, if she's critically ill, of course you can bring her here," Dr. Stein had said.

"We're not goddamned doctors! We shouldn't have to make that decision about Tia. I'll call a damned ambulance and charge it to you!" Steve had screamed.

After the meeting, Priscilla's outlook toward Kaiser-San Rafael changed completely. Although at a subsequent meeting a treatment protocol had been drawn up establishing that in an emergency Tia was to be brought first to San Rafael, Priscilla felt betrayed. Suddenly Kaiser-San Francisco seemed welcoming and friendly, and San Rafael the enemy.

When they brought Tia to San Francisco now, comatose and in deep shock, the staff hurried to set Tia up in her room, hooking her to the mechanical respirator. Mike Applebaum came in immediately to examine her. Sara was on call at San Rafael and had to return there, but she promised to stay in touch. Jim Hutchison had been to the San Rafael E.R. before they had moved Tia—Steve had called him—and he had prayed with them, trying to offer comfort. He was planning to come over to San Francisco later, he told Priscilla.

She wanted friends around her. Tia's room was filled with equipment and only one person at a time could stay with her.

There was no room even to sit down. So Priscilla and Steve alternated, and when Steve was in there, Priscilla had to sit in the tiny Waiting Room at the end of the ward. She didn't want to be alone.

Jan and Jim Doudiet arrived—they were close friends from the baby-sitting co-op. Jan, a nurse, was pregnant with her second child. "Are you sure you ought to be here?" Priscilla asked her after awhile.

"Of course, Priscilla. Don't be silly," Jan said.

"I need you, Jan. You've got so much faith. I need that now."

"She'll make it. Prayers can help. I believe that so strongly," Jan said.

"You know, Tia can breathe on her own," Priscilla remarked. "The respirator's just to assist her."

"That's good, Priscilla. It's possible she could come out of it at any time."

"But they say her condition's critical. They've never said that before." Priscilla began to weep heavily. Jan put her arms around her and hugged. Bob Hamilton arrived. Like the Doudiets, the Hamiltons were longtime users of the baby-sitting co-op. The three families exchanged their children all the time, and they were close friends. Cyndy Hamilton was staying with Erik and Jason. Priscilla and Steve would be here all night.

Dr. Diamond came by. He had been Tia's principal doctor when she had first been hospitalized in San Francisco the previous April. He looked in on Tia and then stopped to talk with Priscilla.

"How is she?" Priscilla asked.

"She's very sick. Do you understand how sick she is?" he said.

"Well, I'm worried about brain damage when she comes out of it. You know she's stopped having seizures, but she's been making this strange noise and arching in a way they say indicates maybe she has brain damage." Priscilla was crying again, the tears a steady unnoticed stream.

"That's quite likely," Diamond agreed soberly. "But these things are unpredictable."

Jim Hutchison returned. Priscilla didn't have to explain anything to him. They stood with their arms around each other and he prayed with them. From time to time a staff member stopped to offer reassurance.

In a while Nancy Dacus came to the hospital. Her daughter

was Erik's age and Nancy had founded the baby-sitting co-op with Priscilla in 1972. She was also a member of Aldersgate, and was involved with the American Association of University Women (AAUW) with Priscilla. And she had lost an infant daughter in 1973, from an unknown virus. She held Priscilla, and then Steve.

"I think you need something to eat," she said to Priscilla.

"No, you go. Take Steve," Priscilla said.

At seven that evening, Priscilla and Steve sat silently in the Waiting Room with the Doudiets. Suddenly the hospital P.A. system came to life, calling a Code Blue in pediatrics. Someone had stopped breathing. At once Steve stiffened.

"It's Tia," he said.

"No, no," Priscilla said calmly. "It's not." But then she saw Dr. Coolman run by.

"I'm going to check," Steve said. He was out and back in a minute.

"It is! It is Tia! They're all standing around her bed working on her. Oh, God!"

Priscilla rushed to Tia's room. It was crowded with nurses and doctors. After a few minutes Lou Guill, the resident in charge, came out to her.

"It's all right, Priscilla. What happened is that periodically the nurse has to take Tia off the respirator and suction her, and when she did it this time, Tia stopped breathing. We've got her going again. But I want you to know that she can't breathe on her own anymore."

Priscilla began to cry. "And her heart wouldn't beat without that drug you've got her on, right?" she asked. Dr. Guill nodded her head.

"Yes, she needs Isoprel to maintain blood pressure," she agreed.

"Can I go in now?"

"Yes, of course."

Priscilla stood by Tia's bed. Tia was hooked up to an IV, a heart monitor, and a catheter. Her mouth was distorted by the ungainly tube exiting from her trachea. Priscilla picked up Tia's hand. It was entirely relaxed and cold. Shakily, Priscilla put her own hand to her face. One of the doctors in the room, a woman Priscilla didn't know by name, turned to her and spoke gently.

"We almost lost her. She's okay now but I'm not sure we'll

get her through the night." Priscilla didn't answer. "So you might want to sit with her," the doctor went on.

"Yes." Priscilla looked around helplessly.

"Here, I'll bring you a stool."

"Lou?" Priscilla addressed Dr. Guill.

"Yes?"

"I want Sara here. I know it's late but—"

"I'll call her. There's a phone right here. You can speak to her yourself." When Sara came on the line, Priscilla took the phone.

"They said she might not make it through the night," Priscilla sobbed. "I need you—please come."

"I'll be right there."

When Sara arrived, she walked straight to Priscilla, taking her in her arms. Priscilla broke into fresh tears and looking up saw that Sara was crying too.

"I'm sorry. I need you to be here," Priscilla sobbed.

"I know. It's all right. I know."

Sara stayed in the room, occasionally leaning over to stroke Tia's face. At one point she turned to Priscilla.

"You do understand how sick she is, don't you?"

"Yes—" Priscilla paused. "But she can't die." Sara turned away.

At one in the morning, Sara finally left. "I'll be in touch, and if anything happens, I'll be back." They embraced again.

But nothing happened. All night long, Steve and Priscilla alternated between the stool and the Waiting Room. Tia lay without moving on a thermal blanket, her eyes half open, their small black pupils fixed and dilated. The IV continued its slow infusion. Once there was a thirty-second period of reduced pulse when the nurse could obtain no blood pressure, but it was quickly restored. Toward morning Tia's icy hand seemed to have warmed a little. Priscilla smiled for the first time when they told her Tia's temperature was up a fraction.

In the morning, Mike Applebaum called a meeting of the doctors involved in Tia's care. When it was over, they summoned Priscilla and Steve. Dr. Applebaum detailed the treatment they intended for Tia.

"First, we want to wean her off the respirator as soon as possible," Mike said. "Also we have to deal with the swelling in Tia's brain. We don't know the state of her brain but we do know there is damage. She is on a drug to combat the edema and we will continue with that. We're going to do an EEG and that will tell us about brain function. And then we want to implant a blood pressure line. For right now she's stable."

After they left, Priscilla turned to Steve.

"They're talking in terms of long-range plans," she said. "We'll deal with the brain damage somehow, if it comes to that. I'll settle for that—just to have her with us. Do you think they're really saying she's going to be all right?"

"I don't know, Pris. I don't think they know either," Steve said.

A little while later Tia's EEG was recorded and shortly afterward a blood pressure line was implanted. For a time nobody spoke to Steve and Priscilla. Finally Mike came up.

"Her EEG is flat," he said. At once Priscilla began to sob.

"What does that mean?" Steve asked.

"Well, it's not good. But I'd rather leave it up to Dr. Leider to explain that when he comes over with Sara this evening. This is his day to be at San Rafael, but he will come over as soon as he's finished there and do some tests on Tia. He'll talk to you then."

"Yes, I know Dr. Leider. He was the pediatric neurologist Tia saw when she was first hospitalized," Priscilla managed. She didn't ask anything more. Beside her, Marilyn Hansen took her hand. Priscilla had called Marilyn this morning to tell her fellow social worker that she wouldn't be coming to work, and Marilyn had immediately come to the hospital to join Jan Doudiet. Jim Doudiet was to return as soon as he got off work. Even Mercedes Murphy had come for a while.

At noon, Jim Hutchison arrived. He went in to Tia and prayed over her for a minute. "I can stay as long as you need me," he told Priscilla.

Jan drew Priscilla aside. "I want to take you to lunch," she said.

"No. I don't want to leave her."

"Priscilla, you have to get out of here. You won't do her any good if you collapse. Nothing's going to happen."

"How do you know? I want to stay." But they persuaded her finally, though she sat over her plate of food and couldn't eat, impatient to get back.

When she turned from the hall into the pediatric ward an hour later, she saw a crowd standing around Tia's door. Screaming, she ran to the room.

"What is it? What is it? What happened?"

"Her heart stopped," someone said.

"Oh, God! I told them! I told them I shouldn't leave!"

"It's all right. We've got her going again."

"I didn't want to go! They made me go!"

"It's all right, Priscilla. She's all right." Jim Hutchison gripped her arm, talking right into her ear. Gradually, Priscilla calmed down. She went back to sit by Tia, but Tia was gray and cold and didn't respond. Steve came in and stood by the bed, the tears streaming down his face. He stared at the EEG.

"Is that some movement there?" he asked once, pointing at the machine, but the nurse shook her head. He left, jerkily.

That afternoon, after Tia's heart stopped and was restarted a second time, Priscilla and Steve finally talked with Jim Hutchison about turning off the machine.

17

His own conversion had its roots in a situation not so unlike this one, Jim realized. Until that time he had avoided religion. His father was a totally rational man who believed that the universe ended at the point his five senses ceased to record it. He was a skeptic and a materialist. And Jim—growing up in Northern Ireland—had seen nothing to persuade him that his father was not right.

But his senior year in nursing school—the week of his conversion—he had been thinking a lot about God's reality and life and death. He remembered this now as he walked with Steve and Priscilla to the pediatric Waiting Room. He recalled it clearly: A woman had come in for surgery on cancer of the colon, and she was absolutely at peace with herself and unafraid. She was like the devout people Jim had known in Ireland. She had what they had, and whatever it was, Jim knew it was missing in him. He wanted to be that unafraid of death. Then he had gone to Westminster Chapel to hear Dr. Martin Lloyd-Jones preach, and Dr. Lloyd-Jones, who had been a famous doctor and then became a well-known minister, preached as if directly to Jim when he talked about those in the congregation who had had questions about God for years. It seemed that in that moment God discovered Jim Hutchison, he often thought. Not in any earthshaking way—it was just that quietly he suddenly believed.

But his fear of death, that had not disappeared entirely until after his extracorporeal experience. He had been pastor at Aldersgate only six months when the doctors discovered the calcium deposit that was pushing on his brain. They had organized a surgical team and operated immediately.

The next thing he remembered was seeing himself on the table with a big gouge in his throat and all sorts of forceps hanging out and someone pushing on his chest and the anesthesiologist squeezing the bag. And he experienced a beautiful sense of well-being as he drifted away from the Operating Room and came to a place where some people were building a little wall. And as he watched them building it, a verse of Scripture came to him, the one where Jesus said, "In my Father's house are many mansions." He knew the true translation of mansions was *caravansaries*—places where caravans were hitched for the night. So he understood the symbolism; he understood that the other side of the grave was not a static thing at all. And as he realized that, it was as though powerful hands brought him back to the operating table. Then the sequence repeated itself twice more. The third time he almost reached the wall-builders and he realized that if they looked up and recognized him, he would never return to the world again, and he realized as well that he did not want to return. He could see the anesthesiologist working on him with the electric paddles, trying to restart his heart, and he felt sorry for the doctor who was trying to save him.

Then when he awoke, he found, as he expected, that they had not done the surgery at all. His heart had stopped three times upon the operating table.

Jim told this story often to his parishioners because he felt that people's attitudes toward death were prehistoric. Even people who faced death every day found ways to avoid dealing with it. When he had started his training at Whipps Cross Hospital, he had once gone to the superintendent to report the death of a patient.

"We don't say 'die,'" he was told. So the next time Jim had to report a death, he called the superintendent and said, "Mr. Smith . . ." and paused.

"What's the matter with him?" the superintendent asked.

"Well, he has no pulse and he isn't breathing and he hasn't

moved for ten minutes," Jim said, adding slyly, "I can't think what's the matter with him!"

Unamused, the superintendent had put Jim on report. "You are to say that his vital signs are imperceptible," he told Jim sternly. It was ridiculous. Jim never hesitated to use the word *die*. There was nothing wrong with the word, just as there was nothing wrong with the fact.

When he turned now to Steve and Priscilla, he held this firmly in mind.

"What do you think we should do, Jim?" Steve asked. Jim looked around the little Waiting Room for a moment, then reached for and took Steve and Priscilla's hands.

"Tia has a flat EEG. As far as I'm concerned she died yesterday," he said. "There's no doubt that she's now being kept alive by machines. We're just holding her here now, and I don't think we should any longer. She'll be far better off. Let her pass on. You both know the passage in the New Testament in which Jesus asked, 'What is life? It is even as a vapor which appeareth for a little while and then vanisheth away.' Death is part of life. In death we affirm the resurrection, don't you see?"

Steve nodded, the tears running unattended.

"She would want us to do it," he said.

"No," said Priscilla. "Not yet. Not until Dr. Leider sees her." And Jim agreed.

"Let's wait until then."

18

Priscilla sat by Tia's bed. It was late that afternoon; Sara and Dr. Leider were expected any minute. Tia lay gray and cold to the touch, like a crack-veined porcelain doll—her dark eyes flat and unwinking. There were tubes and machines everywhere. As Steve came in, Priscilla put her head to the little chest.

"Please, God. I'll do anything. Just don't take her," she said.

Steve stood beside her.

"Jim Hutchison has gone down to the cafeteria to get something to eat, and Jim Doudiet wants me to go to

McDonald's with him to pick up some hamburgers," he said. His voice wheezed in his throat.

Priscilla didn't answer. He touched her shoulder and departed. Jan Doudiet came in and stood with her. Jan had been at the hospital for two days now. Suddenly Priscilla wanted to call Debby and Maria. It seemed very important that they know because they had so often cared for Tia.

"We're going to turn off the respirator," she told them. "I wanted to call you because you loved Tia and I thought you ought to know." And they all cried over the phone.

Finally Sara and Dr. Leider arrived. Steve and Jim were still at McDonald's and Jim Hutchison at the cafeteria. Priscilla stood by the bed while Dr. Leider tested Tia. He poured water in her ear, looked into her eyes. She never moved. He checked her chart. Steve came back then, clutching the McDonald's bag like some pale, pathetic life buoy, and stood next to Priscilla as Leider leafed through the final pages of Tia's thick chart. Finally Dr. Leider turned to them.

"I'm sorry, but Tia's brain is dead. Her EEG is flat. Her pupils have been fixed for over eighteen hours. There are no spontaneous respirations, no spontaneous movements. The only thing keeping her alive is the respirator," he said.

"Is there a chance she will come out of it? Any chance?" Steve asked.

"No. None."

"I want Jim here. We can't go ahead till he gets here. Please, someone get Jim," Priscilla said. She felt her eyes would explode—her whole head pop open and expose to the world what lay within. Steve reached for her and his arm sank like a great weight on her shoulder, pressing her into the floor.

"I'll have him paged," somebody said.

19

Steve watched anxiously for Jim as they all stood around in a little knot, sobbing. No one said anything. Then Jim hurried around the corner and came up to where they waited.

"Dr. Leider says her brain is dead. They are waiting for us to decide about the respirator but we didn't want to decide without you here," Steve said. He could barely get the words out, and he wiped at the tears with both hands. Beside him Jan Doudiet clung tighter.

"I have absolutely no qualms about it. Why hold her here? She has suffered so much. I think we should end it now," Jim said.

"Pris?" Steve wondered for a moment if she could even answer she was crying so hard. But she did, finally, not looking up.

"Yes. Oh, God. All right. Yes," she said.

"Come with me," Jim said quietly. "We'll wait in the Waiting Room." And they all pressed into the room, Priscilla and Jim, Marilyn Hansen, the Doudiets and Steve—all holding onto each other and crying. Sara and Dr. Leider went into Tia's room, and Steve turned his eyes away from there. Maybe when they reached her room, Tia would smile, suddenly look up, and say hi, he thought.

But in just a few moments, Dr. Leider was back. It was 6:45 P.M., February 3, 1977. He nodded slowly.

"She's gone," he said.

Steve felt the ball in his throat swell until he panted for breath. He was squeezed in terrible darkness. He thought he heard someone groan. Somebody tightened an arm around him and they all moved even closer together.

"God has her now," Jan said. "She's totally happy and at peace."

Jim said something. A prayer maybe. Steve couldn't hear or understand it.

"I want to hold her," Priscilla said clearly. "Will they let me hold her?"

"Of course," Jim said. "Come."

Priscilla and Jim and Steve went back in to Tia. The Doudiets stopped at the door but the rest of them entered the room. Sara stood there by Tia's bed, her face a mask. She moved away as they came in. They had removed all the tubes. The three of them stood around the bed. Jim said a prayer. Then he lifted Tia and gave her to Priscilla who sat on the edge of the bed and held her, sobbing. After awhile she gave Tia to Steve.

She was so light and so terribly cold, he thought. It wasn't Tia, and he found he couldn't hold her long. They went back into the hall. Doctors and nurses surrounded them.

"We all loved her so much."

"She was such a special child."

"We're so sorry. If there's any way we can help—"

Rich Coolman came up. The tears were streaming down his bearded face. "We'll always stay in touch," he said. "I owe so much to you three. You've made a better doctor out of me. I never want to lose touch." He put his arms around Steve and Priscilla and they stood there for a long time.

Dr. Leider found them. "There have been other children with similar problems," he said. "If we could do an autopsy, it might help one of them."

Steve looked at Priscilla and they nodded at each other.

"Of course," Priscilla said.

"When will the service be? We want to come to the service," someone said. "Will you let us know? Where is Dr. Applebaum? He will want to know."

"He left when they were going to turn off the respirator."

"He said he couldn't take it anymore," Priscilla said. She hesitated and then looked around. "I suppose we might as well decide on the service right now, so you'll all know."

They went back into the Waiting Room. Steve and Priscilla sat on the love seat, Jim on the chair facing them. Once again, Steve felt shut in. He hunched forward, closing the room off with his hands.

"I think the best thing would be to have a memorial service for Tia rather than a funeral. Then we can have a private committal service later for just the family. We want to emphasize Tia's life, and if the body is there as in a funeral, the emphasis tends to be on the death," Jim said.

"Yes," Priscilla said. "I want to remember the good things. Everyone loved her so much. . . ."

"How soon before they'll be finished with her—with the autopsy? Oh, God!" Steve found himself crying again. He got up and paced the small room. What could God want with Tia? he thought. How could He hurt them so much? But He must—yes, of course, God knew, Steve was suddenly sure.

"I think God understands what's going on here because He too lost someone he loved like this," he said to Jim.

"Of course He does, Steve. And just try to remember that little Tia's suffering is ended now. And even if by some miracle they could have saved her, she would have had extensive brain damage—maybe been in a coma all her life. This is the way she would have wanted it. Now I'll go try to find out about the autopsy."

Jim returned and told them that the autopsy would be tomorrow. Together the three of them decided to set the memorial service for Monday night, February seventh, at seven-thirty at Aldersgate. The committal would be on Tuesday.

"Will you make the arrangements, Jim?" Priscilla asked. "I can't—I just can't face that."

"Yes, certainly. Will you be all right getting home now?"

"Yes. We'll go to the Doudiets."

"Don't forget about the autopsy form before you leave." They went to sign it. Finally the three of them made their way out into the dark San Francisco street. It seemed strange to Steve that no one gave them a second glance, that no one knew what had just happened. It seemed as though what they had lost should be written all over them.

Steve led Priscilla to the car. On the way across the bridge, Steve said suddenly, "I want to adopt another little girl." And although they had fought about so many issues in their marriage, they didn't argue about this. It was right, Steve knew. It was what they needed to do.

THE INVESTIGATION

1

Ted Lindquist

Detective Ted Lindquist pulled his brown VW beetle into the parking lot at the side of the San Rafael Police Department. He levered his six-foot frame out of the car and stood up beside its aging body. He lingered for a moment by the car.

Just thirty, he looked ten years older. A fan of wrinkles at the corner of each eye added the extra years to his age. He had a tight, guarded face that reflected the suspicion with which he regarded the world. He had been a cop for six years and he wasn't trusting anymore. Still, he was a popular butt of departmental jokes because he would blush if his guard was down, and there was a soft side to Lindquist, an ability to relax, which was as valuable in investigative work as his toughness.

The San Rafael PD was not very large—consisting of perhaps 90 employees including the dispatchers, the meter officers, the secretaries, and the cadets as well as the regular officers. Considering that San Rafael's population of 45,000 swelled to nearly 90,000 during the workday, the police department's staff was but marginally adequate.

Ted stopped at the Investigations Room and poked his head in. The detectives' desks were about half occupied. Rock music blared from a stereo system some of the men had recently installed—an excellent system from the Stolen Property Room. Maybe they'd get lucky and nobody would claim it for a while, Ted thought. He glanced at the bulletin boards for recent announcements. One of the blackboards featured a contest one of the guys was running—something about whether you preferred mayo or mustard with your corned beef. Mustard seemed to be pulling ahead. Walt Kosta looked up from his desk at the end of the room and waved, his big basset hound face wreathed in a broad smile. Ted considered Kosta for a moment. In some ways Walt set the atmosphere in the department. He had a gold box he had made from a Shell

125

No-Pest strip, and he had suspended it by a string so that it dangled directly over the chair by his desk where he talked to suspects. He had rigged it so that if he let the string go, the box descended right to a spot in front of the suspect's eyes, whereupon out of it would pop a little toy Pinocchio hanging from a hangman's noose. Walt jerked that string whenever he thought someone was lying to him. Once some lawyer had tried to prove harassment because Walt had pulled the string on his client, Ted remembered. They all had a laugh over that, even the chief.

"The captain wants to see you," Walt called. "Probably wants to tell you to get rid of that VW—bad for the department's image."

Ted gave an answering grin. "Yeah, that must be it," he said. He went off to his own little room across the hall where he worked in the Juvenile Division. It wasn't much of a division as it consisted only of Ted and Lou Foster, his supervisor, and in fact Ted hadn't been doing that much juvenile work lately. There had been a rash of homicides that they were all trying to help solve; Ted was working in Adult Investigations as much as he was in Juvenile. Although he had been assigned to Investigations less than a year, he had learned a hell of a lot precisely because they had been so busy over there. When the new chief had been appointed in 1977, it was decided that Ted was to research the backgrounds on prospective department staff. Benaderet told Ted that there was nothing more important than developing a good department and he wanted his best people handling backgrounds. Despite the compliments the chief handed him on the reports he completed, Ted found it boring work. Sometimes he longed to be back on Graveyard patrolling all alone; in some ways that was the essence of police work for Ted Lindquist.

Things had changed in patrol once he made corporal in January of 1975, because many of his new duties were supervisory and that created personnel problems. They had promoted Ted over a lot of the officers with more seniority, causing a certain degree of friction at first because he was only a three-year veteran. But he knew he couldn't pass up the promotion, not with a wife and two kids to support and a chunk of mortgage payment on a nice older house in San Anselmo.

But since he had moved over to Investigations, new areas of police work opened up to him. For one thing he was able to follow a case from beginning to end.

Ted dropped his leather jacket onto the chair behind his desk and then went over to the captain's office.

"Walt says you have something for me,". he said.

"Yeah. Take a look at this report and tell me what you think." The captain flipped a typed report over the desk. Ted leafed through it, reading carefully. Several pages long, it covered the events of the previous weekend, beginning with the telephone call from a Dr. Carte at Kaiser Hospital regarding a possible child abuse case on Saturday, and ending with Officer Grieve's impressions of Mr. and Mrs. George Stephen Phillips during his visit with them and a Miss A. Jameson from the Child Protective Services. The report sketched the background of the family. Both Mr. and Mrs. Phillips were county employees, it said. It described the contaminated formula discovered by Dr. Carte and summarized a conversation the investigating officer had held with that doctor. The report also made note of the time the apparently contaminated formula had been picked up from Kaiser on Sunday and the fact of its storage in the police department's evidence refrigerator. There was also a reference to an earlier child who had died.

Ted looked up. "It looks very suspicious," he said. "Definitely needs some looking into."

"Yeah. I think so too. I'm going to let you run with it for a while. Normally I'd assign it to Walt, but he's got three murder cases going. Get him to help you for a couple of days. See what you can develop."

"Okay." Ted took the report back into the Investigations Room and dropped it on Walt's desk; then he took a seat under the No-Pest strip and waited for Walt to read it, idly taking in the decor. They had posted some bizarre material. There was a poster on Murphy's Law, under which was written, Murphy Was an Optimist. A picture of Sherlock Holmes sported a big Help written beneath it. Ted considered Kosta's corner decidedly weird. His desk was covered with all kinds of rabbits—a green china rabbit, a candy rabbit from See's, and several stuffed hares. His bulletin board, too, was covered with bunnies. Walt had posted a sign advertising Free Bunny Ears With Wny Purchase. Someone had nicknamed him the Green Rabbit, and he had exploited it to the hilt. The guy made everything a laugh, but he was a damned good cop, Ted knew. He was the "crimes against persons" detective, so all the murders, rapes, robberies—the crimes that involved people rather than property—came to him. It was the most important investigative position in the department.

"Well?" Ted asked. Walt looked up at him with mournful eyes and shifted his weight under a large poster on the wall that warned one and all against playing leapfrog with a unicorn.

"Teddy, my boy, I think you got yourself a case here. It sure looks like someone put something in that little girl's formula, does it not?"

"It does, Walt. It does. Shall we mosey over to Kaiser and see what we can see?"

"An excellent idea. I should have thought of that myself."

In an unmarked car heading toward Kaiser, Ted wondered if he'd have problems over there. Kaiser was a hell of a big bureaucracy. There were something like a dozen Kaiser hospitals sprinkled around northern California alone, he knew, with probably an equal number in southern California and some in other states, too. It was the biggest health maintenance organization in the country. He was a member of it himself; so was most of the department. He and Walt would have to check in with the administration there because they were going to need both Phillips children's medical records. Still, first he wanted to talk to the doctors.

Since Dr. Carte had been the first to contact the police, they decided to start with him. They asked Carte about the formula and he told them about the sodium. It could be ordinary baking soda that had been added, he said. He explained how ingesting too much would cause the sodium level in the blood to rise—just as it had with Mindy, he said. For detailed information, he recommended they see Dr. Shimoda. But there was no question that Mindy's diarrhea and other symptoms could have been caused by the addition of sodium to her formula. And there was no question that the formula contained nearly thirty times its expected content of the element. Carte also described his activities on Saturday: his discovery of the contaminated formula, the controlled experiment he had carried out on a newly mixed batch of formula, the discussions he had held with the parents, particularly the mother. He told them what the mother had said about being a prime suspect.

"But the most important proof in my mind," he said, "was that the child became well in the ICU—as soon as she was separated from her mother. There's a guard on Mindy now, and she's doing just fine. She should be out of the hospital by the end of the week. She could go now except that we're waiting for definite word as to who will pick her up. I imagine it will be the adoption service, or one of their representatives."

After the meeting with Carte, Ted and Walt sought out Dr. Shimoda. She met with them in her small office in the pediatrics wing of the Medical Office Building.

She struck Ted as beautiful and sad and very serious.

"I understand you were away from the hospital last weekend, but I want to inquire about the medical histories of Tia and Mindy Phillips," he began, and she sighed, bringing up one hand to touch her cheek.

"I'll just tell you briefly," she said. "Because it's a very long story—particularly Tia." She started with Tia, describing all the hospitalizations in the different hospitals, the diagnoses, and procedures.

"We never figured out what it was," she said. "Even the autopsy didn't tell us."

"What cause of death was listed on the autopsy report?" Walt asked.

"Secretory diarrhea, etiology unknown. That was just a working diagnosis—an explanation of what we thought was the process of the diarrhea. We don't—didn't—know what caused it. She really died from brain damage probably caused from inhalation of vomit that led to oxygen starvation."

"Could she have been poisoned with sodium, too?"

"I guess . . . looking back on it—" she paused, her voice shaky, "yes. But we never thought of that. The parents . . . the mother . . . was so supportive, so helpful. And the fact that it happened in all these different hospitals, and at home, too. If it had just happened at home and cleared up when she was hospitalized, well, then we might have seen . . . but that didn't happen. Oh, I'll never explain it! It's so hard to believe that she . . . Anyway, it was just in these last few days that I began to think there might be some kind of foreign substance—Epsom salts we thought, or Ex-Lax. And then I was going to speak to the San Francisco coroner on Monday—yesterday—till all this happened. I have been told he's an expert on toxicology. You should really speak to him."

"Boyd Stephens?"

"Yes."

"Thank you. And I think it would be best if you didn't mention to anyone that we've been by to talk with you. We're just trying to get at the truth and we're trying to collect as much information as possible. We're not pointing the finger at anyone," Ted said. It was a standard request at the beginning of an investigation, particularly one as potentially sensitive as this one.

"Yes, I understand."

"Thanks for your help. I'm sure we'll be back to you later."

"Yes," she repeated.

Ted and Walt swung by the administration section of the medical center and talked with Dave Neukom. The administrator wanted to know exactly what they were planning to do in his hospital.

"We're going to investigate this thing," Ted said. "We're going to talk to the doctors and nurses involved—the lab technicians if we need to—everyone."

"I'd like to know when you're going to be here—who you're going to interview. I don't want you bothering the staff while they're on duty here. We've got a hospital to run."

"We appreciate that, sir. But *we've* got an investigation to run, and we're going to run it the way it has to go." Ted let a pause drag out. "You can make it hard or you can make it easy, but we can get search warrants and court orders, and if we have to, we will."

Neukom shrugged and finally agreed, but he insisted he wanted to be in on the investigation as much as possible. Ted wanted to obtain samples of the Cho-free and polycose formulas Carte had mentioned, and Neukom asked him to come back through the administration rather than go directly to the pediatrics ward. Ted agreed to this; it was a minor point to surrender. But he felt strongly that he didn't intend to report to the administration on every detail; it was too complicated and too time-consuming and it was unnecessary. He'd hold his interviews where and when he could. Of course many he'd conduct by telephone. That way he could tape the interview covertly. This was valid police procedure and very valuable because tapes could later be used in court if ever a witness tried to change his story. It also gave Ted a much more complete record than was possible otherwise.

Neukom had given them one interesting lead. He had spoken to the Phillipses' minister. "This Reverend Hutchison said Mrs. Phillips made a rather odd comment to him— something about the police not being able to prove anything," Neukom reported. Ted decided to follow it up immediately.

"What do you think?" Ted asked Walt as they made the two-minute drive down the hill to Aldersgate Church where Hutchison was pastor.

"I think it looks damn bad for the mother."

"Yeah, me, too."

"We'll have to get hold of the medical records on the kids and have somebody look them over—maybe Dr. Stephens or someone he might recommend," Walt said.

"Yeah, and try to track down who made that formula. Also we gotta get an independent lab to run a test on it. I'll call around and see who's the best lab to do it." Ted paused, then sneaked a look at Walt. Walt might not have any kids, but Ted had spent a lot of time with the man: He knew a lot about human nature.

"What the hell makes someone do something like that?"

"I don't know," Walt said. "Maybe this minister can shed some light on the mother."

"I doubt it. He'll probably just stand up for her, say there's no way she could be involved."

"Yeah, probably. The minister and the husband's always the last to know!"

But Ted was wrong. Reverend Jim Hutchison did not stand up for her.

"I had a bad feeling the minute Mr. Phillips called me on Sunday and told me that someone was trying to poison Mindy," he said as he sat with them in his office in the back of the church, Ted's tape rolling. "Everything seemed to come together suddenly—it seemed possible that maybe Mrs. Phillips was involved. And ever since Steve called, I've been thinking a lot about this. I recalled there have been several unexplained deaths of children in the last few years—all young children. And I think most of them involved people in the baby-sitting co-op Priscilla started. There was the little Dacus girl—Holly Dacus—and then Matthew Bloch. I think they diagnosed him as spinal meningitis—he died the same day they found it. I'm sure he was under three years of age. And then Tia—and of course they didn't know what she had. Just last month there was little Cindy Searway. She was sick one day and then died within one or two days and they never figured out what she had either. Her poor father tried to give her mouth-to-mouth resuscitation. And then Mindy, of course. It seemed like an awful spate of infant illnesses within that one tight little group. I don't know if it has any significance, but I thought I'd mention it," Hutchison said.

It was certainly interesting, Ted thought. Maybe nothing would develop but they'd have to look into it. What if this thing turned into a whole lot bigger can of worms than they expected? It was already looking like a possible murder investigation.

Ted wrote down the name of the woman who currently headed the baby-sitting co-op, Mrs. Virginia Gaskin.

"She used to be a pretty good friend of Priscilla's but they had a falling-out over Mindy's illness. You see Mindy has this contagious virus that can affect unborn children and the co-op voted to expel her until she stopped shedding the virus. Ginger Gaskin was one of the main proponents of banning Mindy. Priscilla was terribly upset by it. Anyway, Ginger can give you any more information on the co-op if you need it," the minister said.

"All right. Can you tell me a little about the Phillips family— just your impressions of what they're like?" Ted asked.

"Yes, well, I'd have to say Priscilla's the dominant one in the family. I don't think they have a very close relationship—they seem to argue a lot and compete with each other. Frankly I don't believe Priscilla has that many close relationships because she'd rather talk than listen. However she is very active in the community. In the church she's on the board of the United Methodist Women, and in some other groups as well, I believe. And she's involved in the nursery school and in AAUW. She's on every sort of committee—or she was till little Tia fell ill. Things were very quiet over there after Tia died. Then Priscilla was so excited about Mindy. And when Mindy got sick I couldn't believe it. We all thought, Oh, no, poor Priscilla. It was hard to take in."

"Thanks for your help," Ted said. "We'd appreciate it if you wouldn't tell anyone we've been to see you. This is all very preliminary and we aren't accusing anyone. And considering the status of the Phillips family in the community, we would like to keep everything confidential."

"I understand," Hutchison said as he walked them to the front of the church.

"You know, that's going to be the hardest thing at this point, keeping this thing confidential. I don't want the press to know—it'll blow everything sky-high. Who knows what Mrs. Phillips might do if she knew we were investigating her? If she's unstable enough to poison two kids, she might harm the other two, or kill herself," Ted said as they drove out to the Gaskin house.

"Yeah, and that poses another problem. You're either going to have to get the parents' permission to go for the medical records on the kids, or get a search warrant—"

"And if I get a search warrant I'll have to return it to the clerk in ten days and there goes the confidentiality. It'll be all over the building in ten minutes."

"Isn't the Civic Center where Mrs. Phillips works, too?"

"Yup. Someone's bound to tell her. The press, too."

"Right. You got yourself a problem there, Teddy. Maybe the DA's office can think of something."

"Well, if we can get the parents' permission, we won't have to return the warrant, and nothing gets filed. I think that's the strategy we have to develop."

"Yeah, it's good—if they cooperate," Walt said. Ted lit a cigarette and coughed into the gathering smoke filling the car.

"I'm getting some strong vibes on this Priscilla Phillips," he said. "And none of them are good. I mean assuming the medical stuff holds up, and we've got something to go on with the first child's death, it looks pretty bad for her."

"Yeah, unless there's some deranged nurse or doctor running around," Walt said.

"In four different hospitals?"

"Right. Not too likely, is it?"

"Of course, it could be the father, or the two of them together."

"Yeah. Maybe there was some insurance money in it for them—some kind of financial gain thing. You'll have to look into that, Ted."

"Uh-huh, I will. First I gotta get the medical aspect squared away."

"You got your work cut out for you, kid."

"Yeah, I know," Ted said.

2

One week later, Priscilla wandered around their small bedroom restlessly, the sounds of Jason playing out in the yard a distant distraction. She could look out through the sliding glass door and see him playing back there on the swing set. The boys were grappling confusedly with Mindy's absence. She had explained to both boys that someone had put something harmful in Mindy's bottle at the hospital. Everyone was trying to make certain of Mindy's safety while they figured out who might be trying to harm her, Priscilla said. But she was not sure that the boys had understood.

The appointment with Gary Ragghianti was scheduled for three-thirty. They had finally understood last Wednesday that they were going to need a lawyer. Mary Vetter and Mercedes Murphy of Catholic Social Service had been adamant.

"Priscilla, we don't like to do this, but we have no choice," Mary had said in her croaking, smoker's voice. "The hospital has put security guards on Mindy, and as director I had to make a decision. We're going to recommend that Mindy go to a foster home until this is straightened out. We know you didn't have anything to do with it, but you're familiar with this kind of case. We have to think of the safety of the child first. Now we have a lovely foster mother in mind—she's very experienced and very loving—"

"Oh, no—"Priscilla said tearfully. "How can they believe this of us? We could have just given Mindy back if we didn't want her! Why would we risk such a thing?"

"I know, Priscilla. The thing is, that crazy as it is, they're pointing the finger right at you. And you're going to need to consult a lawyer about how to get Mindy returned to you. We dislike having to take this position, but we are still Mindy's legal guardians, and I suppose in a sense we are now adversaries in that we have Mindy and you want her back. Please understand that we want you to have her. But just at the moment our hands are tied. You do see what I'm trying to say?"

Priscilla nodded. "How often can we see her, Mary?"

They discussed that issue at length. Finally Mary and Mercedes agreed to a once-a-week meeting, every Friday at Mary's office in San Francisco.

"I know it's not very much, but we all hope it won't be for long," Mary said.

After Mary and Mercedes left, Priscilla and Steve discussed their options. They had no lawyers among their friends, but Steve knew of one attorney who had gotten a coworker off on some charge recently, even though Steve maintained the man had been guilty. It was a reference of sorts and Priscilla called Gary Ragghianti and made an appointment with him.

"We'll get her back, Pris," Steve said. "The whole damn world can't be so screwed up they don't see they've got nothing on you. Who the hell do they think they're dealing with? They'll realize soon enough they're backing along the wrong spur. All they have to do is start really checking everything out—all the hospital records and everything. Then they'll see."

"It's not that easy—don't you see? Have you any idea how long Tia's records are? You know every time they ran a blood test or gave her some medication, it was entered somewhere. It would take weeks to go through her records—and then they probably won't understand what they're looking at. That's what I'm worried about. And I'm not even sure they're tying Tia into this. I don't even see how they can do that. Why haven't they even talked to us?"

"It'll be all right, Pris. We can handle it," Steve said.

The next day, she made the suggestion to Steve about the hospital irrigation bottle. Priscilla had been using such a bottle to water Tia's grave. She kept two of the liter bottles at home; both had originally contained sodium chloride, a solution that the hospital used for wound and burn irrigation. Priscilla had discovered other uses for the bottles as well; they worked effectively as containers for ice water on camping trips.

"Steve!" Priscilla had run to find him.

"What?"

"You know those irrigation bottles—the ones that have point nine-percent sodium chloride on them—that we use for camping?"

"Yeah?"

"Some of the nurses use exactly the same kind of bottle to mix the formula with on the ward—only it has distilled water instead of salt. What if by mistake the nurse picked up the wrong bottle!"

"My God, Pris! You could be right! Maybe that's it! Just a simple mistake like that."

"Why don't you call the police and tell them?'"

"I will. Maybe we can clear this whole thing up right now."

"I wonder if Mindy's formula was contaminated with sodium chloride, though. That's the thing," Priscilla said.

"That's what they said, isn't it?"

"No, they just said sodium. That's not the same. I guess they can test to find out."

Steve had telephoned Detective Lindquist, who had promised to send an officer to pick up the bottles for testing. Priscilla had not yet heard from the police. She wondered again why they had not been to see her; she felt she had a lot to tell them. Lindquist had dropped by one day when she was out to deliver some papers for them to sign to release their personnel files. Otherwise there had been no contact. The only thing Priscilla knew was that the police had obtained a search warrant for Tia's and Mindy's hospital records. That she had discovered by accident from Chuck Best, who was a superior court judge in Marin. Priscilla knew his wife from AAUW and it occurred to her that Chuck might be able to help so she had gone to see him.

"I know about it already, Priscilla," Chuck had said. "It shows you how small Marin County really is. There was a detective here asking me to sign a warrant to obtain medical records from Kaiser. I told him that I knew you and couldn't sign it—that he'd better get somebody else. I assume he did."

"I don't know. But I'm not functioning well. I can't stand the separation from Mindy. That's what I wanted to ask you about. Isn't there some way to get her back?" She was crying.

"Yes. You should get a writ of habeas corpus demanding her return. You'll have to hire a lawyer."

"We've got an appointment to see one."

"Good. Well, he'll help you with it. You might think about taking a polygraph test, too. And if there's anything else I can do, just let me know," he said.

But for the rest of that week and the weekend, Priscilla did little but cry. She woke up every morning with a terrible stomachache. She walked around directionless or lay on the sofa, often falling asleep. But at night she was plagued with anxiety and could not sleep. Friday was the low point. Without warning, Kaiser released Mindy to Catholic Social Service. Priscilla could not remember that day without feeling sick, even long afterward. In her journal she wrote:

> Another agonizing morning—finally did get up and went to work, as it was my duty morning. I don't remember accomplishing anything at work. At noon called Mercedes . . . she said that Mindy was to leave hospital this afternoon. . . . Rushed home and packed clothes and toys for Mindy—very painful—and I wanted time to get things together carefully, to plan, etc. Had to cancel appt. with attorney.
>
> Meeting in Dave Rogers's office so painful—I hurt so much—fell apart. Was made clear that from this point forward case involved S.R. police department and Catholic Social Service. . . . I expressed my concerns about Mindy, tried to write down things about her, what she likes, what she can do, etc. Had time to talk at length to Mercedes afterward; she felt my grief. I told her felt worse than Tia's death, which was final. Not knowing if we'll have Mindy hurts. And the point was made that we could lose her solely on the basis of time—if the investigation proceeds slowly—I've never felt so sick, so scared, so heartbroken.

It was nearly noon as Priscilla began to remove her hair curlers and brushed out her hair. She planned to give Jason a quick lunch; he wasn't feeling well and wouldn't be hungry. She hadn't been eating herself, nor had Steve, who was smoking more and more, even though he knew how much she hated it. Every time he lit one, she seethed. Usually he went out to the garage. Communication between them was minimal. For once she didn't feel like discussing anything. She thought that maybe after they saw the lawyer and could mobilize themselves—call the proper people, write letters, whatever it took—maybe then she could talk and work and get on with retrieving Mindy, and put their lives in place. She had recently told a few friends about her predicament; all had reacted with horror and offers of support. But it was the journal that strangely offered Priscilla the most comfort, as though the words took away the reality, consigning it to the pages of a notebook that could be closed, that could be put away.

When the phone rang suddenly, Priscilla felt nothing special, nothing to signal its significance. Later she wondered—and worried—how she might better have prepared herself for it had she known its importance. But at the time it was an unwanted distraction.

ii

She called out for Steve to answer the phone in the kitchen. After a second he yelled to her.

"It's Detective Lindquist," he said. "He wants to talk to you."

Shakily Priscilla picked up the receiver. "Hello?"

"Hi, Mrs. Phillips. Ted Lindquist. We haven't met yet but I wanted to talk to you for just a couple of minutes if I could," he said.

Priscilla couldn't control a little nervous laugh. "I'd love to talk to you," she said as Steve came in to listen.

"Okay. Great. One of the things I'm working on right now is tracing back step by step the formula that was found to be contaminated on the twenty-fifth, and I need to interview everybody and anybody about that. I have interviewed all the nurses and it's come to my attention that you've been a very supportive and helpful person with the care of Mindy by helping with the feeding and spending a lot of time at the hospital, and I was wondering if you could recall how many times you've been involved either in mixing the formula yourself or seeing somebody else do it," he said.

"Yeah." She paused. "Um . . ."

"Can you think of that at all?"

"I can think a lot about it except for those very last couple of days and there's a logical reason for that. Mindy was going downhill. There were all kinds of crazy things going on and I was under so much stress—I was kind of falling apart myself because of the fact that she was worse. I mean I had conversations with the doctor about that and everything. I can tell you exactly when I made it the last time and that was documented. And that is on —okay—wait a minute, let me get my calendar and then I can tell you."

She put down the phone and reached for her calendar— opening it to the previous week.

"What's he asking you—?" Steve began. She waved him quiet and picked up the phone again.

"Sometimes I helped the nurses with the formula if they were busy, doing it myself or putting out the ingredients," she said into the phone. "It was not an off-limits area. Sunday, February nineteenth was the last time I made the formula by myself. On the twentieth Debby Roof phoned me and asked me how to mix the formula. Dr. Carte overheard that and he ordered that only nurses were to make the formula from then on."

"Do you know what his reason was at that time?" asked Lindquist.

"No," Priscilla answered. "He never talked to me about it. Making it had just been a totally innocent, carefree kind of thing. And incidentally the best day Mindy spent at the hospital was the day I made the formula. But after the order— I never made the formula after that," she said.

"Maybe you can run me, then, from the twentieth through the twenty-fourth—what your involvement was with the formula."

"Yes. On the twentieth I opened the can, and another time I helped a nurse assemble the ingredients. Trying to place exactly when that occurred is hard," she said.

"Do you remember what days last week you stayed overnight at the hospital?"

She paused. "Thursday the twenty-third—the day they put down the NG tube, and the twenty-fourth, a real bad night. I remember that no formula was made on the twenty-fourth. What was there had been left out of the refrigerator. That was a mistake by the nurses. And of course there were all the mistakes on the twenty-third—the day two nurses took me to lunch. That was planned long in advance, incidentally.

"I don't know who mixed the formula on the twenty-third— it was such a stressful day," she went on. "And Mindy continued to be very ill while I was out to lunch. There was the consultation with Dr. Applebaum, and all the changes in Mindy's treatment, and Dr. Shimoda apologized to me for making all the changes while I was away at lunch, and then they put the wrong medication in the wrong tube," she said. She told him about that at length.

"What about the formula?" he asked. "Did you use tap water or distilled water to mix the formula?"

"Tap water," she said.

"Have you ever seen anyone use distilled water?"

"Yes, someone—I'm not sure who—used it."

Steve tapped her on the shoulder then. "Ask him about the bottles we sent over—about the sodium chloride."

"Oh, my husband's asking about the bottles we sent," she said into the phone. "Our concern was just the possibility of whether that sodium chloride was used to make the formula, and would that have done whatever was wrong with it?"

"I wish it was that simple. So far the only thing I know about the sodium chloride irrigation is that the percentage of sodium is what would normally be found in the human body," Lindquist said.

"So that's not unusual."

"Yeah. I don't know if that mixed together with the formula would produce a high sodium. I can't answer that question. But I know that the mixture that routinely comes in those is point nine percent."

"I see. I don't know anything about that so it doesn't—it didn't mean enough to me other than that it was a possibility and if that were the case it could have been a total accident. But I guess things don't come that easy," Priscilla said.

"No. I've been looking for lots of easy answers and there just aren't any."

Then he asked her about the afternoon shift change of the nurses on the twenty-fourth, the day before the contaminated formula had been discovered. Did she remember a question about the formula?

"No, I really don't. I don't—I can't think of any kind of conversation at all. I just—I remember expressing a lot of —yeah—like my husband just thinks—fear. I called him in a state of panic and said, 'You know, I can't believe it. She's getting worse and I know you're waiting for me to come home and eat and I can't do it.' I remember that—the only conversation I remember with the nurse at all was indicating that I was upset."

"How about Debby Roof who was working day shift that day?"

"Yeah. I don't re—don't—what—any conversation about formula?"

"Yeah, right. Around the shift change."

"No. I don't re—don't—no—uh-uh," Priscilla said, hesitating.

"Okay."

She didn't remember any formula being made that day, she told him, or anybody asking her how to make it. Because they were all still double-checking with her on the proper amounts to be added to the formula, even on that Saturday when they had moved Mindy to the ICU.

"I don't have any further questions. If you have any questions, I'll try to answer them for you," he said.

Priscilla pawed at her forehead. "I have lots of questions—I don't know how many to even talk about at this point. I'm under a lot of stress because I'm the one who's suffering the most. My family has obviously lost their child temporarily, and we have a lot of questions, but mainly, why haven't we been questioned? There are a lot of things we'd like to point out that somehow may change the—shed a lot of light in our favor if you want to put it that way."

"Uh-huh."

"Like up until Thursday, every time somebody started feeding her, I was cautious—I'd say, 'No, let's wait a little longer.' I was trying to give her the opportunity to get well. And I repeatedly did that—and I can't help but think things like that are important because if I wanted to put something into her, I wouldn't be trying to put less in her. I have a lot of questions to raise like how come it's not significant that our entire family had viruses the three days between the two hospitalizations? And when Mindy went into the hospital, she put out an awful lot in terms of diarrhea and vomiting in a short amount of time, lost a lot of weight—and if that was induced, why wasn't her sodium high at that point? A lot of questions like that. I lie awake all night and those things go through my head and it's like—who do I point this out to—you know, other than you? The one thing I know about medically is electrolytes—because of Tia—that was one of the biggest problems with her. And Mindy—the only thing that really happened before that day or before all that end stuff was that her potassium went really low, but her sodium never went abnormally high to my knowledge."

"Are you talking about Tia or Mindy?"

"Mindy. Mindy. And Tia's a whole other ballpark. I mean I understand there's been some implication at this point—" she laughed nervously.

Then she went on. "To put anything into Tia—that was a medical impossibility. Tia had twenty-four-hour nurses—lots of time there was no privacy for the family because of that. She went weeks without oral intake. And all this is especially distressing because of the loss of Tia—which we've never recovered from. And it was not only our loss but a community loss.

"We had a lot of friends and support, and that implication about Tia is the most painful to me—because if anybody looked back it was just a medical impossibility. There were nights with doctors at her bedside for hour after hour with no oral intake and Tia just continually stooling. Maybe if there had been just one consistent person with her in terms of medical personnel or something, then perhaps someone could have induced something into her."

"Right," Lindquist agreed. "But there are similarities between Tia and Mindy. And given that both had high sodiums, and given the contaminated formula, just based on that twenty-five-words-or-less statement, one could logically conclude that it's possible somebody, involving both children, intentionally induced something into their food supply and it's possible that the parents did, and just on that, it's—"

"But not knowing the medical facts on Tia, that's what—"

"Yeah, but just knowing that much, I have to go into the entire history of Mindy and Tia—"

"So, then Tia is part of this investigation."

"Yeah. That's no secret as far as I'm concerned. It has to be looked into, but no accusations have been made, at least not by the police department."

"The only accusation that's been made to us at this point is by only two doctors," Priscilla said calmly. "But the whole thing about Tia is very distressing—it didn't matter what hospital she was in, or whether she was on oral intake and I don't know—I don't know enough about what—I don't know anything about what you would even give somebody to do something like that—but it seems to me that to induce anything into Tia that caused her to be as ill as she was for as long as she was—somebody would have to find something or notice something, or—ah—seen somebody doing something. It's like my husband says, we brought Tia home with a line in her—a central venous line that went into her heart that nobody's brought a child home with—that had to be taken care of under sterile conditions, injecting heparin daily, that kind of thing. I mean, we went through every—it's like we, at that point, totally donated our lives to her—and every moment was spent protecting her—and when you've lived through something like that and then you have somebody turn around and say you could have done something to that child—ah—"

"That's tough. That's real tough. I wouldn't trade positions with you for a million dollars," Lindquist said.

"That's pretty hard to live with, and at this point—I'm sorry—but at this point the way we look at the whole thing is we've got something like nine years of a perfect record in this community of being nothing but caring, loving people without a spot on our background, and one bottle of formula—and suddenly we're the one."

"Yeah, well, you're not necessarily the ones. All I'm telling you is that—"

"Well, I know you're not saying that, but I know other people have, and I have no reason to believe that the doctors at this point are any less suspect than we are—I just wonder how thoroughly things are being looked into."

"Very thoroughly."

Then she went on. She reminded him about Mindy's viral symptoms, and suggested that the sodium level of 160 in Mindy's blood on Saturday had been a mistake, as she had told Dr. Carte. She told Lindquist about Mindy's CMV, about all her efforts to enroll Mindy in special programs, about having to leave the baby-sitting co-op because of it.

"Why would we have invested so much in Mindy? It just doesn't make sense unless, obviously, unless I'm crazy," she said. "I mean, that would have to be. And that would have to show up in some other aspect of my life, it seems like. And I just—it's a hell of a lot to live with to have invested your life day in and day out to meet Mindy's needs and see a lot of improvements and then see this happen."

"Like I said before, I wouldn't trade places with you for a million dollars. I've been trying to think of how I would feel if knowing in my own mind I've done nothing wrong, to have my child taken away from me—I just don't know how I would deal with that," Lindquist said.

Beside her, Steve was gesturing wildly.

"Look, my husband's upset—he's getting on the other phone," Priscilla said. After a moment Steve came on.

"I was just trying to explain to you why Tia is a part of this. They never could really diagnose her illness—" Lindquist began.

"They did find things wrong—they did find abnormal things," Priscilla said.

"They did an intensive autopsy and didn't find anything," Steve said, at cross-purposes.

"Right," Lindquist agreed. "That's what I just said."

"Well it sounds to me like hospitals being institutions—they're walling up—trying to cover their backsides, and I'm really hot about it—" Steve was nearly screaming. "You know we sweated blood, sweat, and tears with that child and because of one high sodium count—"

"One—that's what we don't understand—" Priscilla broke in.

"Someone put something in a G.D. formula—it's bad enough to have this laid on us for the formula thing and to have two doctors—and I won't mention their names for obvious reasons—lay it on us for her whole illness, and I'm going, 'Wait a minute, man, what about conjunctivitis, what about the flu I had, and what about this?'—I'm not a damn doctor. That's why I go to a doctor—"

"Honey—"

"Steve, let me just give you a simple explanation, make you see the logic of the question—" Lindquist put in.

"I don't see the logic only on the basis that Mindy's sodium only was high at the end when something crazy happened," Priscilla interrupted heatedly.

"I see the logic of a group of doctors trying to—well, I see a different logic—" Steve said.

"Honey, let him—"

"I'm going to listen to what—" began Steve again.

Priscilla broke in. "I just want to ask you one question. It's still my understanding that Mindy's sodium was never abnormally high until the end when they—when they discovered everything."

"That's not the case," Lindquist said.

"But Dr. Carte agreed with me on that point."

"It's my understanding that that was not the first time," Lindquist said.

"I know there was high sodium in her stool—" Priscilla said.

"But her blood—there has never been high sodium—" Steve started.

"—that was Tia's problem. We're coming across pretty upset because the doctors are telling us different things—I know her sodium was high in her stools. And Debby kept saying, and Dr. Shimoda, that it was a relief to know that obviously she's not falling in the pattern of Tia because her sodium's not so high—"

"Well, I see a close similarity—" said Lindquist.

"No. I think you're going to find a medical impossibility," Priscilla said.

"The point is this," Steve said. "You said you had Mindy's medical records. Do you have her entire medical records, or do you have what a certain Chief of Pediatrics gave you?"

"No, I don't," said Lindquist.

"Well, I suggest you get that information—"

"I agree with that a hundred percent," Lindquist said.

"Because I smell a big—"

"Honey—"

"You can shade the information to a certain extent. End of comment. Get the whole record, okay?" Steve said.

"Uh-huh. That's exactly what I'm trying to do, Mr. Phillips. You brought up a very good point—that you can have a self-fulfilling prophecy—or make an assumption at the beginning and then find facts to fit that."

"That's right. And that's what I'm saying a couple of doctors have done," Priscilla said.

"My intention is to come up with all the facts, and I expect the facts will lead me to an inescapable conclusion. And I won't reach a conclusion till I've done that."

"I would like to have faith in that," Priscilla said.

"Well, you can bet on it."

Then they covered the same ground again. Priscilla pointed out that Mindy's illness was different from Tia's if the last three days—when perhaps something was going into her formula—were considered separately. Mindy had not had high sodium before and it would be impossible to induce anything into Tia when she was having no oral intake, particularly at so many different hospitals, she said.

"There just isn't a common denominator," Lindquist said with deliberate innocence. The response he elicited was to prove disastrous to Priscilla.

"Obviously the only common denominator is me—and my husband—as her parents, and that's going to be a common denominator any time there's something wrong with any of our children. There's not a day that we weren't with her so that's obviously a common denominator. I don't mind admitting that there's not a person in the world who wasn't totally amazed that Tia developed and lived a life in spite of her illness; that was attributed to me. She was a remarkable child who stood out in the minds of everyone because we were with her and gave her as normal a life as you can have with that kind of illness. So you know, that common denominator works both ways," Priscilla said in a rush.

"Oh, by the way, thanks for the releases of your work records. They've just been delivered to me."

"Anything you want, we'll gladly give. We have been deeply involved in this community for nine years—not only our jobs but community activity, churches, schools, and everything else, and we have a flawless record, and suddenly our lives are filled with flaws," Priscilla said.

"Okay, listen, I don't mean to cut you off, but I've got to go. We'll be talking again. I know I haven't been able to satisfy you. I'm in the middle and I'm looking at it all, and I've tried to reassure you that I intend to come up with an inescapable conclusion. I feel that I personally have a moral and legal obligation—if I cannot determine the entire answer to this—to at least determine that Mr. and Mrs. Phillips are not responsible so they can go back to being the parents of Mindy," Lindquist said.

"That's all we ask. That's the only thing that matters at this point," Priscilla said in a high voice. Good-byes were exchanged and they hung up. Priscilla checked her watch, her head aching. They had been on the phone an hour and a half. They would be late for their appointment with the attorney.

At his desk at the San Rafael Police Department, Ted Lindquist turned off his tape recorder.

3

Mary Vetter's office at Catholic Social Service was spacious, Steve noted. She headed the place and in her way was a damned impressive lady, sharp as a whip, really, he thought. But she played things by the book, and she was not going to leave them alone with Mindy, even if she did sit off to the side writing reports, her head turned away from them.

Priscilla had collected some of Mindy's favorite toys, and when Mercedes Murphy brought her into the room, she squealed at the sight of them—seeming to recognize them and her family immediately. Priscilla swept her up and hugged her—they all hugged her. Steve blinked hard.

Mindy was doing well, Mercedes assured them. If anything her foster mother was probably spoiling her to death. Mindy had been gone a week now, and for Steve it was one of the longest weeks he could remember.

He dreaded the mornings, dreaded what they threatened to bring. Things just kept looking worse. Priscilla was increasingly anxious, and nobody was sleeping or talking to each other, but for the sake of the boys and their friends, they were all trying to pretend it was going to be all right.

Steve knelt on the floor and rolled the bright plastic ball they had brought to Mindy. She waved at it, her little face creased in two with her smile. Jason grabbed at the ball and sent it back to his sister.

"Not so fast, honey," Priscilla told him. "She can't catch it—"

"It's all right. Relax, Pris," he said. She gave him an irritated look. It didn't take much to set her off these days, Steve thought briefly, with the tension so thick around their house you couldn't see your way clear to the kitchen sometimes. If this damned thing didn't break someway or other pretty soon, they all might crack.

People kept assuring them it was going to be just fine—that after the police finished their investigation they'd see how ridiculous it was to suspect Priscilla. Miss Vetter had made the point this morning when they arrived. Jim and Jan Doudiet were saying it, and the Schaefers—everybody. And Gary Ragghianti, their attorney, had been reassuring, too. While they were sitting in his office in downtown San Rafael, he had called Ted Lindquist to ask him about the status of the investigation.

"I know Lindquist," he had told them. "We used to be neighbors. The guy's straight and hardworking and not apt to go off the deep end. I think he'll tell me what's going on." After he had hung up, he had turned to them.

"It doesn't sound like you have a thing to worry about. You're just a part of the whole investigation—not suspects or anything at this point."

"Oh, that's good—that's great!" Priscilla said.

"The only thing is—I'd be glad to handle this as long as it doesn't come down to some kind of a criminal charge against you. If charges are filed, I'll have to drop out because my friendship with Ted could cause a conflict of interest," Ragghianti said.

"That's all right," Priscilla said.

"But it sure doesn't look like it will come to that. Meanwhile we'll see what we can do about getting Mindy back. I'm not an expert on adoption matters, so if it becomes necessary to appear in court on this, I'll refer you to someone who is. But I can handle the preliminary part."

"Good enough," Steve said.

"Now Ted just mentioned something about a consent to release the children's medical records at Kaiser," Ragghianti said.

"We've nothing to hide," Priscilla said.

"Yeah. We want them to look at the records—all of them, not just the ones some doctors gave them." Steve's voice was heavily sarcastic. "The cops should have them all."

"Well, if you feel that way, I think you should sign the consent," Ragghianti said.

So they had done that, Steve remembered as he helped Mindy play with the push toy they had brought. Lindquist had come over that same afternoon to pick up the releases. He had been polite and formal. Who knew what the guy was really thinking, though?

That was the trouble with this whole damn thing, Steve realized. There was no enemy out there—nobody on the other side of the street wearing a black hat to shoot it out with. It wasn't what he was used to. The threat was there, damn it, he knew that. And if somebody would just admit it, he could deal with it. He understood the face-to-face sort of confrontation he had at San Quentin or at juvenile hall. He could deal with the inmate who came up to you and called you a redneck and then stood and watched how you took it. He knew the rules of that game.

But here people were telling him there was no threat. Carte and Callas wouldn't come out and say directly what they meant; they practically claimed they didn't mean anything when the accusation lay right behind those cold eyes of theirs. Lindquist said there was nothing to worry about—him and his inescapable conclusions. So did Ragghianti and Jim Hutchison. Hell, it made Steve angry. There was a lie there—he knew it if no one else did. But you can't gun down a lie, especially when everyone's telling you it doesn't exist. And he couldn't handle these people who didn't confront him back, who didn't even look him in the face.

There were those railroad tracks again, being laid, tie by tie, right up to his front door. He didn't know how to stop them. Except with the truth. That was all he had to fall back on, he thought as he cradled Mindy for an instant in his arms. It was time to go now, to leave her in the care of some stranger for another week.

Steve tensed until Mindy squeaked with the pressure of his arms. Damn it, though, this time he feared the truth might not be enough.

4

It was too bad he had to lie to Gary, Ted thought as he sat at his desk in the small room opposite Investigations. It was the one thing so far he really regretted. Even though it had been three weeks since that phone conversation with Ragghianti, he hadn't stopped thinking about it. Gary was a good friend and had been Ted's lawyer last year when he had worked out Ted's divorce and custody settlements. One of the lousy things about police work was that sometimes he had to lie and mislead, all for the sake of some other, more important, truth.

He knew it was cornball but Ted was certain that there was some kind of great truth out there: a right way to behave, a correct and moral path. It wasn't necessarily the path everybody followed; he wasn't particularly conventional. And although he would admit to being highly moralistic, he would not accept a conservative label. He did believe in a standard of behavior, and he despised people who assaulted others, whatever form that assault took. If he knew about such a person, he tried to stop him no matter what the obstacles. For Ted Lindquist, the end justified almost any means, as long as they were legal. He considered it damned unfortunate that sometimes he had to smoothe around the edges of the truth. But it was often necessary: That was police work.

In this case lies had proved necessary: If Priscilla Phillips knew how close to an arrest they were, there was no predicting how she might react. She might injure herself or the boys. Ted couldn't take that responsibility. At this point he knew it was only a matter of time before the lid blew off the case.

He had had some luck with the medical consents. Because the Phillipses had agreed to release the records, it hadn't become necessary to return the search warrant, so no affidavit had been filed and the extent of the investigation had not been made public. But the investigative net was spreading, and although he continued to ask for confidentiality, it was inevitable that eventually someone would talk.

Ted lit a cigarette and pulled the Phillips files over; they were growing thicker by the day as the evidence mounted. He had interviewed over twenty-five people, some several times. He hadn't worked on anything else since he had started the case, and it was taking up more than all his time. Thank God for Pam at home taking care of his kids, he thought. She didn't have to do it—they weren't her children—but she was taking up the slack uncomplainingly. He felt they had a damned good relationship. It was just fine as it stood, with no marriage in the works. Neither of them wanted that. Ted was soured on matrimony at the moment. He and Sue had married much too young, while she was still in high school. Her pregnancy made her senior year difficult, especially with Ted off at the University of Arizona trying to make the baseball team.

He had been a pretty arrogant kid then, he knew, thinking he could make the best college baseball team in the country when he hadn't been offered a scholarship and had busted up his knee trying to cut up some eucalyptus the summer before. He hadn't made the team. He had just ended up trying to support a wife and a child, then a second child, and attend school at the same time. Even with Sue working, he had been forced to take a year off just to keep them solvent. But he had finished and graduated with a major in Business Administration and Accounting because he thought that would be practical. But a year of boredom working an adding machine in an accounting firm in San Francisco had changed his mind.

He really had always wanted a career in law enforcement. His father had been a member of the CIA for years—in radio communications—doing secret monitoring in a shack in the woods somewhere. For security reasons, he had never talked to Ted about it. But Ted had been attracted and intrigued, and the unrest of the sixties had focused his attention on social problems. So he had chosen to concern himself with the one problem he thought he could help solve. First he had tried to join the FBI, but for reasons he could never learn, the bureau had turned him down. He was invited to reapply later, but instead, at the age of twenty-four, he had joined the San Rafael Police Department.

He felt at home from the beginning. Even when they had him working Graveyard, patrolling the streets alone, he had been happy, content to return home in the morning to play with the kids. Hell, he thought he had everything. But one day toward the end of 1976, his marriage blew up. He and Sue had grown up in different directions, he had been forced to see that, and suddenly Sue could no longer deal with family life. She had departed suddenly for a job as a police dispatcher in Alaska, and he had kept Teddy and Brenna; Sue had agreed to this unhesitatingly, knowing the kids were the most important thing he had going. They were nine and eleven now—not much older than the Phillips boys.

Ted stacked his files on the desk thoughtfully. Erik and Jason Phillips would be the real sufferers in all this, he realized that. It was always the kids who took the punishment.

Ted had first talked to the coroner on March ninth, nine days after he had been handed the case. He had spent those first days trying to discover who had mixed the contaminated formula. He had talked to the nurses involved and found that a conversation had occurred on February twenty-fourth around the time of the afternoon shift change—a conversation Priscilla Phillips couldn't seem to remember. The other nurses remembered it; Lesley McCarcy and Jan Bond—the nurses' aide who had been on duty—both recalled a discussion about whether enough of Mindy's formula had been mixed to last through the upcoming shift. They both remembered that Priscilla Phillips had come up and said yes, there was enough formula, that she had mixed it herself. That was four days after Dr. Carte had issued his order forbidding anyone but nurses to mix the formula. And it was one day before the contaminated formula was discovered.

Debby Roof had been present at this conversation, too. The first time Ted had phoned her, she had contradicted the other nurses. But she had seemed hesitant, hemming and hawing before finally saying that Priscilla hadn't made any statement at all about mixing the formula. But the next day, when he had called her again to tell her he doubted her story, that it didn't jibe with other people's recollections, Debby Roof had changed her story.

"I don't *recall* any such statement by Priscilla," she said instead. It was pretty clear to Ted that the nurse was covering up. She had even admitted that she and Priscilla had become good friends after Tia's death, that their families were close. And Priscilla Phillips's response on the subject had been interesting.

Although her memory in other areas had been outstanding, she had hesitated when he asked her about the same conversation over the phone. She had suddenly become very vague. That telephone call had proved significant, Ted felt: Priscilla Phillips had certainly made an admission of sorts, confessing that she was the common denominator. And he had it on tape. It might be thought-provoking in a courtroom someday, if he could ever get her there.

By now Ted was sure that she belonged in one. Boyd Stephens had been unequivocal. Ted had sent him Tia's and Mindy's records, and Stephens—a real stickler for detail and hard work—had pulled the slides from Tia's autopsy and talked to the doctors and really done his homework. He had spent several weeks on the case, calling in body fluid physiologists from all over the country. Then he had asked Ted to come to his office to discuss his findings.

Ted had been to the San Francisco coroner's office before: The Hall of Justice on Bryant Street also housed the city jail. The gray utilitarian sprawl of building was in an unappetizing section of town made even less appealing by the freeway overpass which shadowed it. But Boyd Stephen's office was cheerful enough. It was large and cluttered with tagged exhibits from various cases. Ted noticed a shotgun and some spent shell casings, boxes of photographs, a model of a skull.

The coroner himself, at thirty-eight one of the youngest chief medical examiners of a major city in the country, was on the phone when Ted arrived. He waved Ted to a seat in front of his large desk. He was a tall man, well over six feet, with a head full of bushy dark hair and black-rimmed glasses.

"Sorry," he said as he hung up. "It seems like I'm on the phone all day long." The phone rang again and he frowned at it. In a moment someone in an outer office picked it up. "I've told them to hold the calls—otherwise I'd never get to talk to you." Stephens smiled.

"Uh-huh. I know how that is," Ted said. "Well, what have you got?"

"It's an interesting case. As you know, when you first

brought this stuff over, I was pretty sure we wouldn't find anything incriminating against the mother."

"What changed your mind?"

Stephens sat back and folded his hands on his desk. "A number of things. These children showed such clinical swings, swings that are incompatible with any known disease. We did a computer search and could find no disease that fit the pattern of the electrolyte changes.

"But it turned out there were a number of significant findings," he went on. "You have to understand something about cell and body physiology, Ted. The bowel is a semi-permeable membrane across which certain things can pass, and the body always tries to maintain equilibrium on both sides of the membrane. If a very large concentration of sodium is placed into the bowel—on one side of the membrane, that is—the body will try to equalize the charge by shifting sodium away from the bowel and into the body as well as by simultaneously increasing the amount of water going into the bowel to try to dilute the sodium. Now that water goes into the gut very rapidly and causes the diarrhea."

"Would the diarrhea itself be very watery?"

"Yes. And it would contain a high amount of sodium. That's the way the body tries to equilibrate the sodium load."

"How much sodium would you have to give to a child?"

"Not very much. To raise the amount of sodium in the stool three hundred milliequivalents would only take about two or maybe three teaspoons of sodium—either concentrated or in diluted form."

"What would happen if you put sodium into an IV? Would that cause diarrhea?"

"No. But it would cause an increased volume of urine and an increased amount of sodium in the urine. And in fact it is the correlation of the sodium in Tia's blood, stool, and urine that can allow us to conclude that she was deliberately poisoned. There were not many times when all three sodiums were tested relatively simultaneously, but when you see that there were places where the sodium in the stool was greater than that in the blood, you know you've got an ingestion of sodium. And Dr. Holliday over at UCSF—and he's one of the top two specialists in the field in the country—agrees. I presented it to him in as unbiased a fashion as I could."

"So it's pretty obvious?"

"Looking back on it, it is."

"Then why didn't the Kaiser doctors spot it?" Ted asked.

"Because it never occurred to them. They were hung up on secretory diarrhea as a diagnosis, and they were like horses with blinders on. Anything that didn't fit the diagnosis was set aside, I imagine, while anything that did was added to the fuel that supported it. Doctors do that all the time."

"Will you testify?"

"Yes, of course. And I'm sure Holliday will, too. And you can't get an expert with any better knowledge of the field than him. Meanwhile, you've got your work cut out for you, Ted. You're taking on God, motherhood, and apple pie, you know. It's not going to be easy."

"Yeah, I know. But there's little Tia buried out in Novato who's got nobody else to defend her at this point. I'll do whatever it takes."

Ted left soon after. As far as he was concerned, there was no time to play around with. Priscilla Phillips was a murderer. And she was a murderer sitting at home with two other children. The sooner she was in custody, the better. Ted went to work.

"You'd better chart the sodium levels," Stephens had suggested. That had taken Ted days, as had the charting of the presence or absence of the mother at the hospital and their correlation with the children's illnesses. The only way he had discovered to chart Priscilla's presence was through the nurses' notes. The nurses were supposed to note down when the parents were in attendance during their shift, and many of them did. But some nurses just indicated the general presence of the family whereas others wrote down exact hours. It was hard for Ted to tell exactly when and for how long Mrs. Phillips had been present at the hospital.

By now Ted had ruled out Steve's involvement in the case. He simply hadn't been there enough or as consistently as his wife. If he knew about it, or was in on it, he wasn't the main perpetrator and they would never pin it on him.

Ted had also been able to rule out any involvement by Priscilla in the other infant deaths in the community. He had been to see William Dacus about the death of his daughter. And he had visited the Searways about their daughter, Cindy. Priscilla Phillips had not been anywhere near the infants during their illnesses or death, it turned out, although she had paid a condolence call on the Searways following Cindy's death. But there hadn't been anything else to tie Priscilla into the deaths, and Ted had let that part of the investigation drop as unfruitful.

Ted had also run up a blind alley pursuing a possible motive of financial gain in the death of Tia. There had been a small insurance policy—actually three different policies—which totaled three thousand dollars, about double what it had cost to adopt her. It didn't amount to a motive, he decided.

But the medical data was totally damning. And he wasn't going to let Priscilla's standing in the community influence him. Her background and good works weren't evidence. Just like the background material on Munchausen Syndrome by Proxy wasn't evidence. One of the Kaiser doctors had sent him an article on that, and it was interesting and he believed that it might turn out to be useful for establishing motive in a courtroom. But that wasn't what made her guilty. The medical results made it plain that Tia and Mindy had been poisoned. Realistically he knew there was no one else who could have done it. Hell, even she saw that.

Now it was a question of persuading the DA's office to act; that was the latest problem. Ted was on his way over to the chief's office now to talk with Benaderet again about how to approach the difficulty. The district attorney didn't want to issue a warrant. Ted had been out to the Civic Center repeatedly to talk with district attorneys Ernie Zunino and Bruce Bales, who kept stalling, insisting that the standing of the suspect demanded a more complete case. Each time he reported his progress, they asked Ted to go back and talk to others, or wait until a computer check Stephens had mentioned was completed, or finish another chart. Each time he had done what they asked, only to find they had thought of another task for him.

"I think it's ready," he had told them the last time. "The more time we take, the more likely she'll find out we're zeroing in on her, and the more likely she'll do something to hurt somebody. The lady's a murderer. She's unstable."

"The case has to be iron-clad," Zunino said. "After you arrest her we have to be ready to go to the preliminary hearing in ten days, if she wants it. You know that. We can't have any loose ends."

Ted had sighed in frustration. He could arrest her without a warrant, of course. Accepted procedure called for the DA to first file a criminal complaint; then Ted could obtain an arrest warrant from a judge. But he could arrest suspects without a warrant as long as he abided by the technicality in the law that he must arrest them in public or at their place of business, not at home. He didn't want to take that route if he didn't need to. The police were supposed to work with the district attorney, not go behind his back. It was a problem Ted hoped the chief could solve. When he knocked now on the chief's door, Frank ordered him in and waved him to a chair.

"What's the problem?" he asked.

"The DA again."

"Look, Ted, you may have to force their hands over there," Chief Benaderet said, looking across his desk at Ted. "I know I've been telling you to go back and do what the DA asked. You're going to need all those charts, and the computer information, whatever," Benaderet continued. Ted watched as the big man eased himself back in his chair.

"But you may be reaching the end of the rope. I know you're worried about her state of mind—"

"Yeah, exactly. I wouldn't want to have that on my conscience. The thing is, there's no doubt anymore. She's guilty as hell."

"Are you sure you've followed up on everything? What did the FBI lab have to say about the contaminated formula?"

"I just talked to the guy over there last week. He came up with the same results as the Kaiser lab."

"Good. Is there anything else needs looking into?"

"Not really. I've talked to the doctors at Kaiser-San Rafael and San Francisco; Dr. Stephens and Dr. Holliday; a doctor at SF General; numerous nurses. I've got a couple more nurses to see, and the doctor who did the autopsy on Tia—who turns out to be the wife of Dr. Applebaum—and another doctor who ran a cardiac exam on Mindy. But essentially we're ready to go."

"Okay. Why don't you get those, and then I'll go with you to the DA and we'll make another attempt at persuading him to issue the complaint. And if it doesn't work, you'll just have to arrest her without a warrant. Sound reasonable?"

"Yeah," Ted said.

"By the way, you're doing a terrific job on this. You're thorough, you've handled people correctly and intelligently, and it's all going to come together for you. Why don't you try going home at a decent hour for a change?"

"Yeah, I will. It's just that this thing's become kind of an obsession with me."

"We've noticed, Ted," the chief said, smiling.

5

Three weeks later, Wednesday, April 26, 1978, the day started off brightly for Priscilla. On Sunday she had confided to her journal:

> I woke up aching even more—went to the family room to lay down with the boys awhile. I love them so much and hurt so much for them that our family cannot be all together and happy like we should be. They don't deserve to go through this! Sundays are such a horrible day for me—I think and think and worry. I think about what it will be like to get Mindy back, what I'll do with her, etc. I can't wait to fix her sandbox, take her to the pool, the park, etc., to expose her to sunshine and summertime, get out her summer clothes, buy her first pair of real walking shoes, etc., etc. But after those thoughts the fear of being charged and going to court reemerges. If that happens, even though we'll be proven innocent and possibly get Mindy back, life will never be the same. The embarrassment, shame, etc. of such a horrible accusation has already begun to scar me, and I'm sure that after such an ordeal as being criminally charged, I'll never be the same. I'm losing some of my basic trust in people, my love for my fellow man. I no longer accept everyone as basically good, trustworthy, etc. I can only pray that God and the judge will return Mindy to us.

It now appeared that Mindy might in fact be restored to them. Five days before they had filed a petition intended to force her return. A court hearing was scheduled for May fifth. Priscilla was already arranging with her friends to appear in court in case the judge would allow character witnesses to testify for her. Many of them had written letters on her behalf to be used at Mindy's hearing.

Another positive thing had happened. Mary Vetter, the head of Catholic Social Service, reported a contact by Ted Lindquist of the San Rafael Police.

"He wanted to know how many of our Korean adoptees had been treated at Kaiser-San Rafael and how many had been hospitalized," she told Priscilla. "I'm going through our records now."

"I think that's a good sign," Priscilla said. "It means they're focusing on Kaiser."

"I agree. It looks like we'll have this all straightened out in a few weeks."

"I certainly hope so," Priscilla said. "Up until the last few days I've just been so depressed—crying and worrying all the time, aimlessly going through Mindy's things. I've neglected the boys, fought with Steve. For a while I could barely sleep. My stomach aches continually. I've worried so about what Sara and all the other doctors think—that consumes me. And there have been times when I was sure I'd be charged and never see Mindy again. You won't believe what I've been doing: writing endless notes pointing out Tia's real illnesses, reminding myself how her infections used to set off diarrhea episodes. Everything I can think of. I wake up every morning with my mind snowballing already. But I'm starting to feel we'll get her back soon."

"I'm sure you will," Mary said.

This morning's local newspaper, the *Terra Linda News*, had added to Priscilla's new sense of well-being. It featured Priscilla's picture and an article about her recent award. It had just been announced that she had received the American Association of University Women's award for her general service to the Marin County branch, and today's paper ran a short feature about her and her family. It mentioned that she resided in Terra Linda with her husband and three children. As she read the short article, Priscilla wondered if she really did have three children—or whether she ever would again. But she brushed the dark thought aside.

Gary Ragghianti seemed confident. He appeared to be pursuing the matter of Mindy's return in a straightforward way. On the advice of Mary Kilgore, a social worker who had counseled Erik and Jason after Tia's death, and with whom Priscilla herself had talked since Mindy's removal to the foster home, Priscilla had consulted a local psychiatrist. With Ragghianti's approval, she had gone once to Dr. Bernard Bradman at the end of March. Bradman's report—which ruled out any psychosis—was intended to reassure the judge at Mindy's custody hearing about Priscilla's stability as a mother. As soon as the police gave up their investigation, there would no longer be any bar to returning Mindy. Priscilla was sure of that.

It had been difficult for her at work in the last weeks, but she tried to concentrate when she was at Social Services. It helped to distract her from her other problems. When she arrived at her office on the top floor of the building, two floors above the courts and just a few doors down from the cafeteria, she found the phone clerk waiting for her.

"Shirley wants to see you, Priscilla," she said. Priscilla left her briefcase at her desk and hurried to the office of the head of Social Services.

"Hi, Shirley. What's up?"

"I don't know. The director wants to see you in his office. Have you got any idea what's going on?" She lowered her voice. "Is it about the investigation?"

"I don't know. I wouldn't think so."

"I doubt it, too," Shirley said.

Shirley walked Priscilla across the hall to the director's office. He was standing at the door waiting for them.

"These gentlemen are here to see you," he said, gesturing toward his Conference Room. Priscilla peered around the director and saw three men. She recognized only one: Ted Lindquist had been to her house to pick up some consent forms for Kaiser six weeks before. He turned to face her as she walked into the Conference Room.

"We're here to arrest you for the murder of Tia Phillips and the attempted murder of Mindy Phillips," Lindquist said.

Priscilla stood stock still, and then she threw her purse down on the conference table in disbelief.

"We want to make this difficult situation as easy as possible. If you can act like a lady, we'll take you out of here without handcuffs," Lindquist continued, staring right at her.

"If you consider me a lady, why arrest me here in front of everybody?" Priscilla retorted.

"I never said I consider you a lady." He took her by the arm and walked her out, the two other detectives bunched beside her, past the secretary's desk and by some coworkers who stood, shocked, while they stared at the strange procession. The whole world knew what was happening, even without handcuffs. Priscilla knew that absolutely.

As they waited for the elevator, Priscilla said quietly, "It's really not your fault that you don't know I'm innocent."

"You're not innocent, Priscilla, and that's why I'm here," Lindquist said, his blue eyes stony.

They took her down to the San Rafael Police Department and Ted Lindquist led Priscilla directly to his tiny office opposite the detectives' room. He waved her to a chair.

"Would you like me to call Gary Ragghianti for you?" he asked. Priscilla nodded. Reaction was beginning, and the tears were welling in her eyes. Lindquist placed the call and held a brief conversation with Ragghianti's secretary.

"He's at the dentist. I've asked his office to try and get in touch with him. Shall I call your husband for you?"

"Yes," she said, beginning to cry.

"Hello, Mr. Phillips? Ted Lindquist." He was curt and to the point. "I'm sorry to have to tell you but we've arrested your wife. She wants to talk to you." He handed the phone to Priscilla.

"Steve, they think I've . . . mur—killed . . . Tia." She couldn't get the word *murder* out; choked with tears she could barely talk.

"It'll be okay, Pris."

"I need you—"

"I'll get there as soon as I can. Don't say anything to them."

"I know. I won't."

She hung up and sat mutely, watching Ted Lindquist search her purse. She looked down at his desk. There was a press release about her arrest on one corner; she tried to read it upside down. It gave a brief history of Tia's illnesses and her hospitalizations at four different hospitals as well as some information on Mindy's contaminated formula. Priscilla thought immediately that this emphasis on the four hospitals meant they were going to stress child abuse in the case. Her work on child abuse syndrome had taught her that it was typical of abusing parents to take their children to different hospitals as a means of escaping detection. But if that was their slant, how were they possibly going to support a murder charge? she wondered.

Priscilla also noticed a list Lindquist had prepared: In his careful, squared-off printing, he had noted the people he wished to inform at the time of her arrest. Annie Jameson's name was on it, as were Mary Vetter's and Dave Neukom's—the Kaiser administrator. The preparations smacked of a set-up, Priscilla thought, like a carefully thought-out game. She wondered if the arrest at work had all been part of the game, too. If they had just asked her to, she would have come down to the police department.

After a while another officer who introduced himself as Tony Hoke came in to escort her to another room in the department. On the way, they passed a beverage machine.

"Would you like a drink?" he asked.

"Thank you. I'll have a Pepsi."

The officer inserted some coins and gave her the drink. It was an act of compassion she would never forget. Then he took her down the hall.

She was locked in a small room alone to await her lawyer. She could hear a little of what was going on, and once she heard someone mention "special circumstances." The phrase chilled her. She knew enough about California law to realize that a murder charge in conjunction with special circumstances meant a non-bailable, death-penalty offense. She believed there were several circumstances that made a murder "special." They included the murder of a police officer, murder by torture, murder for financial gain, and some others she couldn't remember. She wondered how it could possibly be a special circumstances case, and if she would ever get out of jail. She sat and sipped at the Pepsi, her head down.

When Gary Ragghianti finally came in, he was cold with anger.

"They don't even have a warrant," he said.

"What does that mean?"

"It means the DA wasn't ready to file charges. This whole thing is highly unusual. However I've talked to the district attorney and he *is* going to proceed with this, Priscilla. I'm sorry—apparently Lindquist was afraid you might have a breakdown or something, so he went ahead without the warrant."

"What about bail? I heard something about special circumstances—does that mean no bail?"

"Ordinarily, yes. Lindquist asked that no bail be set. But their not having a warrant works for you on this."

"Why? I don't understand."

"There's no warrant on file and therefore the DA hasn't

declared he's seeking the death penalty. He hasn't declared anything. So bail will be set—but I'm sure it will be steep."

"What happens now?"

"They're going to transfer you to county jail—I'll meet you out there. I'll talk to Steve. I don't think he should come out here at this point. But Priscilla, as I explained to you when you first came to me, I can't handle this case now they've arrested you. I have a possible conflict because of my friendship with Lindquist, and in addition, I'm very overloaded with work and couldn't give you the appropriate time. Now do you know another lawyer, or would you like me to recommend someone?"

Priscilla shook her head. "No, we don't know anyone."

"I have someone in mind—he's very good. An ex-DA named Roger Garety. I'll see if I can get him out to see you at the county jail."

"All right. I just can't understand why they arrested me at work, though. It's really bothering me."

"Without a warrant they couldn't arrest you at home."

"Then why not just ask me to come down here? I would have. There was no call to drag me out like that in front of everyone." She was in tears again.

"I guess it would have been false pretenses. Cops are very careful because of the exclusionary rule."

"But they could even have told me they were going to arrest me. I still would have come."

Gary looked at her kindly. "But they couldn't know that, Priscilla."

"I know it has something to do with Mindy's court date— that's why they're arresting me—they don't want me to get Mindy back."

Ragghianti shook his head. "I don't know. But Lindquist sure led me down the garden path on this one. Look, Priscilla, they're going to take you now—I'll see you over at the county jail. It'll be all right."

She nodded. After a moment Tony Hoke and another officer came in.

"We're supposed to cuff you, but I'm not going to do it until we get out of the garage at Civic Center," Tony said gently.

"Thank you," Priscilla said. The three of them walked out of the station and into the police car for the short drive back to Marin County Civic Center, which contained not only the courts and the Department of Social Services, but also the county jail.

Later she realized they treated her with kid gloves. The proper rituals were observed—she was photographed and fingerprinted, searched, given a shower, and issued prison denim jeans and a bright orange sweatshirt—but each step in the process was handled delicately. Everyone treated her with courtesy.

She was interviewed by a man from Community Health.

"I have been asked to see you because some fears have been expressed about your mental stability. They're worried you may be suicidal," he said, probing.

"You don't have to worry," she sobbed. "All I'm interested in is getting out and proving my innocence. I'm not going crazy or about to kill myself."

After that interview she was placed in another room—it was a cell, Priscilla supposed, although there were no bars. She was left there alone.

"We're keeping you apart because of the nature of the crimes you're accused of. It's for your own safety," she was told.

It was freezing in the cell, and all she could find to put around her were some rough, scratchy wool blankets. The cell contained two metal bunk beds built into the wall, a table—also bolted to the wall—with stools on either side, a toilet, sink, and shower. A television hung at an angle in one corner. By jail standards, the cell was luxurious. Priscilla found out later it had once housed Angela Davis.

Priscilla looked over at the television, wondering if she could turn it on. She was afraid to do so without permission and there was no one to ask, so she left it dark. They had taken her watch and she could not see a clock from the window in her cell. She had nothing to do and desperately wanted paper and pencil to write down her thoughts, to occupy her mind; she had become dependent on her journal. She was terrified.

Gary Ragghianti came to see her; Jim Hutchison arrived, so did the new lawyer, Roger Garety. He was a man in his sixties with a reassuring voice and confident tone. She asked him about special circumstances.

"They're saying Tia's death amounted to death by torture," he said.

"But that's ridiculous! Even if I did it, you couldn't say I tortured her! The only ones who tortured her were the doctors!" Priscilla was sobbing.

"Don't worry—it'll never hold up in court," Garety soothed her.

"I want you to know I'm innocent, Mr. Garety," Priscilla told him.

"All right. I'll be visiting every day. You can tell me all about it," he said. "Bail has been set at a hundred thousand dollars."

"Oh, no!" Priscilla cried. "We'll never raise that!"

"I'm pretty sure I can get it reduced. Meanwhile I'll see you at the arraignment tomorrow," Garety said.

More vistors arrived. A public defender called to see if she required his services. A private attorney, one of a famous legal family, asked if she needed an attorney; a friend of his who knew Priscilla had recommended that he drop by, he said. And Mary Kilgore managed to get in. Priscilla did not realize until afterward that extraordinary visiting privileges had been extended to allow her all these visitors. She still felt lonely, afraid, and terribly cold. That was what she later remembered most vividly about county jail: the cold.

6

On May second, Jim Hutchison made his seventh consecutive visit to Priscilla. The day she had been arrested he had managed only a brief stay with her. Priscilla had seemed dazed and confused and he had tried to reassure her. But he was having difficulties sorting out his own emotions. Bits and pieces of memories kept touching his consciousness and interfering with his attempts to support Priscilla. Over the following six days he remembered the long discussions she had held with him during Tia's illness, and her apparent delight in the most exquisite detailing of the child's symptoms and treatments.

There were other things about her behavior that had struck him at the time as strange. He recalled once watching Priscilla at the hospital as she fed Tia. She had crammed the food in roughly—over the baby's wild protests—scraping the formula from around the tiny mouth and forcing it back in. She was always rough in her treatment of Tia—her pattings were almost staccato buffets, he remembered.

Then when Steve had called him with the news that someone was poisoning Mindy, everything began to fall into place for Jim. He had been so uncomfortable with Steve's call that he had asked Marj Dunlavy, the parishioner with whom he felt most at ease, to accompany him to Kaiser and wait in the car while he saw Steve and Priscilla. He had asked for Marj's confidence and then he had told her what he knew.

Marj had offered some insights of her own.

"Priscilla always seemed to get a charge out of telling all the graphic details of Tia's treatment," she said.

"Yes. And I had the feeling she was trying to upstage me with her medical knowledge. It was a way of making herself the center of attention. And you know, at times, in retrospect, it felt that although Priscilla was always crying and terribly upset about Tia and then Mindy, that she was not truly emotionally involved in their illnesses at all," Jim said.

"What do you mean?"

"It was a strange thing, Marj, but it seemed to me that she was intellectualizing the illnesses and the horrible treatments rather than feeling how awful it must be for those poor babies. It was almost as though she was trying to shock me with the horribleness of their suffering—oh, it's hard to explain. It just seemed inappropriate, somehow."

"I know what you mean," Marj said. "I've noticed other inappropriate behavior. Right after the memorial service for Tia, I had the feeling Priscilla was almost *excited*. And then when we got home, Bill and I talked about her strange reaction, how she went around with a little smile on her face. Bill told me she had come up to him after the service to thank him for getting up to talk about Tia. She was just sort of gaily chattering."

"Like she was a star after a marvelous performance in a play?"

"Yes, like that."

"Well, I've often felt that Priscilla liked to put on little dramas. She tended to display her children—almost set them out with their toys around them and invited you to admire them."

"Yes, and her children always had to be the best at everything—the loudest, the wildest, the smartest, the prettiest—"

"Or the sickest," Jim filled in.

And now Priscilla had been arrested. Jim had suspected that

might happen. He had even talked with Priscilla about the possibility. He remembered that she had shaken her head in disbelief. "If only they'd leave Tia out of it, I could cope with all this," she'd said. Jim wondered now if they would exhume Tia because he knew there was no way she could be left out of it. She was central to the case.

Meanwhile he had to find a way to deal with Priscilla. She was counting on him for support and strength and Jim felt he had to provide those things as best he could. He had been trying to do that since they had taken Mindy away from Priscilla. It wasn't his place to judge her.

"How are you, Priscilla?" he asked now, taking a seat on his side of the screen.

"Oh, I'm doing better. I asked the commander for my watch and they've allowed me paper and pencils and envelopes and things. People are writing me notes, and the commander asked me to tell everyone to stop calling here. The phone's been ringing off the wall, he said."

"Yes, the community's behind you, Priscilla. Steve and Nancy Dacus and the Doudiets have organized a defense fund for your bail," Jim said.

"It was reduced this morning at the bail hearing. It's only forty thousand dollars now," she said with a bitter laugh.

"We'll raise the money. Everybody's pitching in. The church can loan you some." He paused. "You never told me what happened at the arraignment."

"Mr. Garety put off the plea till he could get a gag order—which the judge issued. They were asking for the death penalty but someone in my lawyer's office discovered that Tia died before the death penalty was in force. Thank God I don't have to worry about that, at least! But Jim, I'm really worried about the boys. I've never been separated from them—except when I had the hysterectomy, and they've had so many losses and separations. I've talked to them on the phone and I just—" she began to cry.

He wondered for a moment how Priscilla could claim this was the only time she had been separated from Erik and Jason. He remembered all those nights she had spent at the hospital.

"They're all right, Priscilla. I think Steve is doing very well. He's had to battle off the press—"

"Yes, he's told me." She had regained her composure. "And he's real upset about the police search of our house. Steve said they took away all Tia's leftover medical supplies, the baking soda from our cupboard, a book on Korea we had, my appointment books, the girls' baby books, and even the Merck manual that Steve used when he wrote up disability evaluations—the book with all the medical diagnoses."

"Priscilla, is there anything I can get you—or do for you?"

"No, I guess not. I've been reading a James Herriot book. Oh, and thanks for picking my mother up at the airport yesterday."

"That's okay. She's doing wonderfully well with all this. She's holding on beautifully."

"And the boys? You're sure they're all right?"

"They're fine, Priscilla. Steve has started them back in school. Is there anything else?"

"No—just your prayers."

"Of course, Priscilla. You always have those. Will you be all right?"

"Yes. I've been so cold—they finally brought me a sweater— but it just penetrates everything. And I have a lump in my throat all the time."

"Won't they bring you a drink?"

"Only coffee—and you know how I hate that."

"How are you sleeping?"

"I didn't sleep much last night. I asked them for something and the nurse brought me a pill but she wouldn't let me swallow it. Instead she poured the powder out onto my tongue—I could barely get it down. It's so dehumanizing—" she began to cry.

"Jails are terrible places, Priscilla. We'll have you out soon."

"Jim?"

"Um?"

"I didn't do it! Why are they saying I did this when I didn't? I loved Tia so much—it was like a part of me died along with her! How can they do this?"

Jim, conflicted, hesitated.

"I don't know," he finally said.

With a final murmured word, he left. As he walked distractedly toward his car, he wondered about Priscilla's convincing protestations of innocence. He had majored in Pastoral Psychology, however, and he thought he had an answer. He had learned that most pathological people are convincing not in spite of but because of their pathology: they believed their own stories.

7

One week later, Steve walked up to the clerk at the Marin County jail and handed him a check for $40,000. The clerk looked at him in disbelief.

"This is Priscilla Phillips's bail money," Steve said.

"Hey, man, I can't take this! You gotta go to municipal court with this." Steve slumped. It just seemed like the next in a series of incredible hassles he had faced attempting to raise the bail. From the moment of Priscilla's arrest, Steve realized that finances were going to be a serious problem. Since Jim Doudiet was a treasurer for Pacific Gas and Electric, Steve had consulted him.

"I guess we're talking about big bucks here—by the time we finish with the bail and the attorneys," Steve said.

"Absolutely. Now let's see what you've got in terms of assets. Then we can decide how to proceed," Jim answered.

"We've got about three or four thousand dollars in savings, and the house. That's about it," Steve told him.

"I think you'd better hold the house back. A bail bondsman's going to want collateral, and if you give him the house, you'll have no resources for the lawyer. I think any reasonable attorney's going to need some collateral, too—a second mortgage or something. So we should keep the house in reserve."

"So how do we get bail without a bondsman?"

"We organize a defense fund and we raise it, Steve."

They had done just that. In fact they had raised $50,000. The extra $10,000 was to go to the attorney. The money had trickled in erratically and in different forms. There were checks from Steve's and Priscilla's families on the East Coast, money orders, cash donations. It all had to be collected and cleared and placed in one account before a cashier's check could be issued. Steve could do nothing but wonder at the extent of the community response—he had been so fearful at first about how people might react.

The first night after the arrest, he had walked nervously about the house. Looking back on it he realized that he hadn't behaved totally rationally. At one point that evening, he had loaded his twelve-gauge shotgun and sat up with it across his knee like some old-time sheriff expecting the outlaws to ride in. He was so afraid that when the news got out, a carload of the kids he had been counseling might see fit to come out and blow up the house. Priscilla had been working on the Child Protective Service, writing reports that were taking children out of their parents' houses—there was no predicting how those people might react when they read in the paper what their social worker had been accused of doing to her own children.

But his fears had proved groundless: No one had threatened them. Their friends had rallied in total support, and the boys were doing well, although sometimes Priscilla's daily phone calls reduced them to tears. Visiting at Marin County jail was bleak: glass separated the prisoner from the visitor and communication was by telephone. Since the family was not permitted to use the attorney's room, Steve didn't take the boys to visit, deciding it would be too upsetting for them. Marietta's arrival had relieved some problems, particularly the baby-sitting chores. Steve was worried that Marietta might drop dead of a heart attack when he called to tell her the news of Priscilla's arrest. He and Priscilla had never told Pris's mother, nor any of the family, about Mindy's formula and her subsequent removal to a foster home because they kept telling each other that it would all blow over, that it would be only a needless worry for their relatives. So the news had been a shock. But Marietta had borne it well. Steve knew she was a very strong woman with a religious faith that would support her through anything.

But Steve had other problems. The press was hounding him; Priscilla didn't realize how terrible it was. Television vans and reporters camped on their doorstep, shouting questions at him every time he emerged. Finally Garety gave Steve permission to talk.

"If you give them a little something, it will get them out of your hair," the attorney said. "You can talk all you want about your background—how you met Priscilla, your jobs and community ties—that sort of thing. But stop at the point when you adopted Tia. Don't tell them anything beyond that," Garety cautioned.

"Okay," Steve said. Yesterday he had granted his first interview, determined to be absolutely frank about their family. He had told a reporter from the *San Francisco Chronicle* about meeting Pris.

"She bowled me over," he confided. He reminisced about their marraige and, in an effort to be completely open, even brought out their problems together when he had first worked at San Quentin. But mainly he stressed what a wonderful wife and mother Priscilla had always been. The *Chronicle* had run a front-page story today, a long story with other quotes from their friends and neighbors and even a quote from Jim Hutchison, who had discussed Priscilla's journal of Tia's illness. Steve thought it strange that Jim should mention that—it didn't seem very supportive. Fleetingly, it occurred to Steve that Jim should not be talking to the press at all. But basically Steve was pleased with the *Chronicle* story, which had been accurate and favorable. After he bailed Priscilla out, Steve hoped there would be no further reason for press coverage for a while. The preliminary hearing would be closed, Garety assured them. Maybe they'd retrieve a bit of their privacy; that would be damned nice, Steve thought.

He would never forget the experience of having his house searched—the day following Priscilla's arrest. Steve had been expecting it, but it still rolled over him like a huge invasion, like something out of Nazi Germany. There had been four detectives and a uniformed cop who had left after introducing the detectives. The others stayed for several hours, dividing themselves into two-man teams and working methodically. Steve was glad Lindquist wasn't with them. He couldn't have dealt with Lindquist right then, he knew. Not that he trusted any of those suckers. He moved from room to room with them to make sure they didn't plant any evidence. He could see the whole search was basically a fishing expedition. He laughed grimly to himself when he saw them take the baking soda and baking powder out of the cabinet: as if there was a house anywhere without those boxes! It had annoyed the hell out of him when they wanted to take Tia's baby book; he had fought with them over that. The cops had finally ended up removing it—along with Mindy's—but they agreed to leave behind the album of Tia's photographs. They had confiscated some crazy things, Steve thought: Pris's telephone book and her calendars from the previous couple of years; the can of Korean formula they had been saving to show Tia when she grew up; all eight of Pris's handbags; the numerous formula bottles and cans they had collected; the syringes and sterile gloves they still had from when Tia's central catheter was heparinized; even their copy of Dr. Spock and all the copies of a parents' magazine they subscribed to. Well, he hoped they'd have fun plowing through all of that.

"I don't know when I resigned from the state of California," he told Jim Doudiet later, "but I felt like I had right then. I don't remember signing away my constitutional rights. Hell, they invaded me."

Jim shook his head in disgust. "I know it must feel that way. But how's Priscilla doing?"

"Not real well. She got superdepressed when Garety showed her the police reports. Up until then she kept saying that there was no way they could claim she had done it, but she says those reports have all kinds of damning evidence from doctors—people she thought were on her side. Even Jim Hutchison talked to the cops—steered them around to other infant deaths in the community. It certainly looks like he was helping the cops when he was mouthing off to us that he supported Pris," Steve said in disgust.

"It doesn't seem very ministerial of him," Jan Doudiet said wonderingly.

"You're damn right. And Pris also says there's lots of things in the police reports that are wrong, like a Kaiser nurse saying Pris mixed some formula when she didn't, and some woman over at Kaiser-San Francisco who claimed Pris walked off and left Tia when she was about to die. That really ticks me off! But Pris said she was real shocked at what some of those supposedly supportive doctors like Shimoda and Applebaum had to say to the cops."

"Has she talked to the lawyer about the false reports?"

"Yeah. She asked him how we were gonna fight back on all of that, and he said it wasn't like that—that we have to come up with evidence to dispute their evidence. He's optimistic, though, Pris told me."

"She'll improve once she gets out of there," Jan said.

"Yeah. It's the separation from the boys that's really killing her," Steve said.

Well, now he was going to get her out, Steve thought as he crossed the road from the county jail to the section of the Civic Center that contained the courts. And without spending a penny of their own money, either. He couldn't believe they had pulled that off, but it was damned fortunate. They were going to need every cent of his salary because Social Services had suspended Priscilla the minute she had been arrested. Their income had been cut in half. That was just the least of it.

This arrest has torn Steve apart; there was no other way for him to look at it. When Pris had spoken to him from Lindquist's office the day of the arrest, he thought he would burst with anger and shock. He had hurled himself about the house, kicking at the furniture like a two-year-old. Deep in his heart, he was afraid he would be arrested too. Numbly he arranged to have the Doudiets care for Erik and Jason. Then he sat waiting for the roof to cave in. Ragghianti didn't want him down at the jail, and that made sense to Steve. He knew they wouldn't let him see Priscilla anyway.

Thoughts had raced in his head, darting in and out of his consciousness. He wondered about that damn polygraph Pris had taken a few weeks ago, whether maybe they should have pursued that some more. She had gone in for the test with the attitude that if she passed, it would impress the police, maybe force them to return Mindy to them.

But Pris had been in such a state about everything, Steve was certain every nerve in her body had jumped whenever the examiner mentioned Tia's or Mindy's name. He was positive he could be lying through his teeth and still pass one of those things, that he could make any part of his body lie quiet if he told it to. But Pris was as emotional and wrought-up as hell, and that's where these tests fell down on the job. She had passed most of the exam: Later she had tried to reconstruct the questions and wrote down what she remembered and showed it to him. About half the questions had been control questions designed to establish a baseline for truthful and untruthful responses. There had been four questions directly relevant to the case, and she had done all right on three of them.

"When he asked me whether I *intentionally* induced a *sodium substance* into Tia or Mindy, I freaked out," she told him. "You know I've been going around telling everyone I would never intentionally harm any of my children. I told the examiner that the use of that word was what I was responding to."

"What did he say?"

"He agreed—because I passed the question about whether I had knowledge of what caused the high sodium to occur and the one about whether I felt directly responsible for Tia's death. He said I should probably redo the test and reword some of the questions, that he would talk to Ragghianti about it."

But the test had never been rescheduled. Everyone had focused on that one question, deciding that a report should not be written by the polygraph examiner because the results were inconclusive and wouldn't help Priscilla.

It was the way this whole damn thing was going, Steve thought as he lined up to speak with the municipal court clerk about Priscilla's bail. Here Steve ran into another snag. The court clerk was accustomed to dealing with bail bondsmen and didn't know what to do with a certified check for $40,000. So they danced Steve back and forth in a kind of crazy waltz of frustration. The jail wouldn't release Priscilla without a receipt, and no one would issue one.

Finally the transaction was completed. Then he waited. The processing for Priscilla's release stretched into the afternoon. When she emerged, shortly after five-thirty, she flew into his arms. Ten minutes later they were knocking at the Doudiets' door. Erik and Jason launched themselves at their mother, hugging and kissing and patting her. Everyone was crying. Priscilla was home.

8

The fire flashed, arced, and sped up the flesh of her arm to her shoulder and neck. Suspended for a moment on the point of understanding, Priscilla stared at the flaming cup of white liquid gas that she still clutched, watching it shrivel—the edges blackening and curling like a leaf blown haphazardly into a barbecue fire—in her hand. Then she was on the ground by the campfire, rolling.

"Priscilla!" Steve was by her side at once, pouring handfuls of dirt on her bathing suit as she twisted, trying to smother the flames with it.

Skip Schaefer sprinted across the Lake Berryessa campground to the clothesline and was back in a moment with an armful of wet towels. Nancy Schaefer added a bedspread, and with these they wrapped Priscilla.

"Mommy! Mommy!" Jason and three-year-old Scotty Schaefer were in hysterics. Marietta moved to comfort them, her face ashen.

"Oh, my God," she murmured. "Oh, my God. What more can happen?"

"Someone call an ambulance!" Steve cried.

"Let's get her in the car. It will be faster if we meet the ambulance at the turnoff," Skip said. He helped Priscilla to the car. "Nancy, how is she?"

"She's pretty badly burned," Nancy said. She looked anxiously at Priscilla, watching her chest. "But her breathing is okay."

"Skip and I will take her—you and Marietta stay here," Steve said to Nancy.

"But Nancy's a nurse—shouldn't she go?" Marietta said.

"I'm so cold! Oh, I'm so cold," Priscilla moaned from the car. The pain was suddenly excruciating, focusing in on her right arm. She began to shake. Quickly Nancy rolled up the car windows.

"I think I'd better stay here to help Marietta with the kids," Nancy said. "It's not life-threatening—I can see it's not life-threatening."

Priscilla sat and cried and trembled as Skip drove the ten miles to the crossroads where the ambulance would have to turn off.

"It's going to be all right, Pris," Steve kept saying.

"Oh, it hurts—it hurts so much." She struggled to turn her mind from the pain. This was supposed to have been her last weekend of peace. The preliminary hearing was scheduled to start Monday. The twenty-four days since her arrest had been one of the worst periods in her life.

They had not appeared in court to plead for Mindy's return. After Priscilla's arrest, such a petition was no longer feasible, and they had been forced to abandon the effort. It had been an active pursuit—Priscilla had seen to that. She had asked friends to write to Catholic Social Service recommending that Mindy be returned home; Mary Vetter told Priscilla that she had received over twenty-five favorable letters and not a single negative one. But after the arrest, Priscilla realized the futility of their situation.

Until then, Mary had not been pushing to place Mindy in a new adoptive home, although she indicated that there had to be some reasonable time limit. The foster home arrangement could not be allowed to continue indefinitely; it would not be good for Mindy. But after Priscilla's arrest, Mary called. She was not unkind, but she was firm.

"I'm afraid things have changed now. If you persist with the petition to have Mindy returned, we'll have to take it to court and get some kind of a determination."

"Well, I know how a judge would rule at this point," Priscilla said bitterly.

"Yes, I'm afraid you're right. And in any case, I'm certain you realize it just wouldn't be fair to Mindy—waiting for the outcome of the trial. It could take years. I'll start thinking about a new family for her," Mary said.

Priscilla burst into tears. "She's mine, don't you see? She's mine!" she had said.

The camping trip with the Schaefers had been designed as a quiet interlude between Priscilla's arrest and the furor certain to be generated by the preliminary hearing. Priscilla had vowed not to think about the case. The Schaefers had a sixteen-foot sailboat they could putter about on to help distract her.

That Saturday broke shimmering hot. Priscilla, Steve, Skip, and Nancy drifted on the lake in the boat, baking in the sun, while the boys paddled around on rafts and Marietta sunbathed on shore.

At dinnertime they came off the lake for hamburgers. Priscilla discovered a paper bag of charcoal briquettes in the camper but no one had remembered the lighter fluid.

"Maybe I can just light the bag and start it that way," Priscilla said. She knelt by the fire pit and lit the paper, watching it as it flared and burned quite merrily for two minutes. Then it went out.

"Here, I'll go down to the store and pick up some fluid," Steve said. He started to leave, then paused and came back. "But you have a Coleman stove, Skip. Can't we just use some of your gas?"

"No, no," Nancy said immediately. "We shouldn't; it's dangerous."

"Well, just put a little in a cup. That should be all right," Steve said. Skip crossed to their supplies and returned with a Styrofoam cup. Priscilla took it out of his hand and poured a little on the dead coals.

"Go ahead, pour it all on," Steve said. And so she had.

The ambulance, lights and siren flaring, met Skip's car at the turnoff to Berryessa and drove Priscilla to the Queen of the

Valley Hospital in Napa. The attendants poured saline solution on the burns while Priscilla writhed and shivered. In the Emergency Room, the doctor administered Demerol, started an IV, and washed the burns that covered her right arm and shoulder, her neck, and patches of her chest and abdomen. He charted her burns as first and second degree and arranged to transfer her to Kaiser-San Rafael. It was the last place Priscilla wanted to go, but continued hospitalization in any but a Kaiser facility would not be covered by Steve's hospital plan.

Steve rode with her in the ambulance, back through Napa and Sonoma counties to Marin, but for Priscilla the trip was a blur of half-drugged pain.

"Hang in there, honey," Steve repeated continually in her ear. And under his breath once, she heard him mutter, "C'mon, God, this is enough."

After a stay in Kaiser's Emergency Room, they transferred her into a room and Dr. Ritchings, a surgeon, came in to examine her. She was fogged with pain medication but she could hear Steve.

"Pris, we're not going to leave you. The Schaefers have notified the Doudiets already, and they're setting up a sheet for everybody to sign to make certain you're not alone here—ever. I don't trust these suckers—and I'm going to tell Dave Neukom when I see him exactly why not. Don't worry, he'll watch his backside while you're here."

"Um." Priscilla drifted off. She remembered little of the next few days, but she was vaguely aware of comforting hands. Later she noticed a considerable amount of activity outside her door. People wanting to see the burned murderer, she supposed bitterly. She recognized some of the nurses from pediatrics, but only Debby Roof and Maria Sterling came in. The rest just stared at her. Maria had been in the E.R. when Priscilla arrived, and had brought her up to her room. She had been sympathetic and kind. Of the doctors Priscilla knew, Dr. Arnhold, who had once been the boys' pediatrician, visited several times. Sara Shimoda did not appear.

There had been no contact between Priscilla and Sara for some time. After Mindy's removal to a foster home, Priscilla had agonized for several weeks over what Sara must be thinking. She asked Jim Hutchison to telephone Sara to assure her of Priscilla's innocence. She questioned Debby and Maria about Sara's attitude when they came over one day, but they could not tell her much. It had reassured Priscilla that the

nurses continued to support her, to express shock and
incredulity at the idea that Priscilla might be considered
responsible for Tia's and Mindy's illnesses. But she was
obsessed with wondering about Sara's reaction; several times
she woke from dreams about Sara. Finally she sent her a ten-
page letter. Several weeks later, Sara finally telephoned. The
conversation lasted for over two hours; Priscilla did most of the
talking.

"I just wanted to see how you're getting on," Sara told her.

"It's so hard! I can't stand it here without Mindy—not
knowing how she's doing—where she is. Mary Vetter says she's
with an older woman so they wouldn't have to worry about the
foster mother getting pregnant."

"Because of Mindy's CMV?"

"Yes. But, Sara, it's so terrible! Imagine how you'd feel if
they had taken Elizabeth away!" She wept hysterically into the
telephone.

"I know, Priscilla. I've been thinking about that," Sara said.

The conversation had cheered Priscilla. Still, she was
haunted by fears that all the doctors thought her guilty. Soon
some of the other hospital staff called to reassure her. Rich
Coolman told Priscilla that the San Francisco staff's reaction
had been disbelieving.

"The only thing they can figure is that you must have a split
personality!" he told her hesitantly.

"But you know I don't!" Priscilla answered.

"Of course," Rich said.

Since the arrest there had been no further word from Sara.
Once again Priscilla asked Jim to call her. "Just tell her I'm
hurting so much over this," Priscilla said. But Jim reported
back that Sara had been cool.

And now Priscilla was forced to stay at a hospital where she
knew herself to be hated and feared. But at least she was never
alone.

Several times Jim Hutchison stayed the night with her,
acting as a "special" nurse. He asked her about the status of the
hearing.

"My lawyer had to appear with Dr. Ritchings to get the
preliminary hearing put off. The doctor says I'll be here two
weeks."

"You had a serious burn, Priscilla," Jim said.

Once, in a feeble attempt at a joke, he gestured at the IV

line and said, "Here, I'll just put a little sodium in here!" But Priscilla didn't laugh.

Later she turned to Jim and said, "Now I suppose they'll be saying I did this to myself."

Jim reached for her hand and said nothing.

9

On Tuesday morning, June 13, 1978, three weeks after it was originally scheduled to start, Priscilla Phillips's preliminary hearing began in Municipal Courtroom Eleven at the Marin County Civic Center. The hearing—at the request of the defendant—was closed to the public, and a gag order remained in effect. The only people present were Deputy District Attorney Kathryn Mitchell, Detective Ted Lindquist, attorney Roger Garety, and his associate Sheila Reisinger, Priscilla and Steve Phillips, Judge Gary Thomas, the court reporter, clerk, and bailiff. The courtroom door was locked.

Normally, Kit Mitchell would have selected as her courtroom assistant the district attorney's own staff investigator, Charles Neumark. But at the special session of the Phillips preliminary hearing the week before, she had requested that Neumark be replaced by Ted Lindquist. Lindquist had done all the investigative work on the case and was thoroughly familiar with it. Judge Thomas had agreed to the change.

Ted had anticipated this approval. He had already received permission from the captain and from Chief Benaderet to work full time with the DA on the preliminary hearing. Everyone in the police department recognized the necessity of this. In the last few weeks, Ted had relied upon and received the total support of the department. Without it, the pressures of this case would have overwhelmed him.

But he felt that now he had covered every possible base. He had spent hours working with Sara Shimoda and Evelyn Callas on the medical records, and he knew Kit Mitchell had done the same.

"We've got to organize these records into something understandable—and into something we can present vividly in court," she said. And after weeks of effort, she had succeeded. The charts she had brought to court were simple yet complete.

Ted did not know Kit Mitchell well. Only thirty-one, she was one of the youngest members of the district attorney's staff. She was the juvenile court deputy, and because of that many cops went to her with matters that involved juveniles as victims, even though her responsibility was to handle juvenile offender cases.

Although she had been one of the district attorneys opposed to issuing an arrest warrant for Priscilla, once they had made the arrest, Kit Mitchell had worked on nothing else. Ted was impressed with both her stamina and her intelligence. She had the credentials—he knew that from the Berkeley Phi Beta Kappa certificate framed on her wall, and her Hastings College of Law diploma; but what counted more for Ted was the way she applied her mind.

"You know, math and science were never my strong points," she confided one evening to Ted as they pored over the medical records. "But I'm going to master this stuff if it kills me. It's the key to the case." And she had attacked that data, studying until she understood it.

Last Tuesday there had been a special session of the preliminary to accommodate body fluid physiologist Dr. Malcolm Holliday, who was leaving the following day for a seven-month sabbatical in England and who would not be available to testify at the regular preliminary the following week. And now, seven days later, the preliminary was to resume.

Ted had done what he could: everything now depended on Kathryn Mitchell. In a preliminary hearing, it was the duty of the prosecution to convince the judge that there was reasonable suspicion to believe both that a crime had been committed and that the defendant was responsible. The defense did not have to put on a case and Ted was aware it was very unlikely that one would be offered here, as Garety would not want to tip his hand about the direction of the defense before the actual trial.

Ted looked over at Priscilla Phillips. She was sitting calmly next to her attorney, a yellow legal pad in front of her. During the examination of Dr. Holliday the week before, she had taken copious notes, many of which she had passed to Garety. Sometimes Ted had caught a half-smile on her face.

"You know," Kit had remarked, "she seems almost jolly."

"Almost as though it was happening to someone else," he answered. "She'll catch on soon enough."

10

Roger Garety had been frank with Steve and Priscilla this morning, the last day of a preliminary hearing that had stretched—interminably, it seemed to Steve—eleven days.

"You will almost certainly be bound over for trial," he said to Priscilla. "As Judge Thomas indicated yesterday, today's session is designed to give the attorneys an opportunity to make statements about what the evidence showed, and also about what you should be charged with: first degree, second degree, manslaughter, and so forth. If we can get the charge reduced, that will be a major accomplishment, and about the best to be hoped for at this juncture."

Steve nodded. It had been obvious from early in the proceedings that the prosecution had prepared a very strong case. But as Pris had said over and over to Garety, much of the evidence was slanted and biased and inaccurate. Still some of the medical evidence in particular had given him a jolt, especially the testimony of Dr. Martin Blinder.

Despite Roger Garety's efforts to keep the psychiatrist off the stand, Judge Thomas had allowed him to testify. And he had damned Priscilla. Although he had not examined her—at Garety's insistence—on the stand, Blinder talked at length about Munchausen Syndrome by Proxy. The guy was careful, Steve had to admit. He confessed that he couldn't say Pris had the syndrome, but he sure as hell implied that she did. He described in detail the attention that sufferers of the syndrome hoped to attract from medical personnel. This obsessive desire caused them to hurt their children, he said. It was all ridiculous, Steve believed. Still, the judge had probably bought it: there only needed to be reasonable suspicion in a preliminary, not the proof beyond a reasonable doubt required at the trial level.

It looked like the best that could be hoped was that the charge against Pris would be reduced to second degree or manslaughter. Then some of the pressure would be taken off the trial itself. There would still be plenty of tension to go around. Financial pressures—despite the defense fund—were already beginning to hem them in. Priscilla's income had stopped dead in April. She had not been officially fired, but Steve knew that if she was bound over for trial, she would be. It was as certain as fog in February.

It was time for the session to start finally, and the bailiff came and let them in. Off to his right, Steve saw Kathryn Mitchell and Ted Lindquist conferring. He had come to detest the DA, with her short little skirts and her pointy face and the way she pitched her voice high and strong as if she was leading a cheer. He could tell she thought Pris was dirt under her feet. And Lindquist, who sneaked around taping everybody—like someone in Watergate—Steve couldn't abide the sucker. He stared at the detective with hostility, but Lindquist didn't look up.

Judge Thomas wheeled himself in from his chambers. Steve knew something of his history. The 1970 shoot-out at the Civic Center touched off by Jonathan Jackson's foiled attempt to force the release of his brother George from San Quentin had left Gary Thomas a paraplegic. Thomas, who was the assistant district attorney at the time, had taken a bullet in the back. In the fray, a judge, seventeen-year-old Jackson, and two convicts on trial were killed. Two years later, Gary Thomas had been elevated to the bench. He was a strict and formal judge with a reputation for evenhandedness. He waited now as the bailiff moved to lock the doors and flick on the orange sign that announced the status of each courtroom. Court was officially in session.

The district attorney opened with a request that the court make a holding specifically as to the two charges which had been filed: the charge of murder in the death of Tia Phillips and the charge of endangering the life of Mindy Phillips.

"I believe that a charge of first-degree murder, with implied malice, can be found in the death of Tia Phillips, Your Honor. Particularly as Priscilla Phillips saw the life-threatening situation with Tia, yet persisted, although she must have realized that if the doses increased, the eventual result could only be the child's death," the district attorney said.

The judge looked at Kathryn Mitchell for a moment. "What about Dr. Blinder's statement that persons suffering from displaced Munchausen don't have an intent to kill? That their intention is to focus attention upon themselves?" he asked.

"I don't believe that Dr. Blinder's statements preclude the

existence of both a specific intent to kill or a very conscious realization that one's acts are very likely to cause death," the district attorney responded. Then she summed up her entire case. Steve took Priscilla's hand as the DA recapitulated the events leading to Priscilla's arrest.

"What Tia and Mindy Phillips suffered while in the custody of this woman defies description. She poisoned these two infants with baking soda, and after the first child died, she certainly knew what would happen to the second. Yet she persisted."

"Miss Mitchell, do you believe baking soda is a poison as defined either under the business and professional code or as defined medically?"

"I'm not sure, Your Honor. But in researching that, I found nothing that says it wouldn't fit the definition under *Caljic*."

"Mr. Garety?"

"Yes, Your Honor. I want to say first that the burden of the prosecution at a preliminary hearing is to produce evidence of a reasonable probability; that is, evidence sufficient to induce a strong suspicion in the mind of a person of ordinary caution or prudence that a crime has been committed and that the defendant was the guilty person.

"My query: What crime? I submit first, certainly not murder in the first degree. There is no evidence of willful, deliberate, premeditated killing.

"Next," Garety went on, "baking soda is not a poison, but rather a common household product. Furthermore, if Mrs. Phillips had intended to kill Tia, she could have done so easily by, for example, tampering with the child's central alimentation line. Or she could have allowed Tia to die at home.

"I also suggest that a finding of second-degree murder is inappropriate. There is no evidence that sustains a finding that the activities of the defendant had as their goal the harming of Tia, or her injury or death," Garety added.

"What do you suggest, then, Mr. Garety?" asked Thomas.

"Your Honor, I think a violation of section one ninety-two, subdivision two, manslaughter, would be appropriate."

"And what about the second count of the complaint relating to Mindy Phillips?"

"For the purposes of the preliminary hearing only, I won't address count two of the complaint," replied Garety.

Garety sat down and Steve watched as the district attorney—who was given the last word—reiterated her position.

Finally she was finished and took her own seat in the almost deserted courtroom. The judge collected some papers and then looked out at the attorneys.

"Well, I have thought about this case a lot, and I don't think there has been proved a conscious disregard for life in this matter, as such, that would take this out of second-degree murder and put it up to the category of first degree. And there hasn't been any evidence to show any intent to kill," he added.

Steve in his chair turned to Priscilla, beaming. But she was rigid beside him, her eyes intent on the judge, and she did not turn.

"Priscilla Phillips, please rise," Judge Thomas continued. He waited while she did so. Garety took his place beside his client. "I do believe the evidence does find that such intent— mingling of any harmful substance of any food or drink or medicine involved, of both Tia and Mindy Phillips—was to injure and not to kill.

"Now Priscilla Eichholtz Phillips, I do find that there was committed on or about the third of February of 1977, here in the county of Marin, the state of California, the crime of murder of the second degree, that is, the unlawful killing of a human being, one Tia Phillips. There is reasonable cause to believe that you are guilty thereof. I hold you to answer to same.

"Furthermore, it appears to the court that on or about the times of February third through February the twenty-fifth of 1978, here in the county of Marin, there was committed a felony violation of section three forty-seven of the penal code, in that you did willfully mingle a harmful substance with any food, drink, or medicine with the intent that it be taken by a human being to his injury, that is, with regard to the child Mindy Phillips. There is sufficient cause to believe you are guilty thereof. I hold you to answer to that charge. You must appear in superior court. What date would you suggest?"

From his position at Priscilla's side, Roger Garety answered. "I would suggest the end of the statutory period."

"Make that on July twelfth at nine A.M. Bail is to remain as heretofore fixed."

"Your Honor?"

"Yes, Miss Mitchell?"

"I ask that bail be increased back to the original setting of a hundred thousand dollars."

"Mr. Garety?"

"Your Honor, Mrs. Phillips has made all her court appearances. Her husband, children, employment, and home are all here. I find no reason why the court should change the bail."

"The bail will remain as fixed at forty thousand dollars. And the transcript of this preliminary hearing is to remain sealed," ruled Judge Thomas. He nodded, turned his chair, and wheeled vigorously from the room.

THE TRIAL

Week 1 *Judge*

The trial of Priscilla Phillips began on March 19, 1979, almost exactly nine months after the conclusion of the preliminary hearing. Due to extensive pretrial publicity, the trial was assigned to the largest courtroom in Marin County Superior Court. Justice Louis H. Burke, who was to preside, had recently retired from a fourteen-year tenure as a California Supreme Court justice. He had volunteered his time to the superior court bench, and for his services was paid lunch money and travel expenses totaling $8.50 per day. Burke was a distinguished-looking man with silver hair combed back from a deep widow's peak and marked, arching eyebrows; his small, vivid eyes squinted at the courtroom with wry intelligence. Most of the attorneys familiar with him considered him a judge of the old school: slightly conservative, eminently fair, an authority in the courtroom.

The session began amidst a buzz of whispers and rustles. As one, the prospective jurors rose and were sworn in. A lengthy trial was anticipated, the judge told them, and those for whom that would present a legitimate problem could be excused. Kaiser health-plan members would also be eliminated. Those who felt they should be excused were asked to line up and explain their reasons. About a third of the panel rose and did so.

Then the lengthy process of *voir dire* began, whereby the district attorney and the defense attorney questioned each juror in turn, in order to determine their competency. Priscilla Phillips, with her two attorneys, Edwin Train Caldwell and Albert Collins, faced the journal of prospective jurors, watching them for a sympathetic smile or a sign of distaste. Ed Caldwell had told her that jury selection was an essentially negative process, an attempt to weed out the undesirables and that he hoped to wind up with jurors with warm, sympathetic personalities—perhaps older, more experienced women or salesmen who knew the world and were accustomed to acting independently.

Priscilla felt infinitely more comfortable with Ed Caldwell as her attorney than she had with Roger Garety with whom she had come to a parting of the ways following the preliminary hearing.

"Look, Mrs. Phillips, I think the way to go with this case is a diminished capacity defense," Garety had said.

"You mean say that I did it? Isn't that what you mean?"

"Well—"

"I won't do that, Mr. Garety. I'm innocent," she had protested.

"And she didn't have any diminished capacity," Steve put in. "You sent her to all those psychiatrists. They all agreed she isn't crazy. That whole defense stinks."

"Honey—"

"Well it does, and you know it!"

"I think you should get another attorney, then," Garety said. "Of course I wish you both the best of luck," he had added as he closed his dispatch case.

Edwin Train Caldwell had come highly recommended by Superior Court Judge Chuck Best. He was smart, hardworking, an advocate of defendants' rights, and a dedicated lawyer.

Caldwell was strong-looking, with dark, straight hair combed in a sweep over his forehead, a long, well-shaped nose, and a full dark mustache. He had breezed through the initial interview confidently and attentively, putting Steve and Priscilla at ease with casual facility. Within a few days he agreed to take the case. He also asked an old friend and colleague to assist him. Al Collins was an experienced lawyer and district attorney; he shared space in Ed's nineteenth-floor office, and since his wife was a biologist and medical technologist, he would be able to provide particular assistance in dealing with the medical evidence.

In one of his first pretrial maneuvers, Ed managed to reduce Priscilla's $40,000 bail to $5,000. Although he tried to arrange her release on her own recognizance, the judge—despite a probation report recommending OR—denied this. Still, the lowered bail was a huge relief to Steve and Priscilla. They had promised Ed a $15,000 retainer, but they hoped to avoid a second mortgage on their house. With the return of $35,000, the Priscilla Phillips Defense Fund was able to furnish the retainer.

The summer of 1978 vanished in a haze of pretrial motions.

That summer Steve and Priscilla also officially abandoned all attempts to reclaim Mindy. In July, Mercedes Murphy of Catholic Social Service came to the house to pick up Mindy's visa, explaining that the new adoptive parents were going to need it.

Priscilla packed up all of Mindy's remaining belongings—the few things she had brought with her from Korea, some photographs, and a can of Korean formula.

"We've found a lovely family for her, Priscilla," Mercedes told her. "They've already adopted a Vietnamese child with some medical problems, so they're experienced. They're a very loving family." Priscilla, in tears, could not reply.

Fall sped by. Priscilla, with so much time and untapped energy on her hands, worked hard on the boys' Halloween costumes. In November, a series of events that was later to affect Priscilla directly occurred in San Francisco. Supervisor Dan White resigned pleading that he could not live on his small salary, then changed his mind and asked for his seat back. When Mayor George Moscone refused, White entered San Francisco's City Hall and shot and killed the mayor and a member of the Board of Supervisors, gay activist Harvey Milk. White's trial was scheduled to start in April.

After Christmas, Priscilla began helping to prepare the case for the defense. Every evening she sat down with Tia's and Mindy's medical records, copies of which she had obtained from Kaiser, and pored over them, looking for mistakes or problems or evidence that supported her contention that Tia had died from an undiagnosed illness and that Mindy's illness had been unconnected to Tia's.

At the end of January, as the trial date approached, Priscilla flew back East and drove her mother, Marietta, to California to take care of the boys during the trial.

In early February, Priscilla, Steve, and Marietta—both separately and together—began seeing Dr. Satten, a psychiatrist.

It had originally been Priscilla's idea to see the psychiatrist. Not long after the preliminary hearing, she began asking people, "What if I did it and don't realize it? Could that be?" Jim Hutchison suggested she take a sodium pentothal test.

"It would ease your mind about that, Priscilla," he said. But she did not. Instead she talked to Mary Kilgore, the social worker who had provided Erik and Jason with grief counseling following Tia's death. Mary recommended that Priscilla contact Joseph Satten, a top forensic psychiatrist. But when Priscilla asked Ed about it, Caldwell suggested that she wait.

"I think you should see him later," he said. "He may in fact help the case, but I don't think this is the appropriate time."

In February, on the eve of the trial, Ed recommended that therapy begin.

"We don't know, going into this, whether Satten will even testify for us, whether he can help us," Caldwell told Priscilla. "But it can only be to your advantage to see him."

Dr. Joseph Satten had an admirable psychiatric background, including training at the Menninger Clinic, and positions as director of the law and psychiatry division of the Menninger Foundation and consultant to both the medical center for federal prisoners in Missouri, and the Kansas State Hospital for the Dangerously Insane. He had also acted as consultant to the film version of *In Cold Blood* and had been featured in Truman Capote's book. Since 1971, he had been in private practice in San Francisco, where he concentrated his practice on family therapy. He still devoted about ten percent of his time to forensic psychiatry.

Priscilla liked Satten at once: a small, sweet-faced man with a graying, carefully tailored beard and squared off metal-rimmed glasses, he was warm, interested, involved. He listened intently; he took notes and made tapes. But he took a long time to formulate an opinion, and even as the trial approached, Cadlwell did not know if Satten's findings would help Priscilla or even if he would take the stand.

In February, various pretrial answers and responses were filed. The defendant's motions to dismiss the information and to dismiss on invasion of privacy grounds were denied, but the motion for discovery was granted. This gave the defense the right to examine and copy virtually all of the People's evidence. On the grounds that to allow the prosecution the same opportunity would violate the defendant's right against self-incrimination, discovery was never extended to the prosecution. A list of jurors and their arrest records was also given to the defendant. But a far more important and unexpected ruling was made.

On Priscilla's thirty-third birthday, the court ruled that Municipal Court Judge Gary Thomas, who had presided in the preliminary hearing, had erred in reducing the charge against Priscilla in the death of Tia to second-degree murder. The first-degree murder charge was restored. It was a shocking blow.

"It doesn't mean they can't still find you guilty of a lesser charge, Priscilla—as well as innocent, of course," Ed Caldwell tried to soothe her.

"Oh God! It just seems like every little step forward is followed by a giant step back," Priscilla answered, shaking her head. "You never know where you stand."

"All we have to do is establish reasonable doubt," Ed said. "So many people think we must prove innocence beyond a shadow of a doubt, but that's wrong. Of course, you have to remember there is a presumption of innocence."

"Well, there's reasonable doubt all over the place. All those doctors who treated Tia and came up with diagnoses. She had those elevated VMAs and VIPs. Mindy had CMV. Those doctors had explanations for everything when Tia was sick— including the high sodium levels. How can they be so certain now? I know there's reasonable doubt!" said Priscilla.

"Yes. But I'd like to be able to come up with a doctor or two who can furnish the jury with an explanation other than sodium poisoning. Dr. Holliday and Dr. Stephens make very strong witnesses. I'd like to be able to tear them down."

But in this Ed Caldwell proved unsuccessful. He contacted medical experts in the Bay Area and throughout the country. Essentially they all told him the same thing: if the test results were accurate, the only explanation was an exogenous or external source of sodium. No other diagnosis presented itself.

It was a disappointment but Ed did not give up. He tackled the problem of Mindy's contaminated formula, which was the cornerstone of the People's case. Steve remained certain that someone with a grudge could have been responsible. Long hours were spent locating people—counselees and even a county probation officer—who Steve felt might wish his family harm. This also proved fruitless. Steve remembered that someone at Kaiser had once made an angry comment suggesting that Steve should have adopted an American child. Another dead end. It seemed clear to Ed that the defense could offer no alternative theories to the contamination of Mindy's formula other than a general one: the refrigerator was accessible to all. Anyone might have spiked the formula. Perhaps the formula had somehow arrived contaminated. There was at least reasonable doubt.

After the preliminary hearing in June, District Attorney Bruce Bales had assigned the prosecution of Priscilla Phillips to his assistant, Joshua Thomas. Although Kit Mitchell had done an admirable job at the preliminary, as a matter of course the trial itself was handed over to someone with more experience and more seniority.

Josh Thomas had been trying cases since 1962, first in San Diego's municipal courts, then in Marin county. He was known as a tireless and dogmatic attorney, always well-prepared, never at a loss.

At first, Josh Thomas had voiced skepticism about the Priscilla Phillips case. He was one of the district attorneys who had failed to support Ted Lindquist's arrest warrant. But when the case was formally assigned to him and he began to pore over the medical records and interview the doctors, he changed his mind. As the weeks wore on, Josh eliminated the idea that Tia might have died from an exotic disease and became convinced that there had been a deliberate poisoning for which Priscilla Phillips was responsible. But this was a circumstantial evidence case, and where the case of the People rests chiefly on circumstantial evidence, the jury is not permitted to find the defendant guilty unless the proved circumstances are not only consistent with the finding of guilt, but also inconsistent with any other rational conclusion. Still, Thomas had no doubts, and neither did Ted Lindquist. The difficulty would be proving it to the jury.

"I've got to find a way to make all the medical elements understandable to a lay jury," he told Ted on the eve of the trial. "They're only going to hear it one time around."

"Well, you've got the charts they used at the preliminary."

"Yes, and those should help. I want to make up smaller versions of the charts to give each juror, so they'll be able to follow the testimony about the electrolytes and sodium levels. Blood electrolytes were done routinely each shift—all of that information will go on each chart."

"Dr. Shimoda and Dr. Carte and Evelyn Callas have worked for hours correlating all that information. That much is already done," Ted said, eyeing Josh's cigarette with longing. He had given them up in August, shortly after Pam had discovered she was pregnant, and now he was having a hell of a time keeping his weight within reasonable limits.

Ted turned back to Josh. "I think there's another thing that may trip up Priscilla Phillips."

"Yeah?"

"That's the lady herself. You've seen the baby book she kept on Tia, with all those pictures of the grave and lists of people who had sent cards, like she was making a shopping list—and that notebook page figuring the mileage to the hospital so she could deduct it on her income taxes. You've seen that journal on Tia's illness!"

"Yeah, and the *Redbook* article. What kind of a woman would be thinking about writing up an article on the death of her child for a magazine? I've got to get that all across to a jury, Ted, the kind of woman Priscilla Phillips really is."

"She might just do it for you."

"What do you mean?"

"You didn't see her at the preliminary. She isn't going to sit still and act passive and pathetic. They're going to see her asserting herself and demanding attention. I don't think she's going to help herself out there. Just wait and see."

Week 2

The jury was not complete until Tuesday morning, March twenty-seventh.

The final jury consisted of eight women and four men plus two women alternates. The jurors ranged in age from 20 to 69, with the overwhelming majority in their 30s and 40s. With the exception of the 69-year-old woman—a former librarian—each of the jurors was employed. Three of the women were involved in computer work, three were in secretarial or bookkeeping jobs, and the remaining woman was a teller in a local bank. Of the men, two were engineers, one a manager of a state disability insurance program, and the last a San Francisco fireman. In short, it was a typical Marin County jury: intelligent, respectable, straightforward, and reasonably dull.

On Tuesday afternoon, following the lunch break, Judge

Burke addressed the jury and then turned to the opening statements.

Josh Thomas, a man in his mid-forties, balding, with thin gray hair and a military brush mustache, rose. When he spoke, his voice was pitched evenly.

"May it please the court and counsel, Mrs. Phillips, ladies and gentlemen. As Justice Burke has just indicated, this is my opportunity to outline for you the evidence that we will present in this case. This case is somewhat complex in nature and requires the understanding on your part of certain medical principles that will be explained to you by the various witnesses presented.

"The evidence will show proof beyond any reasonable doubt that the death of Tia Phillips and the illness that Mindy Phillips suffered were caused by the intentional, surreptitious, periodic administration by Priscilla Phillips of a sodium-based compound or compounds.

"There will be evidence that contrary to the impression that Priscilla Phillips has generated in the community, and—no doubt—will attempt to show here in court, of being a dedicated, concerned parent of Tia and Mindy Phillips, the opposite was true." After naming some of the witnesses he planned to call and describing in general terms their expected testimony, Thomas addressed himself to the core of his case.

"There are basically three issues to this case: Did Tia Phillips die as a result of some criminal agency? That's number one. Two: Was Priscilla Phillips responsible? Three: motive. We will present evidence—and to be frank there isn't a complete explanation—of what appear to be the psychodynamics behind Mrs. Phillips as she engaged in this type of conduct. There will be testimony from staff members at Kaiser about the great admiration they had for her ability to bear up under the strain of the constant hospitalizations. And about the continual and dramatic need to bring Tia into the Emergency Room at odd hours of the night, riding with her in an ambulance; and the great publicity about Tia's treatment.

"And we will rule out other explanations of these children's illnesses. Dr. Holliday will discuss that and Dr. Boyd Stephens—coroner of the city and county of San Francisco—will corroborate it.

"We will show evidence that during the course of treatment, Priscilla Phillips became intimately involved with Tia's treatment and management. She was very familiar with the significance of sodium levels. We will also demonstrate the presence of the defendant on various occasions at the hospital and her presence at or about the time of these dramatic episodes of diarrhea.

"It will be indicated that just like Kaiser, Stanford has procedures regarding the participation of the parents in the care and treatment of their children. Tia had a substantial episode at Stanford, ladies and gentlemen, and this is significant because you could always say maybe there was some deranged nurse at Kaiser-San Rafael who didn't like Orientals. Was there one at Kaiser-San Francisco? Was there one at Stanford University?"

Josh strode back to his table, and then turned to face the jury once again. Slowly and carefully he began describing the details of Tia's illnesses and hospitalizations. The exposition continued for over an hour. At each stage he indicated which witnesses he was going to call and to what they would attest.

Following the afternoon recess, the district attorney continued tracing Tia's course of illness. He explained that an autopsy found no trace of a tumor. He mentioned that approximately one week after Tia's death, the Phillipses applied to the proper authorities to adopt another child. He detailed Mindy's illness and treatment and the discovery—by Dr. Estol Carte—of the contaminated formula, and how Mindy's diarrhea stopped in the ICU.

Finally, he returned to the question of motive. "The People are not required to prove motive, ladies and gentlemen. But Dr. Blinder will testify about reviewing all the medical records in the case, and he will explain to you the symptoms of an individual suffering from Munchausen Syndrome by Proxy. And you can reach your own conclusions about whether those symptoms fit this particular case. Thank you, ladies and gentlemen."

The judge adjourned the court and an exhausted Josh Thomas turned to Ted Lindquist.

"How did I do?"

"Fantastic," Ted said.

On Thursday, it was Ed Caldwell's turn. He had spent hours outlining the central arguments of his case. In contrast to Josh Thomas's lengthy, dry, and methodical presentation, Ed's opening argument was short, disjointed, and tinged with the personal. He wanted first to put the trial on a more informal basis. If he was going to win the case, it would be because he was able to make the jury like Priscilla Phillips.

"Sometimes in a jury trial," he began, "you forget the names of the parties. We are the attorneys: myself—Ed Caldwell—Al Collins, and of course Priscilla and her husband Steve." He gestured at the Phillipses, who nodded and smiled.

"Now, medicine is as much an art as it is a science," he continued. "And in this case there are clinical observable signs of unknown origin, such as diarrhea, vomiting, bleeding. And I can give you an example that ties right in with the adoption of Tia and Mindy Phillips.

"Priscilla had two children, Erik, now nine, and Jason, six. And after Jason's birth, she developed severe uterine bleeding whose remedy was a hysterectomy. Now the cause of that bleeding was never known.

"Similarly, when they did an autopsy on Tia, they didn't find anything. And in the case of a boy described by Dr. Sinatra to Dr. Sara Shimoda—Tia's pediatrician—this boy died and had an autopsy performed and in both his case and Tia's, secretory diarrhea was the cause of death, etiology unknown." He paused for emphasis, then moved to another point.

"All kinds of tests and procedures were done on Tia, and Mrs. Phillips was constantly urging the doctors to do them as painlessly as possible. It was as painful for Priscilla Phillips as it was for Tia Phillips for each and every one of those procedures, and there will be a lot more evidence to that effect.

"And the evidence will show that an autopsy was performed with the consent of Priscilla Phillips. Steve and Priscilla gladly and willingly consented.

"The evidence will also show that over the entire medical history of Tia Phillips, not once did any expert, examination, study, or test ever suggest that Tia's condition was caused by either the intentional or accidental ingestion of a contaminant.

"Priscilla Phillips, by her makeup, her character, and her life experiences, was absolutely incapable of even contemplating such acts as have been charged in this case, much less executing them. She has spent a lot of time giving to others in the community, giving to her family. She was active in many organizations dedicated to helping others. She was a giver of life, not a taker.

"Now the evidence will show that Tia—who had been found abandoned in Seoul—arrived in this country in November of 1975, when she was approximately six months old. And there is one medical report that came from Korea showing that she had diarrhea for one month—we don't know when, but it was sometime before she was adopted by Steve and Priscilla. And then she proceeded to have various ear and urinary tract infections.

"The evidence will show that at one time Kaiser-San Francisco released Tia with a central venous catheter leading to her heart, which Priscilla had to inject with heparin daily. Now if ever there was a time that a mother was going to inflict any harm, that would be the time.

"Now, throughout the illnesses of Tia and Mindy, the evidence will show that the mother was very supportive. That support was encouraged by Kaiser, and this support was commendable. It's now taken as very suspicious that she was so supportive and so overattentive, though it's a natural mother's instinct in caring for a sick child.

"The evidence will further show that in the days before Tia's final illness, she had been very healthy, and that other members of the Phillips family had been ill with various complaints. And the evidence will show that although they wanted a healthy baby, Mindy Phillips was suffering from cytomegalovirus, CMV, which can produce mental retardation, and, as it did in Mindy's case, motor coordination disability.

"Now, on the matter of the contaminated formula bottle. Point one: there will be evidence that Mindy's name was not on that bottle. More importantly: the last time that Priscilla Phillips made the formula was on February twentieth, and this bottle was found on February twenty-fifth.

"Subsequently, the San Rafael Police Department obtained a search warrant and, without notice, went to the Phillipses' house, and obviously the purpose was to find remnants of baking soda in a bag that she carried to and from the hospital. They took all her handbags and they sent all this material back to the FBI lab in Washington. And no traces of sodium bicarbonate or baking soda were found." Ed paused to let this sink in.

"I think that the evidence will totally fail to prove any wrongdoing on the part of Mrs. Phillips. Thank you for your attention." With a slight nod, Ed Caldwell sat down.

While he waited for Josh to call his first witness, he glanced back at Priscilla and Steve. They were seated in back of the defense table, in a row of seats separated from the audience.

They wanted to sit together, and Ed thought the picture of them as a strong and loving couple would present a dramatic image for the jury. Predictably, the prosecutor had argued against the arrangement, but the judge had allowed it. The decision meant that Ed could not see Priscilla, however, and later Ed believed that this was a serious mistake.

ii

Josh Thomas called Sara Shimoda as his first witness. During the months following the preliminary hearing, Josh had met frequently with Dr. Shimoda and with many of the Kaiser doctors regarding the care of the two Phillips children. All of them, and in particular Sara and Evelyn Callas, had been invaluable in preparing, correlating, and charting the hospital records.

Sara Shimoda took the stand shakily. She had been dreading the culmination of an ordeal that had dragged on for a year. It had been supremely difficult for Sara to accept Priscilla's guilt; Priscilla's adamant, tearful denials weighed on Sara, reinforcing her doubt. Finally she had come on some level to believe that Priscilla was guilty, that she was mentally ill. The medical evidence was overwhelming and Sara had always been trained to believe in scientific proof. In the end she had to choose between that and what she wanted to believe emotionally. In a last gesture that proclaimed her choice, Sara had handed over to the police the ten-page personal letter Priscilla had written to her after Mindy's removal.

A great deal of her first day's testimony was taken up with a long battle between the attorneys over the admissibility of various Kaiser records and a chart prepared by the prosecution. During the discussion, Josh Thomas asked permission to distribute reductions of his chart to each juror, and this was agreed to. The chart, which was to become a focal point of the trial, contained the histories of Tia and Mindy Phillips on a daily basis. There were columns for the patient's weight, laboratory results, type of intake, presence of mother or father, stool, and emesis. In cases where laboratory results had been abnormal, these were outlined and a color-coded dot placed on the line to indicate the source of the sample. Blood was represented by a red dot, urine by yellow, stool by green.

Using the chart, her notes, and her recollections, Sara

recounted the history and course of Tia Phillips's illness. She described Tia's early bouts with ear and urinary tract infections, the child's hospitalization for possible seizure activity, and the onslaught of her diarrhea.

Finally, just after four o'clock, testimony was halted and the judge, with his standard admonition regarding discussion of the case, excused the jury.

Ed Caldwell was satisfied with the day's proceedings. Al Collins—who was handling the medical witnesses—had pointed out to the jury several mistakes on the People's chart—one a misplacement of a lab result, others misrepresenting Priscilla's presence during a particular shift. Dr. Shimoda had found two errors of her own that she presented to the court. None of the errors was serious, but any errors at all tended to discredit the accuracy of the chart.

Sara Shimoda spent all day on the stand Friday as well.

Josh next led Sara into a more thorough discussion of Tia's treatment. He also felt it was important to show how much Sara had admired Priscilla and the ways in which Priscilla's ego might have been stroked during Tia's repeated hospitalizations.

"Did you begin to feel any admiration or friendship toward Mrs. Phillips because of her apparent dedication to Tia?" he asked.

"I think I identified somewhat with this mother, who was close to my age and who had an infant who was also close to my child's age. I understood the strain of not having your child at home to watch her grow and develop. Well, certainly I felt great sympathy for the situation she found herself in."

"Did you at any time express that sympathy to Mrs. Phillips?"

"I don't know if I did in so many words. I tried to be supportive."

"Did you admire her dedication to Tia?"

"Yes, I did."

"Did you in any way indicate that admiration?"

"I—I think I did in perhaps an indirect way. I don't think I came right out and said, 'I really admire you.' But I felt she certainly was doing the best she could."

"Did you ever observe Tia in any pain, Dr. Shimoda?"

"Yes. There were times—I—I was impressed by the amount of discomfort this child was in. There were multiple times we had to order sedation, or, if that didn't work, Demerol."

"During the course of treatment, did Tia ever give any indications of being hungry or—"

"Well, it was difficult when we had to make her NPO because, in effect, we had to take away what was pleasurable to her, which was to eat. I remember distinctly seeing her sucking on the pacifier like she was saying, 'Don't you dare take this away from me.' She just kept holding onto that because that was the only thing, many times, that she was allowed to have." Sara paused and looked down at her hands. In her seat behind Ed Caldwell, Priscilla put her head down and wiped away tears.

After a moment, Josh went back to the final months of Tia's treatment—the laparotomy, the worsening episodes of diarrhea; the high electrolyte readings present not only in Tia's blood, but in her urine and stool as well.

Sara described Tia's devastating fluid losses during one of her last episodes in December 1976.

"She lost a tremendous amount of fluid. On the third shift of December third, she lost eighteen hundred thirty-two cc's and this was followed by the loss of fourteen hundred ninety-four cc's the next shift. This is a total of over three thousand cc's lost in a sixteen-hour period of time. It corresponds to a loss of forty percent of this patient's body weight. And if fifteen percent is considered life-threatening, she had exceeded that many times."

"Now, Dr. Shimoda, is there anything about the nature of your profession that had any effect on your lack of suspicion of the possibility of intentional poisoning of Tia?" Josh continued.

"In pediatrics we have become aware of child abuse, but it is generally physical abuse. I was not aware of instances of a parent intentionally poisoning a child. I was looking for a disease."

"Did the relationship or rapport you had built up with Mrs. Phillips and your knowledge of her general background have anything to do with your failure to suspect sodium poisoning?"

"Yes, that certainly entered into it. But also I had presented her case to a number of consultants who didn't have a relationship with Mrs. Phillips, and no mention was ever made that this could be intentional poisoning."

"As these various stool and urine samples were obtained, did the significance of those readings present itself to you?"

"Well, it was certainly a puzzling finding. But I had not had prior experience with electrolyte levels on stool. And Dr.

Applebaum felt that for some reason Tia was secreting a lot of sodium in addition to losing water."

Carefully, Josh led the witness through a description of Tia's last hours. All in the courtroom could see how difficult it was for Sara to discuss it. Her voice becoming increasingly clogged, she described the final admission to San Rafael, Tia's worsening breathing problems, her transfer to Kaiser-San Francisco, and the arrival of Dr. Leider to assess Tia's condition.

"Dr. Leider was at San Rafael Kaiser that day. I knew he was going to return to San Francisco to consult on Tia and officially interpret her EEG. I wanted to be there at that time, and after office hours I returned to San Francisco Kaiser and was with Dr. Leider when he interpreted the electroencephalogram reading," Sara testified, struggling now to maintain her composure.

"He confirmed that the brain wave reading was flat and he felt this patient had brain death. He discussed his findings with both parents. And a decision was made to stop all support systems." She paused and tried to gather herself.

"And the patient was declared dead at approximately six-forty-five that evening." Her head down, Sara stopped in tears. The jury shifted in their seats. Priscilla began to cry.

"If I may just have a minute, Your Honor," Josh said, walking slowly back to his seat to allow the witness a chance to collect herself. Soon after, Judge Burke adjourned for the day.

Week 3

Although the direct examination of Sara Shimoda had consumed nearly two and a half days, Al Collins spent only just over an hour with this witness. He began by questioning Sara about a report from the Korean orphanage indicating that Tia had suffered from diarrhea for one month prior to the transfer to America.

"Were steps taken to find out what treatment there had been or what the cause was?" Collins asked.

"No."

Collins paused, then brought up the case Caldwell had

mentioned in his opening statement of the seven-and-a-half-year-old boy with symptoms similar to Tia's. A Stanford consultant, Dr. Sinatra, had mentioned the boy in a letter to Sara. The child had suffered from secretory diarrhea yet his tumor had not showed up in either a laparotomy or on autopsy, Sinatra had written. Collins reminded Sara of this.

"There were differences in the two cases," Sara remarked quietly to Collins. Josh, from his place at the prosecution table, cupped an ear.

"I didn't hear that last statement. There were what?" he asked.

"Differences between the two cases," Sara repeated more loudly. Thomas nodded and smiled.

"What were the differences?" Collins asked.

"The boy had an elevated VIP—vasoactive peptide—reading, where Tia did not. Also the boy did not have hypernatremia but had very low potassium levels and had to be given enormous amounts. Also the sodium in his stool was not as high as Tia's."

After the noon recess, Collins questioned Sara about Tia's VMA. First, he underlined the fact that Tia's VMA level was elevated whether one used Kaiser-San Rafael's normal range or San Francisco's.

In an oblique attempt to discredit the witness and her hospital, he followed with some questions about the Kaiser health plan system.

"Isn't it true that although doctors' salaries are fixed, the income of the system depends on profits?"

"Yes, it is."

"And those profits could be affected by malpractice suits?"

"I suppose."

Then, to separate Tia's illness from Mindy's, Collins raised a significant point. Mindy's serum sodium exceeded a hundred fifty only once, while Tia had elevated measurements many times. He also demonstrated that on several occasions Mindy had exhibited low potassium readings, a condition not commonly true of Tia.

Finally, Collins had Sara repeat testimony about Mindy's CMV and its possible effects, including small head size, and potential liver disease. It was an important part of the defense's case that Mindy be seen as a child who was intrinsically abnormal because that could raise doubt about the cause of her diarrhea.

On redirect, Josh went right to the most telling point scored by the defense.

"Dr. Shimoda, I want to refer your attention back to the question concerning Tia's VMA levels. In your consultations with Dr. Solomon—the endocrinologist—did she give you any information concerning the significance of those levels?"

"Yes. She said VMA could be elevated in a patient with no tumor. There could be other factors such as stress, certain dietary intake, starvation."

On recross, Collins asked only one question.

"Doctor, laparotomies don't always reveal the presence of a tumor, even if the tumor is there. Do they?"

"That would be possible, yes," Sara agreed.

Sara was excused and Estol Carte took the stand, ending the day's testimony with an account of his discovery of Mindy's contaminated formula.

Dr. Michael Applebaum was next to testify. Applebaum had confessed to his wife a certain nervousness about testifying. The jury might legitimately wonder how he could now be so certain that Tia and Mindy had been poisoned and yet originally have diagnosed Tia's illness as an undiscovered disease.

Applebaum had rarely felt comfortable around Priscilla Phillips. He was sympathetic to her and her situation during Tia's hospitalization, but she had a nagging way about her, a certain belligerence, and a loud whiny voice that set him on edge. Even in the care of Tia, he had noticed that she was not warm, but rough and jostling. She was not the kind of parent who accepted the doctor, who told him to do what was necessary and trusted him to act competently. Everything was questioned; every issue a confrontation.

As he began to recount to the jury the treatments Tia had undergone at Kaiser-San Francisco, Applebaum was reminded of his difficulties with the case. In retrospect it seemed a crazy idea, but Mike had decided that Tia's high stool and urine sodium levels were a reflection of what had been in her blood earlier. He knew it was possible to achieve much higher sodiums in urine than in blood without any significance being attached to the finding. So he had bottled all the symptoms together into some insane sodium mixture and concluded that Tia merely suffered a syndrome that included disequilibrium of her salt metabolism. With the benefit of hindsight, he now realized this conclusion had been moronic.

Only after Sara had called to tell him about Mindy's illness
had the seed of suspicion begun to ripen in Applebaum's mind.
But he had not placed Priscilla Phillips in the picture at that
point, nor thought to test Mindy's formula.

And even now, he had to admit to himself, though he had
studied the records and become on some level convinced by
what they revealed, there was a portion of his mind that balked
at the notion that Priscilla Phillips was responsible.

He remembered visiting the Phillipses' house after Tia's
memorial service. The house had been filled with many of the
other mourners, but Steve and Priscilla had taken him aside
and showed him about the house. They had led him into Tia's
room and pulled out pictures they had taken of her during her
healthy periods.

"I am so grateful to you for allowing her to be home as much
as you did," Priscilla had cried.

And Mike remembered the four-page, hand-written letter
Priscilla had written him after Tia's death, thanking him for all
he had done. That hardly seemed consistent with a murderer.

"We were frustrated by the lack of abnormalities,"
Applebaum said now to the court. "The only thing we could
find wrong with Tia was a low pancreatic enzyme. We
eventually decided that this was a secretory diarrhea—it's
related to cholera in that there are fluid losses in the absence of
mucosal damage—and we thought a substance in Tia was
causing diarrhea and there were some candidates. VIP and
prostaglandin were the two most likely. So we did a laparotomy
and removed an adrenal gland."

"Did you suspect that sodium was being administered?"

"No."

"Why not?"

"I was trained as a physician to look for medical causes. And
because it was happening in a hospital setting," he said,
echoing Sara Shimoda.

"I believe we've come to the time for our recess, Doctor,"
said Judge Burke. "As you know, there is no court tomorrow,
so we will reconvene at our normal time on Thursday.
Remember not to discuss the case or form any opinion until
the trial is completed," he added to the jury.

As the courtroom emptied Ed Caldwell stopped for a
minute to talk with the bailiff. It was not uncommon for

attorneys to question bailiffs and court clerks about how well their points were coming across.

"How are we doing?" he asked.

"Okay. But you know your client is hurting herself."

"How so?"

"Well, the way she's always writing those damn notes and passing them up to you, and the expressions she gets on her face when she disagrees with a witness—like she's overreacting or on stage or something. She doesn't act like a defendant somehow. I know you can't see her. . . ."

"Yeah, thanks. She's so intense and hyped up, you know."

The guard nodded in sympathy. Ed crossed to the rear of the room and found Priscilla in the hall.

"You've got to cool it with the notes, Pris—it's making a bad impression."

"But I can't stand it when they make a mistake. It drives me crazy."

"I know, but save it and tell me later, at recess or lunch."

"Okay, I'll try."

Ed smiled and patted her shoulder. He intended to telephone Dr. Satten to ask him how he felt about prescribing a tranquilizer for Priscilla—not enough to sedate her, but just to dull the edge of her anxiety. Dr. Satten was still seeing Priscilla, and he hadn't yet reached a conclusion on her case. His delay was probably contributing to Priscilla's anxiety, Ed thought ruefully. But the next day Ed received a phone call that would take his mind off that problem for a while. A call that would alter the direction of the defense.

On Thursday, Josh completed his direct examination of Mike Applebaum early. Although Collins was supposed to handle the medical witnesses, Ed had been enormously disappointed with his colleague's cross-examination of Sara Shimoda, which he believed had been superficial. As a result, Ed cross-examined Applebaum himself. He took the doctor through a detailed description of Tia's final illness. Applebaum mentioned that on occasion he had seen Priscilla adjust Tia's IV. Later, he described Tia's memorial service and his visit to the house afterward. In contrast to the ninety-minute cross-examination of Sara Shimoda, Ed's cross-examination of Applebaum lasted all day.

* * *

Bonnie Pritzker's direct testimony did not differ markedly from what she had said at the preliminary. She had conducted a more complete autopsy on Tia than was normal because Tia had been her husband's patient; in fact he had given her a laundry list of what to look for in the examination, she testified. She had paid careful attention to the brain, spinal cord, pancreas, and remaining adrenal gland in her attempt to find a small tumor. She had found none and was absolutely certain in her own mind that none was there. She could find no pathological causes for Tia's diarrhea.

On cross-examination, Al Collins established once again that a tumor could be microscopic, and that there was no way to establish by autopsy if Tia had died from sodium poisoning. Since one of the causes of Tia's death had been listed as massive cerebral edema, Collins—in an attempt at introducing doubt as to the cause of this brain swelling—asked whether the edema might not have been the result of incorrect fluid replacement.

"It's unlikely but cannot be completely discounted," Bonnie answered. In his place at the defense table, Ed Caldwell turned to smile at Priscilla.

Josh Thomas then called Dr. John Iocco, Bonnie Pritzker's supervisor, who had reviewed her autopsy results. His own findings agreed with Dr. Pritzker's, he testified.

On cross-examination, Collins focused on Tia's electrolyte imbalances, causing a series of objections by Josh Thomas, after one of which, Josh joked, "I better withdraw my objection because I forget what it was!"

"That's a sure test for Friday afternoon," Judge Burke riposted as laughter rippled through the courtroom. "A juror has handed me a question," the judge went on. "Perhaps you can answer it, Dr. Iocco? 'If a tumor was so microscopically small as to go undetected during an autopsy,'" he read, "'could it have caused the diarrhea problem being experienced by Tia?'"

"I have never been convinced that it is possible for a tumor to be so small that a careful, thorough examination misses it. I'm just not convinced of that."

"In the course of the autopsy, it is true, is it not, that the gross examination of the body does not involve inspection of every cell of tissue?" Collins asked at once.

"Yes," admitted the pathologist.

"And the microscopic examination involves only a selected sample of tissues?"

"Yes."

"Isn't it possible that tissue that has not been examined either by the naked eye or been placed on slides could contain the microscopic tumors that we have been speaking of?"

Dr. Iocco answered as he had before. "I'm not convinced of that," he said.

"What's up next week?" Ted asked Josh at the end of the day.

"The big guns—Stephens and Holliday."

Ted nodded grimly. Those two doctors were the heart of the case because they had no ax to grind, no involvement prior to the investigation. They had convinced him he had a rock-solid case against Priscilla Phillips. Now all they had to do was convince the jury.

Week 4

San Francisco coroner Boyd Stephens led off Monday's session testifying that Tia's and Mindy's high sodium readings could only be explained by an outside administration of sodium.

His testimony on sodium levels explained that material passes from the mouth to the anus of a child with severe diarrhea in a minimum time of two to four hours; that toxic levels of sodium could cause convulsions, high temperature, and death; that serum sodium levels are variable and may or may not coincide with the onset of diarrhea. This last was an important point for the prosecution to make, since with Tia there were many instances of diarrhea without increased sodium levels charted, as well as instances of increased diarrhea and vomiting during which electrolyte levels were normal. On cross-examination, Ed Caldwell went straight to this issue.

Using the charts prepared for the jury, Ed pointed to entry after entry on Tia's records.

"From March eighth to April nineteenth, the sodiums were

not elevated but there was lots of stooling and vomiting. To what do you attribute this?"

"It could be, Counsel, that a bacterial infection or a possible viral infection produced the stool at that time," replied the coroner.

"From June twenty-first to July seventh she had stool and vomiting and it seems to me that the blood serums were normal."

"Yes, that's correct."

"Can you tell the jury what the cause of diarrhea and vomiting was at that time?"

"I cannot give a definitive diagnosis. A urine culture during that time included an increased level of organisms. And a pancreatic enzyme was recorded as low—that can cause diarrhea."

"From April first through May twenty-third, there were a number of incidents of stooling, vomiting, and fluid loss and yet the serum sodiums were not elevated," Caldwell continued.

"The serum sodiums were within normal limits."

"And the sodiums were measured often?"

"Almost daily for part of the time, then every other day."

"And to what do you attribute the multiple instances of diarrhea and vomiting between April twentieth and May thirtieth?"

"There is no specific diagnosis that I am aware of that will identify all of those instances, Counsel," Stephens admitted.

Later, Ed questioned Stephens about Mindy's condition. "Can cyanosis be caused by sodium bicarbonate ingestion?"

"Yes."

"Is CMV in any way productive of cyanosis?"

"It can be—in those conditions where a child's nervous system is affected so that it might not have the normal ability to regulate blood flow."

Ed finished his cross-examination, pleased with the chinks in the wall he had hammered out, and the daylight he could see on the other side.

But Josh Thomas lost no time in attacking the points Caldwell's cross-examination had raised.

"Would secretory diarrhea result in Tia's symptoms?" Josh asked his witness.

"No. The variety of tumors known to cause secretory diarrhea in a child are not associated with this volume of stool or this electrolyte imbalance and are not always associated with either the rapidity of onset or the severity of her symptoms. With secretory diarrhea, usually the potassium goes up, the chloride goes up, and the carbon dioxide goes down—not at all what we saw with Tia."

"What about the decreased pancreatic enzyme?"

"It would not cause the massive stooling we saw with Tia."

On recross, Caldwell introduced several articles from medical journals, one a discussion of a fifty-five-year-old Air Force sergeant whose chronic ingestion of sodium bicarbonate had led to severe hypertension. There was no record of Tia suffering from high blood pressure, Caldwell remarked.

Stephens countered immediately.

"In that case, the man was taking bicarbonate continuously, at the rate of over a box a week, because he believed he had a peptic ulcer. In the case of the Phillips children, the exposure was episodic rather than continuous."

"Did the man die?" asked Caldwell pointedly.

"Counsel, as I recall, he did not. Once he stopped taking the bicarbonate, he recovered and his blood pressure returned to normal."

"Thank you, Dr. Stephens. That's all I have."

Court was adjourned for the day.

Stanford Hospital's Dr. Philip Sunshine took the stand Tuesday morning. He spoke of having received Tia's history from Dr. Applebaum, and of how surprised he was that Tia appeared so well.

"Mrs. Phillips told me that even if she looked well now, that Tia had episodes where she didn't."

"Did Mrs. Phillips appear upset in any way when you indicated to her that Tia looked pretty good?" Josh asked.

"I don't know if she was upset. It was just—I don't know how to describe it. She was just not happy with my response." Sunshine could not completely articulate the strange feeling Priscilla Phillips's attitude had left him with but he still remembered the awkward moment.

He went on to testify about Tia's course at Stanford, explaining that he had ordered a stool sodium test after Tia's bout of diarrhea but that the test had never been run because Tia's diarrhea had stopped and no sample was obtainable.

"Had the test been run and showed high sodium, how would you have explained it?"

"It would have been very difficult to explain. The only thing we could have come up with would be that sodium-containing solutions were being given to her orally," he said.

"What about a diagnosis of secretory or viral diarrhea?"

"In typical secretory cases, the diarrhea is basically continuous. I have had two such patients—and in neither case was there high sodium. Usually the potassium was depleted because it was lost in the stool. And if the diarrhea was the infectious or viral type, you would see the chloride tend to rise—which was not the case for Tia."

"What diagnosis did you finally decide on?"

"We could not explain Tia's diarrhea based on biopsy results or the other tests. We speculated—"

"Did you speculate that it might be a secretory tumor?"

"That was our best bet—but again, it didn't add up—it wasn't a good diagnosis. It was something that we suggested that could be looked for, but we couldn't even use *that* diagnosis as an explanation for her symptoms or her lab findings."

"Other than the reason you mentioned, were there additional reasons why you could rule out viral or infectious diarrhea?"

"Yes. When you have diarrhea caused by virus or bacteria the stool sodium can reach a hundred milliequivalents, but very seldom more. Even in cholera, it's rarely above a hundred twenty."

"Can the stool sodium ever exceed the serum sodium without ingestion of sodium into the gastrointestinal tract?" Josh Thomas asked.

"In my experience I've never had that occur." Then Sunshine continued, demonstrating the classic reason why attorneys ask their witnesses never to expand on an answer. "I haven't reviewed the world literature on this but I can imagine that on occasion this can be found. I'm just not acquainted with it," he said.

At the defense table, Ed Caldwell made a note but Al Collins did not pursue this matter when he rose to cross-examine. Instead he questioned the alternate diagnoses Sunshine had listed on Tia's discharge summary.

"We just listed them because we didn't know what was going on. We never seriously considered them," Sunshine remarked.

Josh Thomas asked only one series of questions on redirect.

"Dr. Sunshine, with respect to the two cases on intractable

diarrhea you mentioned for which you could find no cause; were the serum sodium levels as high as for Tia Phillips?"

"We did not find elevated serum, urine, or stool sodiums," Dr. Sunshine said firmly.

Dr. Malcolm Holliday was relaxed and confident when he took the stand. A man in his mid-fifties, he looked considerably younger despite deep lines running from nose to mouth. A University of Virginia graduate, Holliday had been an accelerated student, soon making a name for himself at Children's Hospital in Boston working under the renowned Dr. James Gamble in the field of body fluid physiology. He was currently the head of the Children's Renal Center at the University of California in San Francisco, and he was the specialist to whom Boyd Stephens had turned for an opinion after Stephens had reviewed the case.

From that very first phone call, when Boyd Stephens had presented him with the facts of Tia's case, Mac Holliday had been certain of the cause of the child's illness. "Jesus, Boyd," he had said, "somebody gave that kid an awful lot of bicarbonate!"

The inconsistencies in the medical records didn't bother Holliday. As he had explained to Josh Thomas, when a child receives a huge load of sodium, this causes diarrhea. A large expansion of fluid is produced and then excreted, and this expanded phase is followed by a period of contraction—or dehydration.

"The body behaves in a very different way depending on whether it is in a state of expansion or contraction," he told the district attorney during a pretrial conference. "Particularly in terms of urine output and electrolyte levels. A spot electrolyte sample taken at any particular point could make the results inconsistent depending on whether the sample was taken during the expansion, contraction, or rehydration period. But the essentials for deducing an exogenous administration of sodium are present and clear to anyone who has the least propensity for suspecting such things." And Mac Holliday—unlike the Kaiser doctors who treated Tia—was trained to look at input.

Holliday came to the stand late on Tuesday afternoon, leaving only enough time for Josh to take him through his medical credentials. Speaking in his careful Virginia drawl, Holliday detailed his extensive background as a body fluid specialist. When direct examination was resumed on Thursday morning, Josh ran Holliday through testimony that was finally becoming repetitive.

After the morning recess, Holliday indicated specific points in Tia's chart where he believed Tia must have had either an extraordinary loss of water or a gain of sodium into her body fluids.

Holliday pointed at the entry of Tia's chart for October eleventh. "The concentration of sodium measured in two different samples here were three hundred fifteen and three hundred forty milliequivalents. Both of these are outside any experience I've had or could find. Now despite a very high replacement input of dilute solution intravenously, there was an *increase* in sodium concentration. There had to be an unexplained source of sodium entering the body and leaving the gastrointestinal tract simultaneously."

Josh Thomas continued after lunch with more entries on the charts, and the same ground was covered until finally the judge spoke up in exasperation. "It seems to me this is cumulative. There has to be a limit," he said.

Josh then turned to Mindy's chart. Holliday drew the identical conclusions he had with Tia.

"I have no further questions, Your Honor," Josh said.

ii

Dr. Holliday handled Collins's cross-examination with casual ease. In an unusual reversal, the witness was perfectly relaxed, while the attorney grew frustrated and upset. The resulting exchanges were not without light moments. At one point, Collins referred to a chart entry that had been circled in green to denote an abnormal stool reading.

"Is it your understanding that the circling in green does not indicate that they're abnormal?" Collins asked.

"No, that green circle indentifies them as stool, I believe," Holliday replied.

"Well, how about these tests, which reads 'stool sodium sixty-two'? You'll observe there's no green box around it."

"That's correct."

"Did those figures appear to you more normal than the ones we looked at a moment ago that did have a green box around them?"

"Yes," Holliday returned gently. "They're more normal—but not because they don't have a green box around them." He smiled sweetly as a wisp of laughter sounded from the courtroom.

During recess, Ed Caldwell turned to his associate to offer condolence. "That Holliday's a tough cookie with his hokey southern accent," he said. "We're not going to get anywhere with him."

"Yeah," Collins answered with a rueful grin.

He was not able to make a dent in Holliday's self-confident armor for the rest of the afternoon, not even when he questioned the doctor about why the Kaiser doctors had not spotted sodium poisoning.

"I had a very different perspective and I had the benefit of hindsight," Holliday said.

"But would you agree that other explanations may exist?" Collins persisted.

"I haven't found one, and I have looked for it."

"What about the one month of diarrhea Tia is reported to have suffered in Korea?"

"Whatever its cause, it would not explain the later findings," answered Holliday imperturbably. And court was soon after adjourned for the day.

But something of significance had happened. During one of the recesses, a woman had approached Josh Thomas. Josh knew her because she was the head of the Victim-Witness Assistance program that was a service that ran out of his own office.

"I just happened to stop by here," she told him, "and I recognize one of the jurors. I'm pretty sure he has been involved in a possible incest charge involving his young daughter. He goes to Parents United."

"Oh, God, that's all we need: a child molester on the jury!" Josh turned to Lindquist. "Ted, see what you can find out about this juror. We're going to have to inform the defense and the judge about this. But I don't know what position I want to take. My gut feeling is that we want him off the jury—that he'd sympathize with another child abuser."

"I'll see what I can dig up."

The session on Good Friday was scheduled to last only until lunch. Monday was to be a holiday. On Friday morning Dr. Holliday took the stand once again and Al Collins resumed his cross-examination. He asked Holliday about the period directly before Tia's death when her serum sodium continued to rise. How was this possible, Collins wanted to know, given that the child was comatose, on a respirator, and attended constantly by nursing staff?

"Either she had a reservoir of hypertonic solution—a solution where the proportion of salt is greater than occurs naturally in the body—occurring in her gastrointestinal tract, or she had some other solute there that was extracting water at a greater rate than it was excreting salt from the body."

Collins walked over to the defense table and picked up a copy of the preliminary hearing transcript that he had marked. Holliday's answer had opened a small hole, Collins realized.

"Now, Doctor, in the preliminary hearing your answer to the same question was different. You said it was either a reservoir *or* that they had made a mistake and given her a hypertonic solution as a replacement."

"I'd have to study her records in detail to see her intake, but the reservoir theory is most likely," Holliday insisted.

"How long would this reservoir of excess sodium be present?" Collins went on.

"Several hours—depending on the state of the circulation, and the degree of peristalsis, which is the motility of the G-I tract. In shocklike states, there is a medical condition known as ileus, in which movement of material ceases—in effect there is paralysis in the gut—in which case the sodium could be there for hours.

"Also with poison—and this is very common with aspirin poisoning, by the way—there is a secondary absorption peak that occurs sometime later, even after respiratory therapy. That could also explain the fact that Tia's sodium level increased twenty-four hours after her final admission to Kaiser-San Francisco."

Collins followed with questions about Dr. Solcia's letter to the Dallas doctor, Dr. Said, whom Sara Shimoda had contacted about the possibility of a pancreatic tumor. Solcia had reviewed the autopsy slides on Tia and had been asked for his opinion as to whether she might have suffered from a condition called islet hyperplasia.

Collins showed Holliday the letter Solcia had written to Said. "This letter does suggest the possibility of another fatal disease, does it not?"

"It keeps open the possibility. I don't think it suggests it," Holliday responded calmly.

"But do you agree with the doctor that unless you do both of the tests he suggests in his letter, you cannot eliminate the possibility?"

"One of the tests could not be done, and it is true that you cannot eliminate the possibility of islet cell hyperplasia without them. But I don't feel the need to eliminate that possibility given the clinical setting in this case."

"I have no further questions," Collins said.

"I have no redirect," added Josh Thomas.

"That's all, then, Doctor. Thank you," said the judge. "We'll take our morning recess at this time. Please bear in mind the admonition the court has given you, ladies and gentlemen."

Ted turned to Josh. "What do you think about the islet hyperplasia thing?"

"I think it's a total red herring. Boyd Stephens already testified that he couldn't do that test because no tissue was available for electron microscopy."

"The doctors were just reaching for some kind of explanation at that stage?"

"Yeah. Oh, anything on that juror?"

"I'll have it for you on Monday. I've found somebody who was in the same group at Parents United with him."

"Good man."

"Who's on after recess?"

"Lesley McCarcy."

"Oh, we're into the nurses now?"

"Yeah, nurse row. Three of them who heard Priscilla Phillips say she mixed that contaminated formula."

"Against one of theirs—that Debby Roof—who says she can't remember. And she's been a friend of Priscilla's since day one," Ted said.

"Right," Josh replied.

Week 5

Josh Thomas had notified both the judge and the defense about the problem that had arisen with the juror, and Tuesday's session began in the judge's chambers. Josh brought in Joanne Stoller, who worked in Marin County's Child Abuse and

Neglect program. The witness was sworn in and began to testify in chambers, out of hearing of the jury.

She had received a phone call approximately a year ago from a woman who identified herself as the ex-wife of the juror, she told the small group.

"This ex-wife said that her daughter had come home after spending a weekend with her father, upset and distraught because she was forced to sleep nude with him. Sometime later, I was attending sessions of Parents United when the father—this juror—walked in. Usually in those groups you say why you're there, and he said that his ex-wife had accused him of molesting his daughter but that it was not true. He was attending the group for his own education on the matter, he said."

"Do you know whether he is still going to the group?" Josh questioned the witness.

"I met him recently and he told me the current things that were happening in the group."

"No further questions, Your Honor."

"Mr. Collins?"

"Are we to decide to disqualify this juror? On what basis? What does Counsel have in mind?" Collins said.

Josh suggested bringing the juror in to tell his story. If there was no explanation offered, the juror should be excluded for cause, he argued. "I don't understand why during *voir dire* this man didn't reveal this—perhaps in chambers if not in open court—because his case is not dissimilar in terms of class of offense."

"I oppose bringing the juror in for interrogation at this late stage. I feel it would prejudice him to vote for conviction," Collins said.

"Well, all we have is rumor," the judge remarked. "And the relationship between the crimes charged is so completely remote."

"I think he's going to relate to the defendant because she feels unjustly accused and so does he—so I feel he would be prejudiced even if he's not guilty," Josh said.

"May I say something?" The witness spoke up brightly. "I support Mr. Thomas because although the juror may not have committed the crime, he may have some denial barriers up in order to protect himself. It would make it difficult, I think, for him to hear this trial testimony without getting his own denial system in the way."

"Well, Your Honor, the point is, there is no way we can dismiss this juror for cause. He did not perjure himself," Collins argued.

After ten minutes of additional argument, the judge agreed with Collins. "There is no way we can bring in this juror to discuss this and then return him to the jury without prejudicing both sides. There is no legal foundation for dismissing him for cause. Your motion is denied, Mr. Thomas. Let us return to the courtroom."

Josh was morose. He had made, in the end, a subjective, emotional decision to try to remove the juror. Ted had been unable to turn up much information on the man, and had not felt secure in expressing an opinion about whether to retain him on the jury. As it was to turn out, however, neither defense nor prosecution had read the juror accurately.

In open court, nurse Lesley McCarcy was followed to the stand by Jan Bond and Christine King, and the same issues were raised with each nurse by the prosecution and the defense.

Josh was able to connect Priscilla Phillips to the contaminated bottle of formula as each nurse swore she had heard the defendant confess to having mixed it. Each nurse also identified the bottle by size and color of the contents.

On cross-examination, Ed worked on the credibility of the nurses. Two of them were found to have made minor mistakes in their preliminary hearing testimony. Bond, the nurses' aide, confused the functions of the NG and the IV and had to correct herself following recess. In addition, the nurses could not agree on exactly how the contaminated formula had been labeled, or whether Mindy Phillips's name had been on it.

Caldwell also raised the issue of how Dr. Carte's order indicating that only nurses were to mix Mindy's formula came to be erased from the cardex the nurses kept on each patient. Carte's order was dated February twentieth. On that same day, Debby Roof had checked off and initialed the order, indicating that she had transferred it to the cardex. The cardex was designed to contain only the most recent orders on each patient. As new orders came in, the old were erased. But although no new order had supplanted Dr. Carte's, by February twenty-fourth, the day before the discovery of the contaminated formula, the order had—in fact—been erased. It was a mystery that was never to be solved, and it was not clear why Ed Caldwell had chosen to introduce it at all; the only person who stood to gain by erasing the order was Priscilla herself.

The rest of Tuesday and most of Wednesday were devoted to establishing the chain of evidence formed and maintained for the bottle of contaminated formula, which became People's Exhibit 15. A police officer stated that he had transported the bottle from Kaiser's lab to the police department. The property clerk at the San Rafael Police Department testified to mailing the formula to the FBI. Two FBI lab technologists discussed their findings. Their test on the contaminated formula bottle indicated a sodium content that was thirty times normal. In addition, the FBI technician testified that a visual inspection of the eleven handbags belonging to the defendant revealed no trace of baking soda. Surprisingly, he had not conducted more sophisticated tests on the handbags, testifying that he believed that a visual inspection was sufficient. Several Kaiser employees completed the chain of evidence by describing their roles in supplying control samples of polycose and Cho-free formula to the police department. These samples had been forwarded to the FBI lab and found to contain appropriate amounts of sodium.

Late Wednesday afternoon, Josh called to the stand Dr. Howard Sussman, a Stanford pathologist and laboratory director. He testified about procedures for drawing and evaluating blood samples, and about quality control in the laboratory. He described the numerous verification procedures used to assure test-result accuracy.

On cross-examination, Al Collins scored one important point. "How are stool sodium tests run?" he asked.

"The Stanford lab does not run stool samples for electrolytes," the witness said. "We send them to a reference lab."

"Why is that?"

"We'd have to set up a whole method for handling it. It would be too expensive."

"Have you ever done a stool sodium test?"

"Not personally, no," the doctor said.

At the defense table, Ed wrote a furious note on his tablet. If mighty Stanford University Medical Center—one of the foremost hospitals in the country, if not the world—did not feel that the expense incurred in designing a system for running stool sodium tests was necessary, they obviously did not have much demand for the tests. How was it that tiny Kaiser-San Rafael's lab found it necessary? Ed wondered, suddenly, whether Kaiser-San Francisco's lab ran their own stool sodium tests. It would be a point worth exploring. He had his chance the following day.

Dr. Pat Hardy, a pediatrician with Kaiser-South San Francisco, opened Thursday's testimony with an account of his treatment of Mindy Phillips following her release from Kaiser-San Rafael. He had seen her once a month between March and June 1978. During that period she gained four pounds and four separate serum sodium tests had been normal.

Dr. Hardy was replaced by Kaiser-San Rafael lab technologist Judith Kehrlein. During direct examination, Josh questioned her on Kaiser-San Rafael's lab accreditation—a point that grew into an irritating side issue he would rather have avoided.

"We are accredited by the Joint Commission on Hospital Accreditation and are attempting to be accredited by the American Society of Clinical Pathology—which is fairly stringent. There are certain requirements as to quality control," she added, leaving an opening for the defense that she was to regret.

"And how many times have you analyzed stool and urine for electrolytes?"

"For fifteen years, at the rate of three or four a week. There is a standard material we purchase as a control substance for urine and stool samples."

Josh asked her what procedure had been used to test Mindy's contaminated formula and she described what she had done—including the decimal point mistake she had made—and the various steps she had taken to protect the formula after its contamination had been discovered.

On cross-examination, Al Collins jumped on the technologist's testimony regarding the accreditation her lab was seeking.

"How long has Kaiser-San Rafael been trying to gain their accreditation?"

"I don't know."

"How come your lab hasn't qualified yet?"

Judith Kehrlein bristled. "It's strictly a prestige thing."

"Have you any idea when your laboratory will manage to gain this accreditation?"

"Not being clairvoyant, no," the witness snapped.

After lunch, Collins asked Judith Kehrlein about the techniques used for running electrolyte samples. She described the function of the diluter and centrifuge. Then there were questions on standard deviation.

"We accept standard laboratory acceptances plus or minus ten percent. But we have a quality control program for sodiums, and the standard deviation for those is considerably smaller. I believe it's two milliequivalents per liter," she said.

"So with a determination on a serum sodium of one-fifty, a standard deviation of ten percent would be between one-thirty-five and one-sixty-five, correct?"

"It would be plus or minus fifteen."

On redirect, Josh established that although theoretically there could be a ten-percent deviation in test results, in practice the Kaiser-San Rafael lab did much better. On each sample, three tests were run, Judith said. She pointed to one series of tests which had been run on Mindy's blood.

"On this one I got serum sodiums of one sixty, one sixty, one fifty-nine. If I got a plus or minus ten percent, I'd be worried. I'd clean out the equipment and start all over."

"Did anyone check your results on People's fifteen—the bottle of contaminated formula?"

"Yes, the P.M. tech. I asked her to check my results and she did; they agreed with mine."

"Thank you. I have no further questions."

Dr. John Iocco, the Kaiser-San Francisco pathologist who had already testified about Tia's autopsy, returned to the stand Thursday afternoon to discuss San Francisco's laboratory accreditation. He was a witness whom Josh called in an effort to strengthen the jury's impression of Kaiser-San Rafael's lab competence and efficiency, but in fact his testimony worked more to the advantage of the defense. For it turned out that Kaiser-San Francisco already had the accreditation that San Rafael's smaller laboratory was trying to acquire, yet—like Stanford—Kaiser-San Francisco did not run stool sodium tests, but sent them to a reference laboratory.

"Why?" Ed asked on cross-examination, finally seeing his opportunity to assail the credibility of Kaiser-San Rafael's lab.

"We don't have the methodology to run stool sodiums ourselves."

"Your lab is approved by the American Society of Clinical Pathologists and you don't have the methodology to run them?" Ed underlined.

"Objection, Your Honor. Argumentative."

"Sustained."

"How many requests does your lab get for stool samples?"

"It's very infrequent," Iocco said, in contrast to Judith Kehrlein's testimony. "I've never seen one come down, and I talked to our supervisor and he told me that we might get one every two months."

Caldwell jumped on this. Kaiser-San Francisco was a much larger facility than Kaiser-San Rafael.

"How many pediatric beds do you have in San Francisco?" Ed asked.

"Twenty to fifty."

"Are patients referred to San Francisco because there is more personnel there, or better care?"

"More personnel and more specialized care."

Satisfied, Ed sat down.

Mary Vetter was called and testified to the adoptions of Tia and Mindy Phillips. The Phillipses had applied to readopt another child thirty-three days after the death of Tia, she testified.

On cross-examination, Ed asked Miss Vetter why the Phillipses wanted to readopt.

"They loved Tia dearly and felt she would want them to do so. They said they wanted to care for another child in need," she said.

At recess, out of the presence of the jury, a motion was made asking that the records of Dr. Alice Eaton be examined and altered. Dr. Eaton was Mindy Phillips's current physician and Josh Thomas was planning to call her to the stand.

"Miss Vetter wants Mindy's new name and the names of her new parents to be blacked out before you turn the records over to the defense," the judge said.

"No problem, Your Honor," Josh said. He had tracked down Dr. Eaton through Catholic Social Service, and after interviewing her, had decided to call her as a witness, even though her testimony might prove damaging. It would be better if Eaton were his witness rather than Caldwell's, he reasoned, despite what she had to say.

The in-chambers session had been convened to deal with a second issue as well: the admissibility of the tape recording Ted Lindquist had made of the telephone call between himself and the Phillipses. The prosecution planned to put Lindquist on the stand and play the recording the following day. But the defense hoped to suppress the phone call because Ed Caldwell felt the prosecution was taking the position that it constituted an admission by Priscilla Phillips.

"I think the court should ban the tape in any event," Caldwell argued. "If the court listens to the tape and does find it to be an admission, then he should ban it. And if it is not an admission, he should ban it because it was not voluntary."

"Certainly it was freely given! She didn't have to talk to Lindquist," Josh replied.

"She only did it in an effort to exonerate herself, and she had no idea she was being taped. She never gave her permission for that."

"Your Honor, as to that, I cite P.C. section six thirty-three, I believe it is, which prohibits an individual from taping another individual without consent, but which makes an exception with a law officer taping pursuant to an investigation."

The lawyers argued about what constituted an admission until tempers were frayed.

"There is no jury here, Mr. Caldwell," Josh reminded his adversary tightly.

"I'm going to put it on the record, Counsel. It's improper for you to indicate that the evidence should be admissible because the defendant doesn't want the evidence in. That's an improper argument and you're supposed to be a prosecutor and law officer for the People."

"Judge, do we have to listen—"

"I'm sorry, I'm tired of listening to you," Caldwell retorted angrily.

"Just a minute," interrupted the judge. "I'll read the transcription of the phone call overnight and see you in the morning."

"Your Honor, I'd appreciate it if you'd hear the statement instead, because part of my objection hinges on Mrs. Phillips's tone of voice. She was very emotional and distraught and her mind was very scattered," said Caldwell.

"Very well. I will hear it here tomorrow morning at eight-thirty. I will see you then."

"Thank you, Your Honor," Caldwell said.

The following morning the judge heard the tape with both attorneys present, and subsequently Ed Caldwell changed his mind, withdrawing his objection to its presentation to the jury.

"After listening to the tape this time, we don't believe it presents a problem. We heard it originally at a different level and Mrs. Phillips sounded hysterical," Ed remarked.

"Your Honor, we will play the tape later today. We have some other witnesses to call first."

"Very well, Mr. Thomas."

ii

From the beginning, it was clear that Dr. Alice Eaton regarded the courtroom proceedings with disdain. The more determined Josh became in his questioning, the more flippant the response from the witness. The fiery doctor, a slender attractive woman in her fifties, began by reciting Mindy Phillips's history while under her care. Mindy had suffered many problems, she said, beginning with a severe febrile convulsion a few days after her adoption. Dr. Eaton had prescribed daily doses of Phenobarbital for that problem. Loose stools had been reported early last August—a week after the convulsion—but a stool culture for bacteria and worms proved negative. Mindy had exhibited an apparent neurological problem evidenced by a wobbly ataxic gait, and because of cyanosis reported by the new adoptive mother, she was worked up at the cardiac clinic at Oakland's Children's Hospital, with negative results. No cause had yet been found for the cyanosis. Mindy had several upper respiratory infections in November that Dr. Eaton had treated with penicillin. Some loose stools had also been reported.

"Did you ever put Mindy in the hospital for any episodes of vomiting or diarrhea?" Josh asked.

"No. We always got by without it. I'm not a hospital pediatrician at all—I don't like it at all. It isn't my cup of tea to go into a hospital with a child."

"Can you recall the number of times that you received reports either from the mother or from Mindy's school that Mindy was having loose stools?"

"Well, they sent her home from school once. I didn't tell you that last night," she said directly to Josh. "Because she had become such a pain in the neck to them. They refused to change her diapers anymore."

"I see."

"So they were calling on me as the good honest pediatrician to do something about it. There were frequent calls. I suppose I did more work on this child by telephone than I ever did in the office. It was two or three times a week that we worked on this problem."

Josh Thomas shook his head in annoyance at the witness's tendency to elaborate and stray from the point. "Now I'd like you to pay attention to the question that I'm going to ask you," he said sternly. "Do you have a recollection how many times between July of 1978 and November of 1978 you received reports of loose stools?"

"Well, you asked me not to conjecture last night, so I can't. I don't know how many times I've had this sort of thing. They're—"

"Do you have a recollection or not?" Josh interrupted angrily.

"Only one sincere recollection. As I described to you, that episode was a real blast. I don't know whether you want me to discuss that!" She shuddered in remembrance.

"Yes. Did you examine Mindy at that time or did you receive a report from her mother? Tell us all about it," Josh retorted, his hands out in a gesture of supplication.

"I received a report from her mother. It was a very cold night and I didn't want to go out. And I take Mindy's mother very seriously because she's a well-trained mother. She probably has the acumen of a well-trained nurse on the subject. She has raised two other kids and one of them has been somewhat of a problem.

"Anyway, the mother reported that Mindy had diarrhea all day and part of the previous day, would not take liquid by mouth, and had vomited. I thought we might have to hospitalize her but decided to wait and see if the mother couldn't get some fluid into her."

"Did you ever go to the house?"

"No, I kept in touch by phone."

"Did the mother indicate that Mindy was dehydrated and lethargic?"

"Lethargic is not a characteristic of Mindy, I assure you. She's not a lethargic kid."

"Does she have somewhat of a temper?"

"Does she! That's one of the big problems. You don't want me to discuss *that*?"

"Yes, I do. Go ahead."

"She started having enormous temper tantrums. I deduced that she had been wrapped up in cotton wool and had had everything going her way, and then she had found herself in a home with two other children and a mother and father who were pretty down-to-earth and were expecting certain things from that little kid. She even hit her head so hard, they had her wear a helmet part of the time."

"Does she wear it now?"

"I think so. I'm still refilling a prescription for Atarax for the child so the parents can sleep."

"Did you ask the mother to keep a running account of Mindy's episodes between February second and March first of this year?"

"Yes. We were trying to work out a logical approach to these temper tantrums and behavior problems. The mother wrote a beautiful running account."

"Would you read that to us please?"

"Yes, well—" she stopped to search through her records. Finding her copy, Dr. Eaton began to read:

"'Saturday—woke up reciting vocabulary. Color: purple lips, hands, feet to knees. Walking normally ataxic. After nap, runny nose. Temperament vile.'

"'Sunday—had screamed intermittently until about two-thirty this morning. Color: normal.' It goes on like this. On the tenth: 'diarrhea started about midnight. Very liquid.' On the eleventh: 'color and temperature normal but didn't want to be touched or open her eyes. Slept for another hour. Seems in a stupor. Lays on floor. In afternoon, seems back to normal. Diarrhea gone but back at five P.M.'"

Dr. Eaton read on. Further entries in the diary chronicled crankiness, cyanosis followed by normal color, nighttime wakings, doses of Atarax, and ataxic—or unbalanced—walking. There were more upper respiratory infections.

Suddenly, Josh interrupted the witness with a question about her medical education.

"I went to medical school at the University of Texas. I don't know how I got here, I really don't," she answered into an explosion of laughter in the courtroom.

"I think we kind of gather that," Josh retorted quickly.

It was time for the morning recess and Josh Thomas badly needed the break. "The woman is infuriating," he said to Ted. "I wonder what Caldwell will do with her?"

If Caldwell had hoped to fare better with Dr. Eaton, he was soon disabused of the notion. He began his examination by asking if Ted Lindquist had seized the doctor's records.

"No."

Caldwell tried another tactic. It, too, was a dead end. "Did the district attorney ask you not to discuss in detail the episodes of diarrhea?"

"No."

"Can you tell me about the adoptive parents' other child?"

"Well, Joey comes from Vietnam, and he was hospitalized at Mount Zion in San Francisco for several months with severe gastrointestinal problems. He came home, developed Salmonella, and had diarrhea pretty constantly. The mother was well trained in the use of Pedialyte."

"Is that the reason why you didn't hospitalize Mindy when she had this chronic diarrhea?" Caldwell asked, setting up the witness for an obvious helpful answer. But she played no favorites.

"I explained that to Mr. Thomas. I don't hospitalize patients," she answered, frowning.

"Now about Mindy's cyanosis. It's your opinion that it is not caused by anything she ingested?"

"I don't think it could possibly be."

"You know Mindy has been diagnosed as having CMV?"

"Yes."

"Has she also been diagnosed as having cerebral palsy?"

"That's tentative."

"She has had seizures—the father called July twenty-fourth to report one. Have there been occasional convulsions since?"

"Not that I know of. We took her off Phenobarbital."

"Has Mindy had any stool sodium tests done, Dr. Eaton?"

"Heavens, no!"

"Is there any particular reason for that? Have you as a pediatrician ever run or requested a stool sodium?"

"No, never. I don't know of any value that would have. We have much better ways of determining body sodiums. As far as I know, I think—well, I'm not going to conjecture."

"You can testify as to something based on your experience, education, and training, Dr. Eaton," said Caldwell, his voice raised just a bit.

"As far as I know it's a pretty variable test and difficult to evaluate. The lab technicians don't run them often enough to be that accurate with them anyway."

"Now, what about other infections? She's had periodic infections, what looks like almost periodic temperatures and so forth, and an ear infection—otitis media?"

"Yes."

"Any other infections?"

"Oh, nothing. I don't think so. I don't have them all down. The mother is so proficient, she wouldn't tell me about them all."

"Well, how many infections has she had since last July?"

"Numerically, that would be hard to comment on. You told me not to conjecture. She's a problem in my practice."

"Dr. Eaton, if you were describing Mindy's condition to a fellow doctor, is it fair to state that Mindy has a continuing virus problem, for example?" Ed asked.

"I don't think so."

"Is it something that comes and goes?" Ed tried again.

"It's the usual pattern in this age group. Between nine and twenty-four months of age, children have reduced immunological levels. They get lots of bacterial and viral illnesses. This is well-documented."

On redirect, Josh asked Dr. Eaton again about Mindy's behavioral problems.

"Can diarrhea be emotional in nature?"

"I doubt it. Though it could have an effect. It's more common to have constipation in that age group. We call it the unlove syndrome."

During recross, Ed went back to this point. "If the 'unlove syndrome' produces constipation, if the baby is receiving a lot of love, that doesn't necessarily mean there's going to be diarrhea, does it?" he asked.

"No."

"I have no further questions."

"No questions, Your Honor," Josh added. Dr. Eaton left the stand.

Priscilla Phillips leaned and whispered to her attorney as the next witness was called. "Do you think her testimony helped?"

Ed Caldwell shrugged. "Not much. She didn't take herself or the whole thing seriously enough."

"And the jury won't take her seriously either?"

"I'm afraid not."

"But the diarrhea—it shows Mindy still has it!"

"Wait till we get Pat Wrigley on the stand," Ed answered with a smile. "I think we'll get a lot more mileage there."

Ted Lindquist finally took the stand following the afternoon recess. He was not nervous, as his only function was to serve as a witness to having made the telephone call to the Phillips house, the tape of which was now to be played for the jury. He sat solidly as the first of two tapes was played. The courtroom was very quiet, the jury angling toward the tape machine as though that would enable them to hear more clearly. In her seat, Priscilla was still, her head against Steve's shoulder. She was not ashamed or embarrassed about what she had said. She did not believe she had made any kind of admission. She *was* the common denominator—anyone could see that, but that was not an admission of guilt. Indeed the whole telephone call was an attempt to exonerate herself, to point out Mindy's legitimate illnesses and the fact that her serum sodium had been elevated only once, to bring up other significant evidence Priscilla felt the police would miss about Tia and her illness. All of Priscilla's nightmares about that had come true, all of her fears about being charged that she had written about in her journal and confided to her friends.

The judge stopped the tape in the middle of the second recording, since the hour of adjournment had been reached. The tapes—People's Exhibit 50—were returned to the clerk to hold until Monday. It was an unfortunate break in the drama as far as the prosecution was concerned. Josh Thomas did not believe that Priscilla Phillips presented herself well on the tape: she seemed self-serving, aggressive in the way she cut off her husband, too quick to point out her status in the community and the ways in which the care of Tia and Mindy had been a hardship for her. But the full impact of her personality would be softened by the intervening weekend—an unfortunate error in timing of the type common in a long trial. Josh sighed. It was too late to worry about that. He had almost finished his case. Next week the truly nerve-wracking part would begin.

Week 6

The People rested their case on Tuesday of the following week. During the final few days of the prosecution's case, considerable time and argument had centered on the admissibility of Dr. Martin Blinder's testimony on Munchausen Syndrome by Proxy.

Ed Caldwell made three arguments against its admissibility. The testimony was to be highly speculative. Munchausen Syndrome by Proxy was not a scientifically reliable diagnosis, and in addition, the doctor had never examined the defendant.

Josh Thomas countered that the doctor's testimony would provide information about motive. As to Blinder's qualifications, he was an expert in forensic psychiatry, and just because a syndrome was new did not mean that it failed to exist. Furthermore, the defense attorney had opened the subject himself, Josh reminded Ed Caldwell, when he had cross-examined Boyd Stephens about an article on the subject. In any case, Josh argued, as had Kit Mitchell before him in the preliminary, the extent of the expert's knowledge about the syndrome went to the weight of the expert's knowledge about the testimony, not its admissibility.

In the end, Judge Burke agreed with Judge Gary Thomas and ruled to allow Blinder's testimony. The doctor took the stand after lunch. An impeccably dressed, elfin man in his early forties, Martin Blinder enjoyed the frequent confrontations testifying in court provided. He was articulate, intelligent, and experienced. Calmly he awaited the district attorney's questions.

As he had with each of his medical witnesses, Josh Thomas began with Blinder's credentials. A 1962 graduate of Chicago Medical School, Blinder had interned at San Francisco General and completed a residency in psychiatry at Langley Porter Neuropsychiatric Institute at the University of California Medical Center in San Francisco. He had authored numerous articles, taught psychiatry at the Hasting College of Law for six years, and testified in hundreds of cases.

Before the district attorney could reach the heart of Blinder's testimony, Ed Caldwell asked to *voir dire* the doctor to examine the validity of his expert credentials.

Ed had done his homework.

"Have you taken and failed certification as a board-certified psychiatrist, Doctor?"

"Yes. I flunked the neurology portion. But the part that I did not qualify on has been eliminated now as a criterion for board certification."

"Have you testified in a previous action that the fact that a doctor fails to attain board certification is a test of his competency?" Ed persisted.

"Well, I think it's a measure among others. I think primarily it's a test of his competence to pass a specific examination. But I will allow—and do on every possible occasion—that I'm a crummy neurologist," Blinder answered with perfect equanimity.

"What about psychiatry?"

"I'm pretty good."

Caldwell moved on to another point. It was one with which he later intended to impeach the witness.

"Have you ever testified under oath in a prior proceeding that you were the chief of the psychiatric service at UC Hospital?"

"Yes, I have."

"And that is the truth?"

"Yes—it was at that time. I was chief of a private inpatient psychiatric service at UC Hospital."

Ed tried a flank attack. "Did you offer your services to the district attorney after reading about the case?" he asked.

"No."

"Are you charging the same rates as you did in 1976: three hundred dollars for half a day, five hundred for a full day?"

"Yes."

"How many hours have you spent preparing yourself for *research*—if that's the proper word—" Ed added meaningfully, "in the syndrome of Munchausen by Proxy?"

"I don't know. Is it your intention, Mr. Caldwell, to include all my files in this case or just the academic literature on Munchausen's?" Blinder responded evenly.

"It's my import to ask you what the taxpayers of the county of Marin and the district attorney has paid you—"

"Your Honor—" Josh broke in. "I'm going to ask that that gratuitous comment on the part of Mr. Caldwell be stricken. I don't think he has to frame his questions in an argumentative fashion."

"Overruled."

The *voir dire* continued for several more minutes. Finally, after numerous arguments between the attorneys about how the foundation should be laid for Blinder's testimony, Josh Thomas resumed his direct examination of the witness.

"Dr. Blinder, I want to pose to you the following hypothetical question, and I'll ask you as part of that question to assume the following facts: number one, that the defendant, Priscilla E. Phillips, did repeatedly and surreptitiously administer doses of a cathartic sodium-type compound over a period of months to first one adopted child and then another, until this poisoning was discovered by hospital officials—"

"I object, Your Honor. It's assuming the guilt of the defendant. That's totally inadmissable. I cite *People* v. *Hardy*—"

"Overruled." Judge and Counsel had discussed this at length in the judge's chambers and the judge was prepared with his ruling.

"Fact number two," Josh Thomas continued. "Assume there were frequent admissions of the victims, usually in a condition that required immediate emergency procedures, including ambulance rides and dramatic life-or-death situations. Fact number three: assume that the mother, Priscilla Phillips, was actively involved in the treatment of the victims, becoming very knowledgeable about their treatments, and that she became friends with, and received the sympathy and admiration of, the hospital staff—"

"I object to the form of the question. It's confusing. Also, Your Honor, this is a hypothetical question and he's attempting—by using the name of the defendant—to make it not hypothetical."

"I believe that objection is well-taken, ladies and gentlemen. Please disregard whenever Mr. Thomas has mentioned the defendant."

"Number four," continued Josh Thomas inexorably, "assume that the defendant appeared to be stable, competent, and extremely concerned about the welfare of both children, and that all the doctors were confounded as to the cause of the victim's illnesses. Now assuming these facts, Dr. Blinder, do you have an opinion as to whether these facts indicate behavior on the part of the defendant that is consistent with that exhibited by mothers affected by Munschausen Syndrome by Proxy?"

"I have an opinion. Your hypothetical person evinces symptoms consistent with that syndrome."

"Now, Doctor, could you describe the symptoms of Munchausen Syndrome by Proxy?"

"Yes. The illness is typically a dramatic one. Every case I've read involves the mother, who is typically outwardly devoted to the child. By contrast, the father tends to be peripheral—it

Description of disease

is clearly the mother's show. Often these mothers have unmet needs from their own parents, and they transfer these to the authority figures represented by the doctors, nurses, spouses, maybe even the community. There's another side of the coin in that there is a certain amount of anger and depression in the mothers, and they punish the parent-surrogates—that is, the doctors and nurses—by making the child more ill despite the best efforts of the physician to save the child.

"The mother will flourish on the ward, and the concern and competence of these mothers and their apparent strong motherliness makes it hard for the doctors to suspect them. The mother may have an underlying depression or suicidal inclinations, but they're well hidden behind all this activity.

"When the mother is confronted with evidence, she cannot accept responsibility, even when the evidence is incontrovertible. This is largely an unconscious process with a great deal of denial," Blinder added.

"Are these persons psychotic or mentally ill?" Josh asked.

"The literature describes some mothers who are frankly psychotic. But a great number of mothers who do this are not overtly mentally ill."

"What is usually the primary intent involved on the part of the mother regarding attention?"

"To become the focus of attention themselves. To win sympathy and acclaim for being 'supermom.'"

"Now, without a clincial examination, are you able to say with reasonable certainty that this defendant was or was not suffering from Munchausen Syndrome by Proxy?"

"No. Without a clinical examination I cannot."

At least he had been honest on that point, Ed thought as he stood to conduct his cross-examination. Ed had studied all the articles on Munchausen Syndrome by Proxy—only one of which actually mentioned the syndrome by that name—with a great deal of care. And he had found significant differences between the mothers described in these articles and Priscilla Phillips—or rather, the hypothetical mother in the district attorney's questions.

"Let us look at the article on Munchausen Syndrome by Proxy that appeared in the British journal *Lancet*—an article by Dr. Roy Meadow. There are two cases in that article, one a girl named Kay, the other a boy named Charles?" Ed began.

"Yes."

"Now I want to ask you whether the following facts about

Kay's and Charles's cases fit our hypothetical mother. In Kay's case, the mother was not as concerned as the doctors about Kay's illness. Did you find that in the history of the hypothetical mother, Doctor?"

"No." An experienced witness, Blinder did not amplify.

"Many times Kay was taken to the hospital during holiday periods. Similar?"

"No."

"Kay's mother reported false medical history. Similar?"

"That was implied but not explicit in the hypothetical."

"Kay's mother added her own urine or menstrual discharge to her child's sample. Similar?"

"No."

"Kay's mother had an extensive medical history that she concealed. Similar?"

"No."

"Kay's mother felt her husband was more interested in Kay than in her. Similar?"

"No."

"Charles's mother was a nurse. Similar?"

"No."

"After Charles died, his mother attempted suicide. Similar?"

"No."

"Charles's mother was an hysteric. Similar?"

"No."

"Charles's mother interfered with wounds healing. Similar?"

"No."

Ed continued in this vein with several more medical articles that Blinder had used as a basis for his opinion. Blinder agreed that his hypothetical mother had not battered her children, had not lacked family support, nor been hospitalized for depression. It was an impressive litany of differences that Ed continued following the afternoon recess.

Judge Burke, meanwhile, in an attempt to underline its seriousness, read and then reread to the jury the instructions concerning hypothetical questions. It was vital, he told them, that they understand how hypothetical questions functioned in a court of law.

"Hypotheticals are allowed only with *expert* witnesses," he said. "That witness may assume a set of facts and give an opinion based on them. The assumed facts need not have been proved, but must be within the probable or possible range of the evidence. If the jury should find that the facts assumed have not been proved, it should determine the effect of that failure of proof on the value and weight of the expert opinion."

Then Caldwell continued his cross-examination, moving to a more crude *ad hominem* attack on Martin Blinder's character. He tried to paint the doctor as a flake, asking him about some of his extracurricular activities. In addition to once serving as mayor of San Anselmo, writing a book on psychiatry and the law, and lecturing on jury selection, Blinder had been involved in several less conventional activities.

"You've written a cookbook, I believe, have you not?"

"Yes."

"What's the name of that?"

"Lucretia Borgia Cookbook."

"What kind of cooking is that, Doctor?"

"Very rich cooking," Blinder answered, drawing a laugh.

"And you play the piano?"

"After a fashion."

"And you in fact had professional engagements as a pianist locally?"

"Yes."

"Dr. Blinder, as we know, Munchausen's Syndrome was named after a famous teller of tall tales. Have you ever been described by any of your colleagues as having some of the same attributes as Baron Munchausen?"

"No."

"I ask that that question and answer be stricken," Josh broke in angrily.

"It may go out," the judge ruled.

"Now, Doctor, if I understand correctly, the conclusion that you reached both in the preliminary hearing and today is that in the absence of a clinical examination of Mrs. Phillips, you cannot say whether she is or isn't the subject of this disorder?"

"Not in a court of law."

"And there had been no clinical examination of Mrs. Phillips?"

"There has been none."

"Thank you. Your Honor, I would ask that the entire testimony of Dr. Blinder be struck and that the court admonish the jury to disregard it."

"The objection is overruled. Motion denied," returned the judge.

* * *

It had been an exhausting day for both sides. Josh was particularly pleased because he had prevailed on the admissibility of Blinder's testimony, but he was to lose an important admissibility argument the next morning.

Ted Lindquist had prepared extensive charts designed to show the correlation between Priscilla Phillips's presence at the hospital and the illnesses of her children. He had gathered his data from the nurses' notes in their progress reports. But Judge Burke disallowed the introduction of the charts because Lindquist had made some assumptions that the court felt were unjustified. If a nurse had noted the presence of the defendant during a particular shift, Ted's chart showed her as present during the entire shift. And this, the judge ruled, was an unwarranted conclusion, and could possibly deceive the jury. It was a significant victory for the defense.

As his last witness, Josh Thomas called Dr. Betty Shreiner, a pathologist on the staff of Kaiser-San Rafael. Josh felt he needed to bolster up the reputation of the San Rafael lab, which had suffered under the cross-examination of several of the prosecution's witnesses.

On the question of the accreditation by the American Society of Clinical Pathology (ASCP), Dr. Shreiner testified that her lab did not have such accreditation because it was expensive. "Lack of that accreditation does not reflect on the quality of the lab or its people. We are accredited by the state and by the Joint Hospital Commission," she said.

"Isn't it true that your lab is trying to get ASCP accreditation?" Collins asked on cross-examination.

"Not to my knowledge. We are not attempting to get ASCP accreditation for the lab as a whole," she answered.

"Thank you," Collins said.

"Your Honor," Josh Thomas pushed himself to his feet. "The People rest."

ii

After his *pro forma* motion for acquittal was denied, Ed Caldwell opened his case with Pat Wrigley. She was a surprise witness, and one with whom Ed hoped to win the case.

Catholic Social Service had been very secretive about Mindy's whereabouts after she left the Phillipses, but Mindy's new adoptive mother had called the Marin County courthouse a few weeks before and asked to speak to Priscilla Phillips's attorney.

"I'm Mindy's new mother—Mindy is Sarah Wrigley now—and I've been reading a lot of lies in the paper about Sarah being well now. She isn't," Pat Wrigley had said in introducing herself on the phone.

Ed lost no time in going across the bay to Vallejo to meet Pat and her husband, Harry. Pat had been impressive. She was small and overweight, but she struck him as warm, motherly, homespun. In addition she was extremely knowledgeable medically, particularly because there were problems with her first adopted child, a Vietnamese orphan named Joey.

Pat began her testimony by describing her family and her background.

"When did you receive custody of Mindy Phillips—now Sarah Wrigley?" Ed asked.

"July 19, 1978."

"And since that time, has she experienced any diarrhea?"

"There have been thirty cases of severe diarrhea in the past nine months," she answered as the courtroom audience stirred in astonishment.

"Can you define diarrhea for us?"

"It's primarily liquid bowel movements that occur more than twice a day."

"Now, Mrs. Wrigley, can you describe what happened when Sarah had one of these bouts of diarrhea?"

"Well, typically they came very suddenly. She'd be sitting in a high chair and then suddenly it would pour out of her diaper, through her rubber pants and her clothes, down the chair, and onto the floor in a puddle."

"And how long would these bouts last?"

"The explosive part about an hour. It could go on for the rest of the day or even a week."

"Were there any prior indications of when Sarah was about to have an attack of diarrhea?"

"No. And we tried to plot it out, link it to allergies and so forth."

"Mrs. Wrigley, what did you do to deal with these bouts of explosive diarrhea?"

"Well, to control the convulsive motion of the bowels, we

put her in warm water, and if that didn't work, we gave her some Donnatal elixir, which calms the bowel," she answered.

"And how much fluid would Sarah typically lose during one of these explosive bouts?"

"Typically one pint during each explosive incident," Pat answered firmly. "She would lose maybe a quart an hour."

In his chair, Josh Thomas wrote himself a note. Then he looked over at Ted, who was shaking his head in sick disbelief. His case was unraveling before his eyes.

"Do you remember the dates of these explosive bouts, Mrs. Wrigley?" Ed went on.

"There was one right after Thanksgiving. I remember because I lost sick leave staying home with Sarah. Also on St. Patrick's Day we had an incident, and one about the time of Joey's birthday, which would be February twelfth."

"Now, can you tell us a little about your experiences with Joey, Mrs. Wrigley?"

"Yes. Joey arrived from Vietnam at the age of six weeks, very sick. He was critically ill in three different hospitals. The longest hospitalization was at Mount Zion."

"You learned about diarrhea because of Joey's numerous bouts?"

"Yes. I always kept Pedialyte with me because Mount Zion told me to do so. We had one and a half years of severe diarrhea with Joseph."

"Is that why you didn't go to Dr. Eaton each time that Sarah had diarrhea?"

"Yes, definitely."

"Does Sarah still have cyanosis—blue coloration—Mrs. Wrigley?"

"Yes. She had it yesterday. She also had severe seizures. Three days after we got her she had her first major seizure—a full convulsion—seven minutes long. We took her right to Dr. Eaton. Sarah has been a very sick child. Up till last month you would almost have to say she'd never had a well day. She is gradually getting better."

"Now, tell me a little about your educational background, Mrs. Wrigley."

"Certainly. I have a Master's in the education of the physically handicapped and a teaching credential for teaching the physically handicapped and health-impaired. The children I teach are afflicted with such conditions as cerebral palsy, osteogenesis imperfecta, and severe asthma."

"Would you be able to determine that Sarah has cerebral palsy?"

"Yes. Sarah has ataxic CP. It is characterized by imbalance, which is commonly called the drunken sailor's gait. Sarah is ataxic and falls frequently. She wears a helmet to protect her from those falls."

"Now, about those bouts of diarrhea that were not of the explosive type—that is, the other twenty-six times. What were their characteristics?"

"There was a sudden onset and no known cause. They might go on for several hours or even several days."

"Has Sarah ever had this type of diarrhea while she's having breakfast and still goes to school?" Ed asked. It was a question he was subsequently to regret.

"Yes. This is very typical. If she's not dehydrated and is acting normal, we send her to school. My husband, Harry, is a custodian at the school Sarah attends and he can watch over her."

"And you say that during Sarah's explosive episodes, she can lose up to a quart an hour?" Ed repeated.

"Yes."

"Now, you say that Sarah had an attack of cyanosis yesterday?"

"Yes. And yesterday evening she went into a severe otitis media problem—her teeth were chattering and she was running a fever of a hundred four degrees—so we took her to Dr. Eaton for penicillin. Through the night her temperature stayed down and this morning she was ready to go, fit as a fiddle, and we put her on the bus to go to school."

"Going back to the severe attack around Thanksgiving, Mrs. Wrigley, can you describe that for us?"

"Yes. We had to put Sarah in the bathtub. She was losing about a pint at that time, and maybe in an hour altogether she lost a quart. She became very lethargic, wouldn't even crawl. She started to become dehydrated and we called Dr. Eaton. Her skin was parched and dry but she was not feveral. She vomited a few times and we couldn't get her to drink. Finally we got her to take some Coke."

"Now, moving back in time a little, Mrs. Wrigley. What was Sarah's condition when you first got her last July?"

"She was not walking; she was drooling some, unable to drink from a cup. She had a tremor on her left side and paresis—that's a weakened muscle condition—on the left side of her face. She spoke about three words."

"And she was how old?"

"Sarah was eighteen months old."

"Do you have any photographs of Sarah when she was Mindy Phillips?"

"Yes—they're in my briefcase." She handed her case to Ed Caldwell, who struggled with it for a moment.

"I can't open it."

"It takes a Master's degree," Pat answered lightly. The audience laughed and even the judge smiled.

"How does Sarah relate to you as daughter to mother?"

"We have a very close relationship. She's very affectionate to other women. She has had only two strange reactions: one to a woman at her school, and the other to medical personnel—she has an hysterical reaction to them."

"Mrs. Wrigley, have you ever talked to Mrs. Phillips prior to recess in this courtroom?" Ed shifted emphasis.

"Never."

"Now, has it been your practice to stay with your children when they're hospitalized?"

"Yes. They've been hospitalized five times and I've moved in each time."

"And do you keep detailed records of these hospitalizations?"

"Oh, yes. In their baby books, of course, and I have kept diaries of their hospitalizations day by day. These reflect in some cases the medical care or very often their emotional reactions."

"Thank you, Mrs. Wrigley." Ed Caldwell was finished with direct.

In his chair, Josh Thomas collected the pages of notes he had made. This whole ruse involving Pat Wrigley—and Josh was convinced it had been a ruse—infuriated him. Both Dr. Eaton and Mary Vetter had insisted that the district attorney examine all of Dr. Eaton's records prior to giving them to the defense and painstakingly delete each reference to Mindy Phillips's new name. Josh was sure that that exercise had been a ploy to keep him away from the Wrigleys so that Caldwell could spring this witness on him. Because now it turned out that Ed Caldwell not only knew her name, but he was using Pat Wrigley as his star witness.

And what a damaging witness. The parallels between Pat

Wrigley and Priscilla Phillips were astonishing. The defense could not have found a better witness had they invented her, Josh thought. Yet these very similarities that would work for Priscilla Phillips might be turned around to the detriment of Pat Wrigley, and Josh realized this almost immediately. If he could suggest this to the jury, and at the same time convince them that at the very least Pat Wrigley was not an impartial witness, he could undercut the effectiveness of her testimony. During recess he had noticed Pat throw her arms around Priscilla Phillips, hugging her like a long-lost sister. He wondered if some of the jurors had seen it, too. Just to be sure, Josh planned to point it out to them.

But he would begin by airing his suspicions about the fortuitous arrival of Pat Wrigley at the trial. Josh was not sure about who had contacted whom in this little scenario he believed the defense had worked out, and he wanted the jury to share his doubts.

"Mrs. Wrigley, you testified that you contacted Ed Caldwell on April fourth?" he began.

"Yes. After nine months of trying to keep Sarah in hiding, I thought it was time to bring the truth out into the open."

"You're certain you called Mr. Caldwell and not the other way around?"

"Definitely. I called Ed."

"Ed—you mean Mr. Caldwell?"

"Yes."

"Did you have any conversation with Dr. Eaton after she testified in this case?"

"I saw her last night. Sarah was sick," Pat snapped.

"But you advised her, prior to her testifying, that you were going to be a witness, didn't you?"

"I told her I had called Mr. Caldwell."

"When your adopted son Joey was in Mount Zion, Mrs. Wrigley, what was the matter with him?"

"He had scabies, Salmonella, diarrhea, and malabsorption."

"Did you move in with Joe at Mount Zion?"

"Not permanently. I spent every day with him."

"At the time he left the hospital, was he well or still sick?"

"Still critically ill."

"And you removed him from Mount Zion against the wishes of the doctor?"

"Yes."

"How was he critically ill?" Josh had the witness on his line now, and very carefully he began to reel her in.

"He had severe diarrhea. He still had active Salmonella. At that point his prognosis was very poor."

"How many doctors advised against taking Joey home?"

"Two."

"And what was Joe's condition after he came home?"

"He didn't have a normal stool for a year and a half. He was on Cho-free, distilled water, MCT oil, and polycose. For one and a half years he didn't have a bowel movement you could hold in your hand. Sometimes he had diarrhea ten times a day. He was a severely, critically ill child."

"Was he ever hospitalized for diarrhea?"

"No."

"Would you characterize his diarrhea as massive and voluminous?"

"Yes. He was on Cho-free until he was thirteen months old. At that point he was getting obese from the formula and it was obvious he no longer needed it. He was put on regular food even though he still had diarrhea."

"So he was gaining weight?" Josh asked pointedly.

Pat was oblivious. "Oh, yes."

"Have you had any experience in determining what are life-threatening symptoms in a child the age of Sarah?"

"With Joseph, yes."

"Have you had any formal training in that area?"

"Before they let us take Joseph home from Mount Zion, they went over and over again the signs I had to watch out for and how to measure the formula."

"Did you ever mix his formula in the hospital?"

"I was never allowed to. If you overdose by one cc of polycose you can cause severe diarrhea."

"Is that because polycose is a sugar-based compound?" Josh readied his gaff.

"Yes."

Josh paused maliciously, then he jabbed at his catch. "Is that why you gave Sarah all those Cokes?"

The witness grimaced angrily. "I just gave her a small amount," she answered.

"How much?"

"Probably about a quarter of a cup diluted with water."

"And that was sufficient to overcome the extreme dehydration she was suffering from at that time?" His voice dripped sarcasm.

"It started her drinking again," Pat protested.

"Now during that episode of *severe diarrhea* that you described, when she was in the high chair. What happened?"

"She was eating her dinner. There was a loud sound and it just started pouring out of her. We immediately took her out of the high chair and put her in a warm bath."

"And did her diarrhea continue in the bath?"

"It's sort of like labor. The convulsiveness comes in a big whoosh and then stops. You can feel her belly tighten and rise and then it pushes out."

"And you kept putting her in and out of the bathtub when she had these explosive periods?"

"Yes."

"And then at the end of the hour, you dispensed with the bathtub treatment?" The disdain in his voice almost choked him.

"Yes, she was coming out of it," Pat answered resolutely.

"Did she appear to be in any pain?"

"No."

"Even while she was going through these convulsions?"

"No. She was chatting away."

"Ah." Josh paused meaningfully. "And after this episode you indicated that you sent her to school the next morning?"

"Yes, I did. I would send her if she was having controllable diarrhea."

"Did the school authorities ever complain because they were tired of changing her diapers?"

"No."

"Did anybody ever make complaints of that type to Dr. Eaton?"

"I believe they may have."

"Now you testified that Sarah had a feveral episode last night, with a hundred-four degree temperature, yet you sent her to school?"

"Yes. She had no temperature this morning. I called the school and talked to her teacher, told her how to get in touch with Dr. Eaton should anything occur."

"We have reached the hour of our afternoon adjournment," Judge Burke interrupted. "We will not be in session tomorrow. We will meet at the regular time Thursday."

Josh and Ted Lindquist walked out together.

"Josh, we blew it. We should have followed up on Mindy's new parents." Ted was furious with himself.

"Yeah, I just about dropped dead when this Wrigley woman took the stand."

"I'm damned if I don't think there's some kind of conspiracy going on. I'd almost believe Catholic Social Service and Priscilla Phillips were all involved somehow, that all these people knew each other. Maybe Priscilla and Wrigley even met at the Vietnamese babylift or something," Ted said.

"Yeah. I'm going to call Vetter and Eaton tonight—"

"They'll deny it—you watch."

"Yeah. Look, Ted, we've got to get out to Vallejo tomorrow and talk to Mindy's teachers, get her school records. If she was in school most of the time, how sick could she be? Oh, and another thing, we'd better talk to Mindy's foster mother. You know, the woman who had her before the Wrigleys. Find out her name. Maybe she can help."

"Okay, I'll call Vetter."

"She won't want to tell you."

Ted smiled grimly. "Don't worry, Josh. I'll get the name."

iii

The next day Josh and Ted met and drove over to Vallejo to the Carol Loma Vista School for the orthopedically handicapped. Carol Loma Vista had ten students, including Sarah Wrigley, all of whom had some handicap that prevented their participation in a regular school.

Josh headed for the principal's office to obtain Sarah's attendance record while Ted went to interview Sarah's teacher. There he met resistance: Kamala Schwartz refused to be interviewed until she had consulted a lawyer.

"Miss Schwartz, we are not investigating *you*," Ted said after a few minutes of exasperating conversation. But she would not budge from her position.

Ted's luck improved with Edith Horne, Sarah's teacher's aide, who agreed to be interviewed that evening. She told Ted that Sarah had suffered numerous episodes of diarrhea while at school, but she tended to minimize their seriousness. Sarah had never been sent home early due to diarrhea, Edith said. Their practice was merely to change Sarah's clothes—she kept three changes at school because of the problem—and send her about her business. It was no big deal, just a nuisance.

"What about the attendance records?" Ted asked Josh when they met later.

"Take a look for yourself," Josh answered with a grin. He held out the records. "Sarah Wrigley hasn't missed a day all year. Hardly a life-threatening sort of diarrhea!"

"Just what I was thinking. Oh, I got the name of Mindy's foster mother out of Mary Vetter—had to threaten her with a charge of obstructing justice, though!"

Josh laughed grimly. "Well, at least you got through. She won't even take my calls anymore! Who is it?"

"A Mrs. Portillo."

"Where does she live?"

"San Francisco—the Mission district. I've got an appointment with her tomorrow. And I'll follow up with this Miss Schwartz after she gets a chance to consult her lawyer."

"Okay. Did you know Dan White's trial began today in the city?"

"Yeah."

"Blinder's testifying in that one, too. They're going for a diminished capacity and Blinder's their star witness." He paused and then shrugged. "C'mon, let's go home."

On Thursday morning, Pat Wrigley arrived early and waited on the witness stand for court to begin. But one of the jurors was absent and it took some time to track her down at home where she was in bed with symptoms of the flu. Judge Burke finally called off the day's testimony, but not before Pat Wrigley had a chance to show her disdain for the district attorney by sticking her tongue out at him while his back was turned. She also passed the time by talking in sign language to her sister, who was attending the proceedings.

"Another nail in her coffin," Josh remarked to Ted after he heard about Pat Wrigley's various gestures. "She ought to be taking this trial a lot more seriously—someone's life is at stake."

"What have you got for Wrigley's cross?"

"All the records she brought in her briefcase—I've had a chance to review them. Nowhere in the Mount Zion discharge summary does it say that she took her son out against medical advice, nor that he was critically ill."

Ted nodded. "The lady likes to exaggerate."

"Yup. Well, a lot depends on what this Mrs. Portillo has to say. What time's your appointment?"

"Four. Stop worrying, Josh."

But Josh frowned grimly. "Sure," he said.

At four that afternoon, Ted walked up the steps of Mrs. Margie Portillo's Park Street house and rang the bell. It took longer than usual for a response, and Ted immediately saw why. Mrs. Portillo, a middle-aged, dark-haired woman with thick glasses and a kind face, was on crutches.

She led Ted to her front room and he sat gingerly on one of the three upholstered pieces of furniture and took out his tape recorder. The room was heavy with knickknacks and pictures of Jesus.

"I have seven children and fifteen grandchildren," Mrs. Portillo told Ted. "After my husband died in 1967, I started taking in foster children. I have had twenty-six. And Cindy—we called her that because Catholic Social Service asked us not to call her Mindy—was the last."

"Was Cindy sick with diarrhea while she was with you, Mrs. Portillo?"

"No. She was very shy at first and everybody—my family's in and out of here all day—everybody thought she was retarded, but then after a few weeks she was lovable and friendly. She played with my children—they used to like to take her to the swings at Holly Circle Park."

"Was she walking?"

"Oh, yes."

"And did she have diarrhea?"

"No. She was constipated once. I gave her Milk of Magnesia."

"Mrs. Portillo, may I ask why you're on crutches?"

"I was mugged a few years ago. I needed some surgery," she answered simply. "It's hard for me to get around now and I don't think I'll have any more foster children." She looked at the floor. "Cindy was the last."

"Thank you for your help. You'll be receiving a subpoena in the mail, and on the day you'll testify, I'll come pick you up and drive you over to Marin and then back."

"all right," she said.

Later that afternoon, Ted drove back to the Civic Center to report to Josh, who was working late in his office. Ted was on his way down the long hall leading from the elevator to room

155, his footsteps loud in the deserted corridor, when Josh leaned his head out and saw him.

"Well? Well?" he said eagerly. "What happened?"

Ted put on the longest face he could muster and hung his head, shaking it as if in total disappointment.

"Well, Josh, you're just not going to believe it," he began.

"What? What?" Josh was frantic.

"I'm sorry, but we've got a real problem with Mrs. Portillo," Ted went on, his voice a mournful dirge, his eyes on the floor. And then he looked up and gave a huge grin.

"Wait till you hear this!" he said.

On Friday, Josh Thomas went on the attack against Pat Wrigley.

"Did you hug the defendant during recess?" he asked.

"Yes."

"While you were waiting for an absent juror yesterday, did you stick your tongue out at anybody?"

"Yes."

"Who?"

"You."

"Now you testified that you took Joseph out of Mount Zion against medical advice?"

"Yes."

"Did you sign a form acknowledging that?"

"No."

"You said Joseph was critically ill when you took him?"

"He was still in very serious condition."

"You used the term *critical* on Tuesday, didn't you?"

"All right, critical."

Josh handed the witness a copy of Joseph Wrigley's discharge summary from Mount Zion. "Does this summary say that Joey was 'critically ill'?" he asked.

Pat Wrigley shrugged. "No, those words do not appear here," she acknowledged.

"How much formula was Joey getting at discharge?"

"Seven hundred to eight hundred cc's a day, to be given ad lib, or without restraint."

"Can a patient who is critically ill be receiving that much formula, Mrs. Wrigley? That's your definition of critical, isn't it?"

"That is not my definition of critical."

"Your Honor, I object—argumentative," Caldwell interrupted.

"Sustained."

Josh now turned to a paper Pat Wrigley had written about Joey as part of her master's thesis.

"Didn't you write that because of the love and affection your family bestowed on Joseph, that his gastrointestinal problems started clearing up immediately and were completely gone at the end of approximately four months?" he asked.

"Those words occurred on a paper I wrote but they're out of context the way you're stating it. I was referring to his problems of explosive diarrhea and malabsorption. Later in the paper I said the diarrhea continued."

"Mrs. Wrigley," Josh asked as he shifted to a new tack, "was Sarah walking when you first got her?"

"No. Just one or two steps."

"Did Miss Vetter relate any diarrhea problems Sarah had suffered when she was with the foster mother?"

"No—she didn't relate it, but that doesn't mean it didn't exist."

"Did she relate any problems with convulsions?"

"No."

"Any problems with balance or ataxia?"

"No."

"Did she wear a helmet the first time you visited her while she was still with the foster mother?"

"No."

"Thank you, Mrs. Wrigley."

On redirect, Ed Caldwell tried to salvage his witness. Mrs. Wrigley had brought in a photograph of Joey Wrigley at his most emaciated, and this was entered as evidence. Ed then asked her about the difference between malabsorption and diarrhea as symptoms of severe gastrointestinal problems, and how these could be distinguished from simple diarrhea.

"Malabsorption is life-threatening because you can't absorb nutrition. Diarrhea can be life-threatening if the child is not gaining weight," Pat said. "Joey's malabsorption cleared up in four months, so that his condition was no longer life-threatening. But the diarrhea—the ordinary diarrhea—continued for two years," she added in explanation.

Proudly, Pat Wrigley held up a newspaper clipping of Sarah winning a blue ribbon in the twenty-five-yard dash during the

Special Olympics held the previous week. This, too, was entered as evidence.

"Sarah will be legally ours next Thursday, May fourth, at nine A.M." she added, smiling.

In her seat, Priscilla Phillips put her hand over her face and dropped her elbows into her lap.

"That's all, Mrs. Wrigley," Ed Caldwell continued.

"Do I have to leave the room?" Pat asked.

"Yes," the judge replied.

With a shrug and a disappointed grin, the defense's star witness left the stand while Ted Lindquist gripped Josh Thomas's hand in congratulations.

That evening, Pat Wrigley told Dr. Eaton about the proceedings at some length.

"That district attorney twisted everything I said!"

"I warned you. Don't say I didn't."

"And boy, were you right! I thought our system of justice was after the truth, though. Naive little me. I mean that could just as easily be me up there instead of Priscilla—I keep thinking that. If they could accuse her, they could just as easily accuse me, or anybody! And I didn't do anything. It boils my blood! I don't think I helped Priscilla much at all."

Ed, too, was disappointed. He had to admit that Josh Thomas had done a hell of a job belittling Pat Wrigley. And there had been another setback. Ed had asked that Pat let him know the next time Sarah suffered from diarrhea so that he could obtain a stool sodium, and Pat had done so. Ed had stopped over at the Wrigleys to pick up the sodden plastic diaper for testing. But the sodium content had been normal, so that was a dead end. But he still had some ammunition. He had a string of character witnesses on tap—as many as the judge would let him put on the stand. He also planned to call four nurses; a surprise witness designed to cast doubt on Martin Blinder; Dr. Satten, he hoped; and, of course, Steve and Priscilla Phillips. Priscilla was to testify last. By that time, the jury should have formed some kind of attachment for her— if they were ever going to do so. Ed had worked it out. The end of the trial was the point at which she could best help herself.

Week 7

Many of Priscilla Phillips's friends had volunteered to take the stand as character witnesses, and Ed Caldwell and Al Collins had picked and chosen among them for those they felt would best impress the jury. In the end, Judge Burke allowed the testimony of only seven of these witnesses, ruling that the testimony was cumulative and that additional witnesses would not add to the quality of the testimony.

During the week, interspersed among other witnesses, Jim and Jan Doudiet, Marilyn Hansen, Nancy Dacus, and neighbors Bob Hamilton and Russell Mayhew testified, as did the director of the nursery school Erik and Jason had attended. A foundation was laid to show how each character witness knew Priscilla—and for how long—and then each was asked for an opinion as to the truth and veracity of the defendant. One after another, these witnesses insisted Priscilla was truthful, that they had upon numerous occasions entrusted their children with her, that they believed in her absolutely.

The defense also called four nurses to the stand: Debby Roof, Maria Sterling, and Susie Torrence from Kaiser-San Rafael, and Pat Middleton, a nurses' aide from Kaiser-San Francisco.

Debby testified to her close friendship with the defendant, which—she said—had developed after the death of Tia. She admired Priscilla's concern for, and commitment to, her children, she reported softly. On the matter of the contaminated formula, Debby insisted that Priscilla had never said that she had mixed the formula, although the nurse did remember that there had been a conversation at shift change about the formula. Debby testified that Priscilla may have said that there was enough formula and that it was in the refrigerator.

Debby also described how upset Priscilla had been over Mindy's admission to the hospital. "I stayed forty-five minutes past my shift to try to comfort her," she said.

On cross-examination, Josh Thomas asked her again about the formula.

"Your testimony is that Priscilla Phillips did *not* come up to you, Lesley McCarcy, and Jan Bond and say, 'I've mixed the formula and it's in the refrigerator'?" he asked, his voice pitched to indicate disbelief.

"Yes, I can honestly say that she did not say that because I would have questioned it—it would have been a violation of a doctor's order," Debby replied firmly.

Nurse Maria Sterling had cared for Tia the first day she was admitted to the hospital and on many subsequent occasions. In her testimony, she too described Priscilla Phillips as loving and concerned.

"Mrs. Phillips was often very upset and crying over Tia. She was very concerned about the IVs, very involved in the treatment. She worked very closely with the doctors," she added. "Toward the end of Tia's life, it was getting very hard, I think."

"Did you feel sympathy and admiration for Mrs. Phillips?" Josh asked on cross-examination.

"Yes," said the nurse.

Susie Torrence, the Filipino nurse who had often worked day shift at Kaiser-San Rafael, was used by the defense to point out and emphasize some of the mistakes made by Kaiser hospital personnel during the treatment of Tia and Mindy.

She testified to unusual incidents involving both Tia and Mindy. The wrong bottle had been hung for an IV, so that Tia had received 12.5 milligrams of potassium chloride per 500 cubic centimeters instead of per 1,000 cubic centimeters, she explained. And two different medication errors were made involving Mindy. Medication was administered at the wrong time, and then, in an unrelated incident, via the wrong tube.

Pat Middleton testified that for much of her stay at San Francisco, Tia Phillips had been on one-to-one nursing care, with the nurse remaining in the patient's room. Pat also explained how much she liked caring for Tia.

"I asked to care for her. In general she would come in real sick and start to perk up after a few days, and then she was so happy and lovable."

On cross-examination, Josh scored some points when Pat Middleton acknowledged that even when one-to-one nursing was ordered, there was some flexibility about whether the nurse was in the room the whole time.

"I was not there one hundred percent of the time," she admitted.

Ed Caldwell then called Dr. Daniel Chaffin, a psychiatrist in private practice who had worked with Blinder at Langley Porter Neuropsychiatric Institute, to the stand.

Chaffin testified at some length about the *Diagnostic and Statistical Manual of Mental Disorders*. *DSM–2* (the second edition) was used by hospitals and insurance companies to list official psychiatric diagnoses, Chaffin explained. *DSM–1* had been published in about 1957, and *DSM–2* in 1968, with a major revision issued in 1972.

"Is Munchausen Syndrome by Proxy listed in *DSM–1?*"

"No."

"Is it listed in *DSM–2?*"

"No."

"And for hospitals and insurance companies, you must have a diagnosis that is listed in the *DSM?*"

"That is correct."

"And did you make a study of Munchausen Syndrome by Proxy, Dr. Chaffin?"

"I could find only one article about it, and that's the article from *Lancet*. I also asked my colleagues if they had ever heard of Munchausen Syndrome by Proxy and they had not," he answered.

"Now, Dr. Chaffin, I understand that you supervised Dr. Martin Blinder at Langley Porter. Was he ever the chief of an inpatient service there?"

"Dr. Blinder has never been chief of any clinical service or any other known service at UC or Langley Porter," came the response.

Josh Thomas sent a hurried note over to Ted Lindquist, who nodded his head in response. Lindquist rose and quickly left the courtroom as Caldwell continued his questions.

On cross-examination, Josh belittled Chaffin's research methods. Chaffin admitted that he had not instituted a computer search for the literature on Munchausen Syndrome by Proxy.

"Why not?"

"It's costly and I did not feel it was justified because the literature on the subject is so scanty."

"In your research, did you come across an article called 'Munchausen Syndrome by Proxy, Definition of Factitious Bleeding in an Infant' in the February 1979 edition of *Pediatrics?*"

"No."

"Did you research child abuse in general, Doctor?"

"No. It was too big a task."

"How long did you spend reviewing the case?"

"Eight to ten hours. And I am strongly convinced that Munchausen Syndrome by Proxy does not have the scientific merit to justify its use in a court of law, and most especially in trying to justify the motive in a person," he said.

That evening, Josh talked to Ted. "What about Blinder?" he asked. "Did you ask him about the inpatient service?"

"Yeah. He's madder than hell—says Chaffin's lying. He called it scurrilous. It should be easy enough to track down whether Blinder was or wasn't the head of that clinic."

"Yeah, get on it."

"I'm on it; I'm on it!"

On Friday, Harry Wrigley took the stand. A man in his middle forties, Wrigley walked with a cane. The custodian had reason to dislike the Kaiser health care system as he believed that a misdiagnosis on their part had almost killed him, and because of this, Ed had hesitated about calling him. But after his wife's fiasco, the attorney decided to risk it: Pat Wrigley's testimony needed shoring up.

And Harry provided strong support for his wife's testimony. He described Sarah's diarrhea as virtually constant. As Pat had testified, Harry indicated that Sarah had suffered at least thirty episodes of diarrhea, with five episodes more severe than the others. He testified that once he had been forced to put Sarah into the shower in order to clean her after an episode of diarrhea. He described a bout that had occurred the previous day. And finally he mentioned that Sarah's adoption had become official May first.

"There was a front-page article in the Vallejo *Independent Press*, with a picture of the whole family," he said, showing the article.

Ed Caldwell next called Edith Horne to the stand. The teacher's aide from Carol Loma Vista School described her function.

"My job is to take attendance, work in the physical education program, assist the instructor, change the diapers, and feed those children who can't feed themselves," she said. Then she testified to Sarah's perfect attendance record at school.

"Is there a place on your attendance form to mark if a student is sent home after she arrives?" Ed asked.

"No."

Ed asked how many times Sarah had diarrhea in school.

"About ten times. Most of the children have one change of clothes, but Sarah has three. Once the diarrhea filled her socks and shoes and we had to send her home without shoes. But she has never been sent home early because of diarrhea."

"When was the last time she had diarrhea, Mrs. Horne?"

"Last week—on Wednesday and Thursday."

"Was Sarah ever sent home ill from school?"

"Yes, twice. But she was not marked absent because she arrived at school in the morning."

"Thank you."

On cross-examination, Josh asked about Sarah's diarrhea.

"Has Mrs. Wrigley ever told you of any explosive diarrhea episodes where Sarah lost a quart of fluid in an hour?"

"No."

"Thank you, Mrs. Horne."

Steve Phillips followed Edith Horne to the stand. He was pale and nervous. He was enormously frightened of making some terrible mistake or forgetting something vital. He and Al Collins had even worked out a system to enable him to remember key events, and a hand signal to be used during cross-examination if he felt in need of a breather.

Carefully, in one of his most effective examinations, Al Collins led Steve through the background of the illnesses of his daughters. Steve began by describing the adoption of Tia, giving a brief history of Priscilla's problems with pregnancy, her hysterectomy, and their attempt to adopt a Vietnamese child. Then he testified about Tia's first hospitalization. He pointed out that he had been the one to feed her just prior to her episode of projectile vomiting, and he went on to describe her staring spells that he attributed to the pain medication she was receiving.

"I never went more than a day without visiting Tia," he said quietly. "I spent one whole night with her—the night before her hyperalimentation—just holding her and rocking her. She had an IV in her scalp where it could easily come loose, and I didn't want that to happen."

Steve also noted several other times before Tia became sick at home when *he* had fed her and not Priscilla. This included January seventh, when she had been admitted to the Emergency Room at Kaiser.

"I prepared and fed her her formula that entire day," Steve said firmly.

"*I* raised the subject of adoption on the way home from the hospital after Tia died," Steve also testified, to dispute an earlier suggestion by the district attorney that it had been Priscilla's idea.

He described at some length the police search of his house, focusing in particular on the bag of syringes they had taken from the garage.

"I pointed those out to the police," he said. "The needles and syringes were by prescription from the Kaiser pharmacy for use in heparinizing Tia's central venous catheter. We had a lot left over because the line she ended up using didn't need them. I always disposed of the needles we did use by cutting them with wire cutters before putting them in the garbage," he added.

In an attempt to establish a possible alternative to the prosecution's contention that Priscilla had contaminated Mindy's formula, Al Collins asked Steve about his job as a counselor at juvenile hall.

"I'm responsible for the physical safety of the boys and girls, aged eight to eighteen, and for preparing written reports, and for some crisis therapy. These kids are put there if they are considered a danger to themselves or to the community."

"And which unit do you work in, Mr. Phillips?"

"The senior boys' unit. It's a maximum security unit for boys accused of serious crimes such as assault and battery, rape, and so on. I have to prepare behavior-observation reports that are used by the juvenile court as a recommendation for disposition. Some boys are sent to the California Youth Authority as a result of these recommendations and the boys and parents know this."

On cross-examination, Josh Thomas asked, "Have you received threats to yourself or your family as a result of your job, Mr. Phillips?"

"Yes, about twelve to thirty verbal threats. And there's always the possibility that they'll carry them out. The parents sometimes make threats, too."

"And have you passed these threats on to the police?"

"On occasion I've passed them on to my supervisors, but not to the police. There's nothing they could do."

"Well, in view of these threats, you've taken all possible

steps to keep the existence and whereabouts of your family secret, then?"

"No, that's not a fair statement."

"And did you publicize the hospitalizations of Tia and Mindy?" Josh continued, in an effort to counter the theory that some crazed juvenile had poisoned Steve's children.

"No. But a note on Mindy's arrival—with our address—was in the *Terra Linda News*. We made no attempt to keep our address secret," Steve replied.

In an effort to underline Steve's violent reactions to some situations, Josh Thomas asked him questions about the meetings with Carte and Callas and with Dr. Stein, during which he had made threats.

Steve admitted that he had made a comment about throwing someone through a wall. Although he could not recall threatening Dr. Stein, he did agree that he sometimes talked quite violently.

"But I have a tendency to verbalize stuff rather than do it. I do remember getting upset with Stein when he told me from then on Tia was to be treated at San Francisco. I said I wouldn't drive to San Francisco, but rather to Marin General and then bill Kaiser for it. But I never did that," he added.

Josh ended his cross-examination with a question regarding the list of Kaiser employees that Steve had asked Dr. Carte to send him so that he could check for potential enemies. Carte had refused, and Steve had never followed through.

"After you called Dr. Carte and he refused to send you the list, did Mr. Caldwell ever have a subpoena *duces tecum* issued for that information? Did you ever suggest to Mr. Caldwell that perhaps he ought to issue such a subpoena so you could study the list for potential enemies?"

"No, I didn't. I assume the subpoena you're talking about would get the records? Is that—"

"You've heard of a subpoena *duces tecum*, haven't you?" Josh was needling him now.

"Yeah, oaky. I understand the word now. You said it a little slower. The answer is, no, I did not."

"All right." Josh had a final question. Steve had talked about Priscilla's burn on direct examination, making it sound accidental. Josh believed there was another possibility. "Now, do you remember how soon prior to the preliminary hearing Mrs. Phillips was burned?"

"I believe it was the weekend prior."

"And she was scheduled to start the preliminary hearing on Monday, is that correct?"

"To the best of my knowledge, that's correct."

"Thank you. No further questions."

Shortly afterward, Steve Phillips was excused and court was adjourned for the weekend.

"You did fine," Ed told him as they walked out.

Steve turned to Priscilla.

"Pris?"

She nodded in agreement.

"Thank God," Steve said.

Week 8

The second week in May was to be the decisive one in Ed Caldwell's overall plan for the defense. He had scheduled only two witnesses: Dr. Joseph Satten and Priscilla Phillips.

Dr. Satten, after sixteen hours of interviews with Priscilla, Steve, and Marietta, had finally reached a conclusion, and it was all that the defense had hoped for. Caldwell believed Satten would make a powerful appearance, not only because of what he intended to say about Priscilla, but because Ed felt he would make a strong contrast to the prosecution's psychiatrist. There was no artifice about Joe Satten. He was not the type of forensic psychiatrist—and unfortunately Ed knew several in the field—who would sell out to the highest bidder.

Furthermore, Satten was experienced. He was unlikely to become flustered on the stand, even under the battering cross-examination techniques the district attorney liked to practice. So Ed Caldwell entered the final week of his case with confidence.

Caldwell had asked Satten to focus primarily on the issue of whether Priscilla could be suffering from Munchausen Syndrome by Proxy. In his background research on the case, Satten testified that he had reviewed the medical records of Tia and Mindy; police tapes of Priscilla Phillips and others; Martin Blinder's preliminary hearing testimony; and articles on the syndrome. In addition, he had completed a lengthy evaluation of Priscilla Phillips's mental status.

"And what did you conclude, Doctor?" asked Al Collins, who was handling the direct examination.

"I found an essentially normal mental condition and specifically none of the distortions of thinking or emotion that have been described in the articles of Munchausen Syndrome by Proxy, or that one might expect if Mrs. Phillips had committed the alleged acts," Satten answered firmly.

"What are the elements that make up Munchausen Syndrome by Proxy, Dr. Satten?"

"There are two. One, somebody deliberately creates symptoms in the illness of a child and then lies about them. Two, the mother has a history of Munchausen Syndrome and in addition has a severe mental disorder that is described by some as psychotic and by others as hysterical."

"And does Mrs. Phillips evince either of these symptoms?"

"No. She has no severe psychosis nor a history of Munchausen Syndrome—that is, fabricating her own symptoms in a hospital setting. Nor does Mrs. Phillips have the symptoms of an abusing mother," he added.

"Now, Doctor, I would like to list some attributes and ask you whether these could be used to diagnose Munchausen Syndrome by Proxy: capable, responsible, and devoted to her children; and telling church members that her daughter was ill."

"No. Those are not the attributes of a person with Munchausen Syndrome by Proxy."

"Thank you, Dr. Satten."

As soon as the doctor was called to the stand, Josh had motioned to Ted to investigate Satten's previous record as a witness. Ted had made a couple of calls to district attorneys in the East Bay and made a rather significant discovery. Dr. Satten was known on occasion to forget to bring his notes with him, and this could prove to be a significant lapse. A district attorney was allowed to examine all the material an expert witness had used to form a conclusion, including notes, tape recordings, and articles. If a witness failed to bring such material, the prosecutor would be badly hampered in cross-examination. And if an expert witness—particularly one who had testified numerous times in the past—neglected to bring such material, it could be construed as intentional. It suggested a way to cast doubt on the witness's impartiality. Josh intended to find out whether the doctor had brought his notes, but as it happened, Satten's answers to his very first series of questions opened up a different source of attack—one which horrified Ed Caldwell.

"When you first met with Mrs. Phillips, Dr. Satten, what background did you have on the case?"

"I had a verbal report from Mr. Caldwell."

"And what happened in this first meeting?"

"Mrs. Phillips denied the allegations. She told me about her past. I did not tape this interview, but I did tape six or seven others, beginning with the second," he added. Taping his patients was a technique Dr. Satten used often, as he had found in the past that the accused's own words could make a very powerful and direct statement. He believed that more often than not this openness worked to the advantage of a client: in fact, frequently such a tape, when played in court, convinced a jury more clearly than anything else of the mental state of a defendant. But of course this case was different than the norm. Usually Dr. Satten was called in to establish that a defendant's mental condition had prevented him from acting rationally. On this occasion he had been called upon to assert the mental health of the defendant.

When he heard Satten's answer, Ed Caldwell squirmed in his seat and almost put his head in his hands in despair. He could not believe that an experienced forensic psychiatrist had actually taped a patient. Satten should have recognized how dangerous this could be! Ed wondered what was on those tapes. Priscilla had believed she was in a confidential doctor-patient relationship with Satten, as indeed both Ed and Satten had encouraged her to think. There had been no reason for her to hold back. Ed knew Josh Thomas would jump all over this information, but it took the district attorney a few questions to arrive there. He was still intent on the doctor's notes.

"Do you have the notes for that first interview with Priscilla Phillips, Dr. Satten?"

"Not with me. I brought a copy of my CV and a list of the articles I studied in connection with this case and my review of those articles."

"Are you aware that your notes would be something asked for—that I would want to review those?"

"No, I was not aware of that."

"You didn't realize I would want to have access to them?"

"No. I just brought what I had relied upon to form my opinion."

Josh looked up at the judge. "Your Honor, I would like a court order that Dr. Satten be required to produce all the material he reviewed so that I can effectively cross-examine him."

"Yes, I will grant that. You may, of course, exclude all the documents furnished to you by the police and prosecution, Doctor."

Pausing from time to time to look down at his notes, Josh Thomas continued to question Dr. Satten, skipping from point to point. He established that it was not necessary to examine a person to diagnose Munchausen Syndrome by Proxy. Then he moved on.

"Did you make a written report to Mr. Caldwell about your findings?"

"No, but we had phone conversations and three conferences in my office. I formed the opinion early on that Priscilla Phillips did not show the mental disturbance associated with a child abuser, but I did not formalize the opinion until after I interviewed Mr. Phillips and Mrs. Phillips's mother."

"Did you review Mrs. Phillips's medical records?"

"Yes, the records of her two deliveries, her hysterectomy, and the burn."

"Were you informed about the proximity of the burn incident to her scheduled preliminary hearing?"

"No. But I don't think the burn incident was unusual. I would characterize it as a stupid accident."

At the noon recess, Steve went up to Dr. Satten and the two men walked off to the little lake behind the Civic Center.

Steve had grown fond of Satten. After meeting with the doctor for a formal interview at the beginning of April, and again—with Priscilla this time—two weeks ago, Steve found himself relying on the older man as a kind of touchstone for his own emotions. Stretched this way and that by bitterness, anger, fear, and confusion, in the last few days Steve had begun to distrust all his emotions, uncertain which—if any—were appropriate anymore. Unashamedly he reached out to the father-figure for reassurance.

The two men stopped by the water's edge. The hills beyond were dusky brown, burned dry by the hot May sun and two years of drought from which the county was only just now recovering. Dr. Satten turned to the younger man.

"Look, Steve, Priscilla does not have, nor has she ever had, any mental problems. She's a strong, determined woman, with plenty of community support and emotional strokes from you, her friends, and others. She isn't needy in the way that is typical of a child-abuser. She has plenty in her life that is tangible and real to satisfy her. She had no special sick need to live through her children, or to punish them. Her personality is part of what makes her special."

Steve shook his head despondently. "But sometimes I feel we're not gonna make it. Our whole world is caving in on us, you know? And I don't know who to trust anymore."

"It's frightening—opening yourself up—I know that. No one likes to risk that."

"Yeah. And suddenly, all the stuff we've tried to build for—" Steve stopped, then gamely went on. "It's all starting to go—" and he pointed at the ground. "And I think it's just gonna continue in that direction."

Satten put an arm around Steve's shoulders. "That could happen, Steve. But I want you to trust your instincts about Priscilla at least."

"Okay. I guess I just gotta come to terms with the fact that I may have nothing when this is all over, that if the four of us can just walk away from this—even with no resources left—we'll be damned lucky. If I come to terms with that, that's a helluva weight off my shoulders."

"I think you just did come to terms with it, Steve."

"Yeah."

"Come on, let's get back. We're not dead yet, you know. There's life in the old horse left," Satten joked gently. "And you're a strong family. You're going to handle whatever comes along."

"Whatever comes down the pike?"

Satten smiled and nodded. "Right," he agreed.

After lunch, Josh Thomas questioned Satten about the articles that he had reviewed on Munchausen Syndrome by Proxy.

"In about half the articles I read, the mother expressed relief at being found out," Satten remarked.

"But in some cases the parents denied involvement?"

"Yes. But in all but one article—the Kurlandsky article called 'Munchausen Syndrome by Proxy: Definition of Factitious Bleeding in an Infant'—the women were described as being severely disturbed. And I believe that only a psychotic or a near-psychotic could commit the acts involved in this case."

Josh Thomas rummaged through the pile of material on his table and came up with the Kurlandsky article.

"This says that 'to date the psychiatric evaluation of the parents has been unrevealing,'" he read. "Does it not also say that there was a healthy male sibling, and that during the time of the second child's illness, the mother lived in at the hospital and gained the respect and intimate friendship of the staff because of her helpfulness?" Josh asked.

"Yes."

"Were there any psychiatric tests done on Mrs. Phillips?"

"Yes. Dr. Lowell Cooper, who is a psychologist, prepared a psychological test report."

"And do you know what psychological tests he used to evaluate the defendant?"

"He prepared a report about her testing with a Rorschach, Wechsler IQ, Draw-a-Person and Thematic Apperception Test."

"Did you bring a copy of that report?"

"No," Satten said. Josh Thomas shook his head in disgust.

"What were the results of those tests?" he asked.

"No severe psychopathology was found. In some tests, she was overly cautious and self-abnegating, with some feelings of loneliness and feelings of being badly treated."

"Now when you evaluate somebody psychiatrically, what do you look at?"

"Basic personality factors. In the defendant I evaluated her capacity to express feelings of warmth, to express anger and keep in control, her capacity to relate herself to others and have feelings about them, her capacity to evaluate reality, to experience loss and to grow from that experience."

"Would you say that Mrs. Phillips has a need for attention, praise, and sympathy?"

"No, she thinks well of herself."

"I thought you indicated that she tends to put herself down?"

"Even so, she thinks well of herself, though she has self-deprecating tendencies," Satten insisted.

"Now a patient, unless they're completely hallucinating during your examination, can choose to withhold information from you, can they not?"

"That is true."

"So that your evaluation of Mrs. Phillips is dependent in large degree on the material she revealed to you?"

"No. It's based on the kinds of interactions I saw. I'm assuming there was a fair amount of truth in many of the things she told me. But misstatements about one thing or another were not especially important. It was the pattern of her emotional responses I was looking for."

"Isn't it a fact, Doctor, that persons who have committed certain heinous offenses that they do not want to face psychologically, bury them and rationalize their behavior or deny that it ever existed?"

"That frequently happens."

"Did the author of the article we were just referring to on factitious bleeding in an infant indicate that there was usually a denial by the parents of the motives involved in the commission of the acts on the child?"

"Well, he described that the parents in the case had denied the acts."

"In that particular article, the parents' behavior was described as exhibited by their concern for and devotion to the child. Is that correct?"

"I believe so."

"Thank you. I have nothing further," Josh Thomas said.

On redirect, Al Collins asked Satten to define the psychiatric term *hysteria*, which had been used by some psychiatrists to characterize the mothers suffering from Munchausen Syndrome by Proxy.

"It has two meanings in psychiatry. One has to do with a particular form of illness called hysterical neurosis, which is characterized by a patient blocking his feelings so that he feels relatively comfortable and without overt anxiety. Hysterical is also used to describe a personality type that is characterized by excitability, emotional changeability, irritability, and a high degree of seductiveness, as well as self-involvement and attention-getting. In my opinion, the description of the patients in the literature on Munchausen Syndrome by Proxy referred to the second sense of the word."

"Did you find this type of hysterical personality that is identified with Munchausen Syndrome by Proxy in the person of Mrs. Phillips?"

"I did not."

"Doctor, do you have with you the summary you made of the articles dealing with the abuse of children with drugs and/or Munchausen Syndrome by Proxy?" Collins asked awkwardly.

"Yes."

"Did you find any correlation with respect to the mental conditions?"

"A high degree of correlation. There were twenty mothers described. Nineteen of them were either psychotic, hysterical, or severely disturbed with a history of Munchausen."

"I have no further questions."

Dr. Satten was excused subject to recall at a time when he could bring his notes. While the jury took its afternoon break, Josh Thomas made a motion that he assumed would fail, but for which there was some legal precedent. He asked that Priscilla Phillips be forced to submit to an examination by prosecution psychiatrist Dr. Blinder.

Josh argued that Blinder had already requested permission to examine the defendant prior to the preliminary hearing and been denied. And that until Dr. Satten had been brought forth as a witness for the defense—thereby putting the defendant's mental state at issue—the prosecution had not pursued the matter further. If the court preferred, Josh added, he could appoint another psychiatrist in lieu of Dr. Blinder to examine the defendant for the People.

The judge, in response to arguments by both Ed Caldwell and Al Collins, asked for the research cited by all three attorneys before he would be ready to rule.

After recess, the jury filed back and took their seats quietly. Into the expectant hush of the packed courtroom, Ed Caldwell spoke clearly.

"At this time, the defendant will call Priscilla Phillips to the stand."

ii

The passivity forced on Priscilla throughout the weeks of testimony had taken its toll. She perceived it as a sort of punishment that no one remembered events as clearly as she did, and that when the witnesses did recall accurately, often the emphasis drawn from their testimony—even about the most innocuous of her actions—damaged her character. Her naïveté had been stripped from her like a bandage drawn suddenly from a wound. The trial was not about what had happened. Not even her own lawyer cared about that; he cared about the theater of the trial, the presentation of his client. The trial was about nuance; the trial was about what she wore.

Now it came down to Priscilla's performance. She welcomed the opportunity to speak for herself, but she had not lost sight of the difficulties she faced. Essential to the defense she and her attorneys had adopted was the principle of her normalcy. But under the theory of Munchausen Syndrome by Proxy, the desirable qualities of a caring, concerned mother became, by definition, abnormal qualities, and all the characteristics usually valued by society turned into indexes of depravity. So how was she to appear normal? If she suffered from Munchausen's, then Priscilla's intense involvement with her children—for which she had been praised by friends and doctors alike—became a plea for attention, as did her interest in community affairs.

Indeed, everything about the situation was double-binding. Priscilla had to toe an invisible line on the witness stand and present to the twelve jurors an impossibly complex series of characteristics. On the one hand, she had to persuade them that she was sane, competent, and self-assured. On the other hand, she must seem appropriately upset by her circumstances without appearing emotionally needy. It was necessary to express some emotion—so as not to appear cold and calculating—yet she must not seem hysterical. She could be assertive but not aggressive. And in the matter of her children's illnesses, she should seem concerned with their welfare yet not meddling or attention-seeking.

Except for a bout of weeping that interrupted her controlled narration only once—when she described finding Tia in a bed of vomit and diarrhea just before her last admission—Priscilla maintained her composure. Even under Josh Thomas's occasionally savage cross-examination, she raised her voice only once. Josh asked her about the *Redbook* article she had once planned to write on Tia's life and death. Priscilla had written a notation in one of her notebooks concerning the type of article *Redbook* was interested in. The notebook had been among those seized by the police in their search of the Phillipses' house and thus had ended up in the hands of the prosecution.

"Your notation on this article reads 'Five Hundred Dollars for Young Mother's Story—practical and useful information about a mother solving problems of marriage and family life, one thousand to two thousand words.' Correct?" the district attorney asked.

"Yes. And I copied that directly from the magazine."

"And you already had a title—"

"No, I did not."

"The words here: 'Adoption had always been a part of our family plan, so it was natural? . . .'"

"That was not a title but a leadoff sentence, and that's as far as I ever got."

"When did you first put that in the notebook, Mrs. Phillips?"

"Sometime after Tia died."

"You were considering writing an article about Tia's illness, the progress of her illness and death?"

"I was considering writing an article about the beauty of Tia's life, and my decision at that point was that we had decided to adopt another child, so I wanted to wait until Mindy arrived and then write an article so that it would have a happy ending, and that's why I never did it."

"Wouldn't it have been extremely painful for you to review the course and progress of Tia's treatment and the agony she went through?"

"That's not what I planned to write about. I planned to write about the beauty of her life in spite of her illness."

"Well, the beauty of her life, Mrs. Phillips, was that she spent about eighty-five or ninety percent of it in one of the Kaiser facilities, isn't that a fact?"

"That is not the beauty of her life," Priscilla retorted angrily.

"How soon after her death was it that you first thought about writing an article?"

"I can't say exactly." Priscilla was in control again. "I had a lot I wanted to share right from the moment she died. It was sometime after that that I read an article in *Redbook* about a child who had problems like Tia. And it touched me deeply and that's what made me select *Redbook* as a possible place to write about Tia, because they had very touching articles similar to the experiences I had. They were often about ill or hospitalized children or how adoptions or that sort of thing had touched a family."

"And what about those other notes you kept at the beginning of Tia's illness—this daily journal?" He lifted and waved another spiral-bound notebook.

"That was for a different purpose. That was just something the nurses suggested I do, to write up how to cope with a hospitalized child, that sort of thing. I had to drop that after a few weeks because it was so painful."

"And do these entries reflect the beauty of Tia's life, Mrs. Phillips?"

"Objection—"

"Sustained."

The questions and answers continued for hours. Priscilla was on the stand over the course of three different days. In a phenomenal display of memory, she recounted the histories of Tia's and Mindy's illnesses, remembering without notes exact dates for procedures and treatment, names of diagnoses and chemicals, which elbow or ankle had been sites for cut-downs. Medical terms flowed effortlessly from her lips, and she never stumbled over the occasionally complex terminology. It was an impressive display, but it, too, held a negative potential because the ease and familiarity with which she discussed medical treatments also emphasized the unusual extent of her involvement in, and understanding of, those treatments.

At the end of Priscilla's testimony, neither Ed Caldwell nor Josh Thomas was certain how she had come across to the jury. Ed had tried to bring out her qualities of warmth and concern, and to paint her as naturally gregarious, religious, deeply depressed by the loss of her children yet bravely struggling to continue on. Josh had sketched a different portrait: that of a cold, interfering, attention-seeking woman, callous enough to detail Tia's illnesses in her baby book and list at its back all the people who had sent contributions to a memorial in Tia's memory or who had written in condolence. Neither attorney felt that he had completely succeeded.

Meanwhile, controversy was brewing about Dr. Satten's notes and the tapes of his interviews with Priscilla. Ed Caldwell had stayed up all night Monday listening to the tapes, deciding that four of them were prejudicial because they recorded some derogatory remarks his client had made about attorneys and the judge. He also found that Priscilla had revealed to her psychiatrist the planned strategy for her case. On Thursday morning, in the judge's chambers, Caldwell explained his findings to the judge and to Josh Thomas, who had not been permitted to hear the tapes. At that time, the judge ruled that the noncontroversial tapes and all of Satten's notes be turned over to the prosecution while he reviewed the four tapes Caldwell believed were prejudicial. In a separate action, Burke also ruled that there was no legal reason for

Priscilla Phillips to submit to a psychiatric exam by either Dr. Blinder or by a court-appointed psychiatrist.

By the time Dr. Satten returned to the stand on Thursday, Josh Thomas had studied the doctor's notes and reports. Josh concentrated on one report that Satten had never mentioned during his earlier testimony: that of Dr. Paul Berg, the Oakland psychologist who had actually tested Priscilla Phillips.

Josh picked up Berg's report, instructing Satten to read excerpts that the district attorney believed were damaging. The jury heard how Priscilla had reported to Berg her belief that she was the more dominant in the relationship with her husband. They heard about her earlier marital problems, including numerous arguments and some physical fights, which she usually started. In her interview with Berg, Priscilla had also described Tia as more like a friend than a daughter— someone who gave as much as she received.

"I loved her so much. My relationship with Tia was the most gratifying I ever had in my life," she had told the psychologist.

Josh ended with a point he felt needed more emphasis than it had yet received.

"Don't you think that the fact that Mindy Phillips was hospitalized on the anniversary of Tia's death is significant from a psychological point of view?"

"No. I think it's a strange coincidence," came Satten's response.

On redirect, Al Collins cut to the heart of Paul Berg's report. He asked Dr. Satten to read aloud a paragraph from Berg's summary.

After considering all the historical, clinical, and testing materials, I must admit that the situation is very enigmatic and baffling to me. My simplistic conception of this kind of situation is that when a person murders their child, one invariably finds a significant and serious degree of emotional disturbance. I have within the past year evaluated four such situations and in every one found extreme mental illness—save the case of Priscilla Phillips. I am even more surprised not to find this in her case, since according to the charges that have been leveled, a single or momentary act is not being discussed. It is apparently continuing and repetitive behavior. That kind of conception would either have to be seen in a thoroughly malevolent creature or at least someone whose emotional condition precludes them from normal human feelings and restraints. I find none of that present in Priscilla Phillips.

Satten finished reading and looked up.
"Thank you, Doctor," Al Collins said.

Week 9

Josh Thomas had saved Evelyn Callas's testimony for rebuttal. She was terribly nervous as she made her way to the stand, far more so than she had been at the preliminary hearing. She felt the trial was a culmination of all the hell she and Sara—the entire staff—had suffered at the hands of this woman. She did not begrudge the endless hours she had spent charting, recharting, collating, organizing, and reorganizing the records of the two Phillips children. It was an atonement of sorts. She should have realized the significance of the stool sodium; she knew that. She had tried to trade her guilt for anger at Priscilla Phillips, and to a certain degree she had succeeded. But the extent of her nervousness now reflected her anxiety that in some way she might fail again.

Evelyn began her testimony with a detailed account of the conversation on February twenty-fifth in the ICU Quiet Room. She described her fears that the Phillipses would remove Mindy against medical advice, her hopes that the situation would not escalate uncontrollably.

Her most important testimony centered on the conversation that she had held with Steve Phillips about the relationship between Tia's condition and Mindy's.

"There was a conference with the parents and Miss Jameson, and after the meeting, Mrs. Phillips and Miss Jameson started into ICU and Mr. Phillips and I were standing in the hall and he asked me, 'Is this what Tia had?' And I answered, 'The two cases are just the same.'" Evelyn testified.

Steve, in his seat by Priscilla, looked astounded. Priscilla turned to stare at him and he returned a baffled frown. At first he could not remember asking Dr. Callas that question; later, when he recalled the conversation and recognized the misunderstanding, it was too late: the damage had been done. Dr. Callas's testimony made it appear that he was willing to link Tia's illness with Mindy's contaminated formula, but that was not the truth. He had meant only that if Tia's high sodium had been attributed to the normal consequences of diarrhea, why couldn't Mindy's?

By Steve's side, Priscilla penned a quick note and passed it up to Ed Caldwell.

On cross-examination, Caldwell's first question reflected Priscilla's observation. "Did you ever tell Detective Lindquist about Mr. Phillips's remark in the hall?"

"I'm not certain."

"Why didn't it come out in the preliminary?"

"I was never asked any questions in reference to it."

"Have you ever related that conversation to anybody else before testifying in this courtroom—other than Mr. Thomas?"

"Yes. Other people know, including Dr. Shimoda," Evelyn answered evenly. "It was the strongest statement made that weekend. It was the only time Tia's name was mentioned to me. I am sure I told Dr. Shimoda because I had very strong feelings about the question."

"Prior to February twenty-fifth, did you ever bring up to the Phillipses the similarities between Mindy's situation and Tia's?"

"No, I did not."

"Thank you, Dr. Callas."

The following day, Josh Thomas recalled Sara Shimoda in an effort to rebut portions of Dr. Alice Eaton's testimony concerning her treatment of Sarah Wrigley. Josh had given Sara the transcript of Dr. Eaton's testimony and asked her to study it, and Sara had come up with several points.

"Dr. Eaton says she treated Mindy on six different occasions with Streptomycin," she told Josh.

"And—?"

"And Streptomycin is not used in pediatrics any more. I have never had occasion to use it. In fact the only time I have ever seen it used is to treat tuberculous meningitis. The drug is highly toxic to the nerve that's involved in hearing and balance."

"Could it have caused Mindy's ataxia?"

"Maybe. In any case, it's certainly not the drug of choice—to say the least—when dealing with minor respiratory infections or ear infections. It's like killing a bug with a cannon."

On the stand, Sara discussed this issue and raised another. According to her records, Dr. Eaton had removed Sarah from Phenobarbital abruptly, whereas a gradual decrease in dosage over a period of about a month was the advisable procedure, Sara said.

On cross-examination, Al Collins tried to establish that Dr. Eaton had not acted incorrectly.

"Streptomycin has not been ruled by the FDA as unsafe to use, has it, Doctor?"

"No."

"Isn't it true that most drugs have side effects?"

"Yes."

"Can CMV affect balance?"

"Not to my knowledge."

He tried an alternate approach. "Is cerebral palsy on occasion a result of CMV?"

"No."

"What correlation or connection would you state exists between the two?"

"I don't think anybody could make a direct correlation between the two. They are two different entities."

Finally, Collins hit upon a winner. "Can cerebral palsy cause unsteadiness?"

"Yes," Sara Shimoda said.

Without question, the star among Josh Thomas's rebuttal witnesses was Mindy's foster mother. Josh had done little to prepare Mrs. Portillo for court. He agreed with Ted that she was a natural witness: calm, straightforward, a comfortable grandmother to whom Catholic Social Service had entrusted numerous children over the years.

Under Josh's gentle questioning, she told her story to the jury.

"Mindy was in my custody from March third to July eighteenth of last year. I never noticed any blueness while she was with me. She didn't vomit or have diarrhea or convulsions. She was walking when she left."

"Did she ever have temper tantrums?"

"No. But if anyone said, 'No, no' to her she'd kind of pout and cry. We didn't dare say 'No, no' too often," she added engagingly.

"Did you ever take her to the doctor?"

"Yes, to Dr. Hardy once for a sore throat."

"Did she cry when she saw doctors or nurses?"

"Yes. But mine have always cried when I took them to the doctor."

"Was there ever a time when you were waiting in the Waiting Room for the doctor when Mindy had loose stools?"

"Yes. Once we had to take her for a checkup, and I had given her a little Milk of Magnesia because she was going hard the day before, which I had forgotten. While we were waiting, her bowls moved, but it wasn't diarrhea."

"Did Mindy ever wear a helmet while she was with you?"

"No."

Josh had asked Mrs. Portillo to bring some photographs of Mindy that she had taken at her house, and these were entered as evidence. Then the district attorney singled one out.

"There is a plaque in this photograph you've brought, Mrs. Portillo. What is that plaque?"

"It is the Last Supper," she said.

"Thank you, Mrs. Portillo."

"Mr. Caldwell?" the judge asked. Ed paused. He was afraid a cross-examination might turn the jury against him and damage the case even more than this witness already had. He knew Mrs. Portillo had made a strong contrast to Pat Wrigley; she was not only an older woman, but on crutches. He did not want to antagonize the jury by badgering her.

"No questions, your Honor," he finally said, taking a step he would later regret. Josh looked at Ted and smiled.

On Tuesday, Jim Hutchison was asked to appear in the judge's chambers to discuss his upcoming testimony. Jim had been approached by both sides in the case to appear as a witness, and for a long time he had hedged. Finally, Ted Lindquist had cornered him in a bowling alley and handed him a subpoena.

"I don't think I can help you much," Jim had said to Ted. "There is a penitential relationship after all."

That was only one of the factors in this increasingly uncomfortable relationship. Jim had come to terms with one thing: he believed that Priscilla was capable of committing the crimes. But this did not relieve him of his responsibility. He remained her pastor and he believed his duty was to support her. But given his feelings, this was difficult. It was an increasing struggle to hide what he felt. To further complicate their relationship, he knew that Priscilla and Steve both had learned of his involvement with the police; after her arrest,

Priscilla had read Lindquist's report of his interview with Hutchison. And Steve, in particular, had taken that interview as a betrayal. Still, Priscilla had continued to solicit Jim's support and advice, and he knew his absence from their house had hurt her.

Finally Jim had decided to let the court make the decision. He had suggested in church that his parishioners do likewise since the congregation was deeply upset and divided over the case. Priscilla's supporters were both legion and vociferous. But there were perhaps just as many who could not abide Priscilla in their midst, who resented the way she walked around pretending her life was unchanged.

"I'm not guilty. Why should I behave as though I am?" she had said to Jim and to others.

In the judge's chambers it was decided that the confidentiality of penitential communication was not in force when a third person was present. Jim Hutchison could testify to conversations that had taken place at Kaiser-San Rafael on February twenty-sixth in the presence of both Priscilla and Steve Phillips.

As it turned out, however, Jim's testimony was uneventful. There were more objections on various issues other than his testimony. Jim described Priscilla's uncontrollable weeping on the occasion of their meeting in the ICU Quiet Room. He went on to mention Priscilla's fears that people would believe Dr. Callas's inferences about Mindy's illness. But he left the stand feeling that he had neither hurt Priscilla nor helped her with his testimony, and that this was all to the best. Priscilla had given him a tremulous smile as he left.

Since Judge Burke was attending a conference in Williamsburg on Thursday and Friday, the last day of the week's testimony was changed to Wednesday. Most of the day was given over to *in camera*, or private discussions on three issues: first, the admissibility of a witness Josh Thomas wanted to call; next, Dr. Blinder's credentials—which had been questioned by Dr. Chaffin—and finally, the admissibility of Satten's tapes.

Josh wanted to call Marcine Johnson, who was the Kaiser psychologist Priscilla had visited in 1969, when—pregnant with Erik—she was afraid that her arguments with Steve would harm her baby. Ed adamantly opposed allowing the witness to testify, and the judge, deciding that the testimony was too remote in time and in scope, agreed with him, so Dr. Johnson was excused.

"Your Honor, I had Detective Lindquist verify that Dr. Blinder held the title of supervising psychiatrist for the private inpatient psychiatric service at the University of California, and that his duties were to perform the function of instructor and administrator to the staff of the inpatient psychiatric service. He held this position from October 1967 to October 1968. The hospital involved was Moffitt Hospital at the University of California," Josh then told the judge.

"I will stipulate to that," said Caldwell.

"I want it read to the jury," Josh insisted.

"Agreed," Caldwell said. "It looks like there was some semantic confusion about Langley Porter and Moffitt Hospital. I guess both are connected with UC Med Center," he added in explanation of his witness's contradictory testimony.

"Yeah—it's confusing," Thomas agreed.

The issue of Satten's tapes could not be decided. Judge Burke had listened to them and felt that there was a considerable amount of material that would be prejudicial— negative comments about the attorneys and the judge, in particular—and that the tapes should be laundered before presentation to the district attorney.

"Your concern is the issue of Munchausen Syndrome by Proxy," he told Josh. "Anything else is extraneous and will be removed from your copy of the transcript of the tapes."

"All right, Your Honor," Josh took defeat with a wry smile. The judge and attorneys then returned to open court.

The last witness of the trial was an Aldersgate parishioner named Beverly Smith. Josh called her to testify to the numerous times Tia's name had been mentioned in church and the extent to which the congregation had been involved in Tia's illness. The district attorney hoped to demonstrate Priscilla's need for attention.

"I attended three quarters of the Sundays between late 1975 and the middle of 1977, and something about Tia was mentioned every Sunday during Tia's hospitalization. There would be specific information given, like she was back on IV or NPO," the nurse-practitioner testified.

"How many times did you actually talk to Priscilla Phillips during this time?" Ed Caldwell asked pointedly on cross-examination. He knew that Priscilla had attended church only five times during Tia's eleven months of illness, and only once while Tia was hospitalized.

"I don't remember," Beverly Smith confessed. And on that weak note, the trail of witnesses ended.

The stipulation regarding Dr. Blinder was read to the jury and court was adjourned. All that remained were the final arguments and the jury instructions.

Week 10

On Monday, May 21, 1979, Deputy District Attorney Josh Thomas began his closing arguments. He had prepared very carefully and very thoroughly for these last moments before the jury.

"There are two issues in this case," he began, "perhaps three, if you want to look at it that way. Number one: Were Tia's symptoms caused by sodium poisoning? Number two: Were Mindy's? And number three: If so, was Priscilla Phillips responsible?"

Step by step, the district attorney led the jury through an elaborate rerun of the evidence that he believed provided unequivocal affirmative answers to the questions he had posed. He reminded the jury of the testimony of Dr. Malcolm Holliday and Dr. Boyd Stephens; both had stated that no explanation existed for the children's symptoms other than an exogenous source of sodium.

"And there were no rebuttal witnesses by the defense," Josh pointed out to the jury.

Because it was a point of inconsistency and might bother the jury, Josh covered two of Tia's admissions—and there were others, he admitted—during which there were high sodium levels recorded in her blood yet little diarrhea. He reminded the jury that Dr. Holliday had provided an explanation for that, as well as for the times when there was increased diarrhea and vomiting without elevated sodium levels.

Then Josh touched on some of the defendant's peculiar emotional responses. Her reactions to the placement of Mindy in ICU were strange, he said, as were her curious lapses of memory about crucial issues.

"Contrast those with her IBM memory when it came to incidental details of no consequence," he said.

"For instance, during her examination she corrected Mr. Caldwell when he said, 'Wasn't a hyperalimentation line installed on the twenty-sixth or the twenty-first?' And she said, 'No, no. That was the twentieth of April.' And she did not even refer to her notes. That was *three* years ago, let me remind you! But I'd like to contrast that with her conversation with Detective Lindquist on March the seventh when he started zeroing in on the question of whether this statement was made about the formula—whether Mrs. Phillips had mixed it—and suddenly she couldn't recall, although that conversation had only taken place two weeks before."

After recess, Josh moved to the issue of Munchausen Syndrome by Proxy. He impugned the objectivity of Dr. Satten, reminding the jury of the psychiatrist's failure to bring his notes for cross-examination and of his failure to mention Dr. Berg's report about the defendant.

Then he attacked Pat Wrigley, his voice deep with sarcasm.

"What did you think of Pat Wrigley, ladies and gentlemen, when she testified on the stand? Well, it became apparent to me, as I hope it did to you, that she was exaggerating. One thousand ccs of fluid in an hour, pouring down a leg onto the floor? And this occurring repeatedly? Picture Mindy convulsing in a bathtub, but playing around with her toys. Does this seem reasonable? And would you send your child to school the next day if she lost a quart of fluid like that?

"Mindy never had a well day, Mrs. Wrigley testified. Well, she must have had an iron constitution because she never missed a day at school, either. And I'll never forget a statement Mrs. Wrigley said when she was describing the adoption of Mindy. You know there are some people who look upon children as possessions. 'Sarah, in a couple of days, will be completely, irrevocably, forever ours or mine,' whatever it was she said. I think that statement says a lot about Mrs. Wrigley.

"And I will submit to you also—and I may be stretching a point here—it seemed to me that the evidence showed a striking similarity between Mrs. Wrigley and Mrs. Phillips. They got along famously, didn't they? As a matter of fact, during one recess Mrs. Wrigley went over and gave Mrs. Phillips a big hug. And didn't you think they seemed to see eye-to-eye on the development of children? And the desire to make themselves look good? Contrast that with Mrs. Portillo. No esoteric child-rearing programs there—just a basic down-to-earth person, an honest person, and very loving. Remember that newspaper article the Wrigleys submitted into evidence on Sarah's adoption? That got a little bit of publicity and beating of the drum—as if to say, 'Boy, we're really great folks. We adopt these kids. We're the saviors of the earth!' That's the Pat Wrigleys. That's the Priscilla Phillipses."

Josh's voice was ragged with exhaustion. Because he knew he had ninety minutes of argument remaining, he requested and was granted a recess for the day.

That afternoon, as a hushed audience listened to Josh Thomas in Marin County Superior Court, the verdict in the trial of Dan White for the murder of Mayor George Moscone and Supervisor Harvey Milk was announced in San Francisco. Dr. Martin Blinder—one of several psychiatrists called by the defense in that case—had delivered a remarkably cogent and believable argument on the stand to the effect that a variety of factors, including White's diet of Cokes and Twinkies, had affected his behavior in the days leading up to the murders and had diminished his capacity to plan his actions.

To the shock and surprise of virtually everyone, the jury found Dan White guilty merely of voluntary manslaughter, and that night the San Francisco gay community reacted in outrage. Furious riots broke out and continued throughout what was to be dubbed White Night.

In his office on Van Ness later that evening, Ed Caldwell looked out at the dome of City Hall—scene of the murders six months before, and of the riots that night—and despaired. This verdict could only rebound negatively on his client, he believed. *His* jury would not wish to live through the recriminations White's jury was facing now. A lawyer could control only so much of his case, he thought briefly. And no matter what he did, how effective he was in the courtroom, there were always the extraneous elements: a juror whose past history of possible sexual molestation might cause him to decide unfavorably; another juror's flu that had given a bored and undignified Pat Wrigley an opportunity to stick her tongue out at the prosecutor; a mild verdict in the White trial; an upcoming holiday weekend that might pressure the jury into a quick, undeliberated verdict. Caldwell sighed. He still hoped the verdict would hinge on the jury's perception of Priscilla Phillips. In the end, it all came down to that. The client was the center of the case. If they believed her and liked her, they would let her go. If not, they would convict her. But now, with critical reaction mounting against the White jury, a manslaughter verdict for Priscilla seemed remote.

The case went to the jury on Wednesday afternoon. The weather had turned very hot the last few days, with temperatures into the eighties, but the Jury Room to which the twelve men and women retired was air-conditioned and comfortable. The bailiffs had brought in all the trial exhibits.

The four-man, eight-woman jury did not so much file as slouch into the room. The last few days had been dramatic and emotional. After Josh Thomas had finished his oral argument on Tuesday, Ed Caldwell followed with an impassioned argument of his own. While Thomas had been systematic, complete to the point of redundancy, and logical, Caldwell relied more on drama and rhetoric. As he had in his opening argument nine weeks before, the defense attorney skipped from point to point, underlining those holes in the prosecution's case that he felt provided the jury with reasonable doubt.

He reminded the jurors of the presumption of innocence. "In this situation," he said, "you have sworn that you would follow the standard of the law that holds the prosecution to the burden of proof, and that you will not return a verdict of guilty unless you are convinced beyond a reasonable doubt of Priscilla Phillips's guilt."

As Josh had foreseen, Caldwell made much of the medical inconsistencies—the times when elevated sodiums were not accompanied by diarrhea and vice versa. Caldwell also pointed out a nurse's note on Mindy Phillips dated February 27, 1978—two days after her placement in ICU—indicating that Mindy's stool on one occasion had been liquid enough to cover her bed and clothes. This occurred after Mindy had supposedly recovered, Ed said. And, he reminded the jury, Mindy had never been well.

He discussed the difficulty Priscilla Phillips would have had in introducing foul-tasting baking soda into an NG. The syringes were locked up, he reminded the jury, and no traces of sodium compound were found in any of the defendant's purses. He brought up the legitimate illnesses suffered by Tia and Mindy. He reminded the jury that the medical world was not infallible, that mistakes had been made and acknowledged on the witness stand. A wrong decimal point here, an incorrect medication there. He defended Pat Wrigley and invited the jury to study the photograph of Joey as a skeletal six-month-old—the condition she had brought him home in and cured him of. And in an emotional and rhetorically skillful argument, he attacked Munchausen Syndrome by Proxy as a half-baked theory that twisted a loving mother's acts to look like the works of the devil.

"What inference would you draw, ladies and gentlemen, if Mrs. Phillips had been neglectful, careless, indifferent, or unloving to Tia and Mindy? Would that suggest innocence? Would that suggest she did not have this syndrome—if such a syndrome even exists?

"If she didn't lift a hand for a neighbor; if she didn't have a baby-sitting co-op; if she didn't participate in it and organize it; if she didn't go to church; if she didn't seek the peace and solitude of the minister; if she didn't participate in this community life at all; if she did nothing for anybody else— would that be an inference of innocence?

"In any event, ladies and gentlemen, no witness in this case testified that Mrs. Phillips had Munchausen Syndrome by Proxy. As a matter of fact, all of them testified that she was quite normal. Dr. Blinder did not examine Mrs. Phillips, and without such an examination, he could not and did not render an opinion about Mrs. Phillips. Dr. Satten spent sixteen hours with the family, most of it with Mrs. Phillips. Conclusion: normal. Dr. Kennedy, a Marin County psychiatrist referred by an earlier attorney, examined her. Conclusion: normal. Dr. Bernard Bradman: normal. Dr. Berg: normal. Dr. Cooper: opinion, normal."

"Priscilla and Steve and I and Mr. Collins will be awaiting your decision."

But no decision was reached that afternoon. The case was given to the jury following a lengthy jury instruction, at two-thirty, and the jurors had time only to elect a foreman and structure the course of their deliberations before they were brought back to court and asked if they had reached a verdict.

"No, Your Honor," replied Bob Chapman, the silver-haired manager of state disability insurance the jury had selected as their foreman. "And there is no verdict in sight," he added.

"In that case you will be excused for the day," said Judge Burke. "You will report at the usual time tomorrow for further deliberations."

"I'll see you tomorrow at ten o'clock," he said.

In the Jury Room the following day, deliberations continued: Bob Chapman laid out their structure according to Josh

Thomas's plan. There were three considerations, or questions to be answered, and they would take them in order, he said. First, had there been a crime? Second, if so, who had committed it? Third, if they concluded that the defendant was guilty, of what was she guilty? Murder in the first degree? the second? manslaughter?

All four men were of the opinion from the beginning of the deliberations that a crime had been committed, that Priscilla Phillips was guilty, and that she should be convicted of first-degree murder.

But among the women there was sharp disagreement. One woman in particular, a sixty-nine-year-old librarian named Rose Bristol, was convinced the defendant was innocent. A church-goer like Priscilla, she believed the defendant to be warm, concerned, and caring. Rose passed the baby books around the table.

"How can a woman so lovingly fill out books like these and still be guilty of murder?" she asked the others. Another woman-juror shrugged.

"Yes, those show she loved the children—but even mothers who love their children sometimes abuse them," she answered.

Rose shrank back a little. She felt intimidated by these other jurors—all young people. During breaks, they had played cards and chatted with each other while she had sat working her crossword puzzle. She was an outsider.

"Look, let's go around the table and have each person say what he or she thinks," the foreman suggested. The others nodded and complied. There was still disagreement.

"Can we agree, at least, that a crime was committed?" asked one of the men.

"I don't know—"

"But remember what the coroner said?" They were all talking at once suddenly.

"Look, let's ask for Stephens's testimony to be reread. The judge said we could do that."

"Yes, all right. Good idea. Everybody agree?"

The jury filed back into the courtroom after sending a note to the judge.

Burke asked the court reporter to take the part of Dr. Stephens and each attorney to play himself as most of the coroner's direct testimony was reenacted to the jury. Following this reading, the jury broke for lunch, and afterward, Foreman Chapman sent a note to the judge.

"The jury has heard all they need to of Dr. Stephens's testimony," Burke read from the paper handed to him.

"Well, we can't force the jury to read what they don't want to, but I'd like them at least to be provided with a copy of the cross-examination of Dr. Stephens because a lot of points were countered on cross—" began Ed Caldwell furiously. Perhaps his most effective cross-examination had been of Dr. Stephens.

"I'd object to that," Josh broke in.

"Well, I know of no precedents in my own experience for sending in the transcript for the jury to read. We'll note your objection for the record, Mr. Caldwell."

Some hours later, the jury requested a rehearing of Dr. Carte's testimony about his meetings with Priscilla. The jury once again returned to the courtroom and this testimony was reenacted. At four-thirty, the jury, still deadlocked, was excused for the day.

Out in the corridor, Steve cornered Ed Caldwell and whispered to him tensely. "What do you think? I think it looks bad that they only wanted to hear Dr. Stephens's direct testimony."

Ed shook his head, his face a mask. "You can't tell from that, Steve. I've long ago given up trying to second-guess juries. You never know what's going through their heads. They could just as easily be ruling things out as ruling them in, you know."

"I guess you're right. Hell, I wonder if we'll ever get through this."

At two o'clock on Friday, May 25, 1979, on a day when the temperature reached ninety, the jury returned to Courtroom Three with their verdict. They had deliberated for ten hours over two days. Word that a decision had been reached gradually filtered through the Civic Center and out to the numerous friends of Priscilla Phillips who had regularly attended the trial. Reverend Jim Hutchison came over, and Jan Doudiet and Nancy Dacus. But Josh Thomas could not locate Ted Lindquist, who was looking for a witness to an old homicide case and thus missed the finish.

The courtroom hummed with nervous activity as the jurors entered from the rear of the court and picked their way to their familiar place behind the mahogany railing. Expressionless, most of the jurors looked right at Priscilla as the foreman handed the verdict to the bailiff, who passed it in sequence to the judge and the court clerk. The clerk knew Priscilla, as did many of the Civic Center employees, and as she read the verdict into the hush of the room, her voice broke with strain.

"We, the jury in the above-entitled cause, find the defendant, Priscilla E. Phillips, guilty of murder in the second degree; that is, the unlawful killing of a human being—whether intentional, unintentional, or accidental—which occurs as a direct causal result of the commission of an attempt to commit a felony, namely the crime of willfully mingling any harmful substance with any food, drink, or medicine with intent that the same shall be taken by any human being to his injury, and where there was in the mind of the perpetrator the specific intent to commit such a crime.

"And in count two, we find the defendant, Priscilla E. Phillips, guilty of endangering the life of Mindy Phillips."

Priscilla reacted at once.

"God, I didn't do it! I didn't do it!" she screamed hysterically, her voice so loud that it was heard outside in the corridor where an overflow crowd had gathered. She began to cry in great, whooping sobs, her face buried against Steve's chest. He held her to him, tears streaming down his own face. Sounds of weeping broke out in the audience and the jurors shifted in their padded blue seats and looked away.

AFTERMATH

1

When news reached him that the verdict was in, Jim Hutchison hurried to the Civic Center. He, Priscilla, Steve, and some of their friends rode together in the small elevator, the hunched little group silent. Jim knew neither what to expect nor what conclusion he really hoped for.

He had murmured some supportive words as they met and clustered by the elevator doors. But more and more he had come to accept Priscilla's guilt. There were moments during the early part of the trial when he suspected Priscilla was using him for dramatic effect. He was known to be a minister, and on several occasions Priscilla had rushed, weeping, to his seat among the spectators, to throw her arms around him. He thought this had happened most conveniently once or twice just as the jury was filing in. It was as though every emotion she displayed was artifice, every gesture calculated.

Later he remembered what happened after the verdict. Shrieking, "I didn't do it! I didn't do it!" Priscilla had turned to Jim, still screaming, and added hysterically, "God knows I didn't do it. How could you do this, God?" She had clung first to Steve, then to Jim, sobbing.

Jim sought out the bailiff. "Is there some way I could take her out?" he asked the officer.

"Yes, through the judge's chambers."

Jim gripped Priscilla firmly by the arm and led her behind the bench. Marietta followed, her eyes swollen behind their thick glasses.

"Priscilla, I really care about you," Jim said loudly into Priscilla's ear after they reached the judge's chambers. At once she stopped crying. Instinctively, he felt he had pushed the right button: that was what she needed to hear.

Afterward he wondered if that might not be the key to the whole affair: Priscilla's need for reassurance that she was loved and needed. Tia had needed her desperately and continually,

285

and never more than when she was sick. The same was true for Mindy.

Jim could recall something Marj Dunlavy had told him once; its strangeness haunted him. Marj's daughters customarily helped out in the church day-care center during Sunday service. One of them had described to her mother some behavior on Priscilla's part that she could not understand. Marj had passed it on to Jim.

"Claudia told me that when Priscilla comes into the church nursery after the service," Marj had said, "she always asks after the boys. She wants to know if they've been crying for her. When Claudia says no, Priscilla seems disappointed. If she says yes, Priscilla smiles. Claudia's having trouble understanding her reactions."

But to Jim, Priscilla's behavior was beginning to manifest a horrible sort of consistency, a pathological progression that had apparently ended in tragedy. Jim had yet to figure out a way to deal with the pathology, but it was not an immediate concern. For now he had to get Priscilla home.

Somehow, Jim and the women found their way downstairs. Steve was waiting with the car, his face set. Behind them they left a crush of reporters gathered expectantly by the Jury Room, hoping for insight into the deliberations. The reporters would be after him soon enough, Jim knew.

Friends were clustered in tight knots on the patchy brown front lawn of the house on Woodbine when they arrived. Jan Doudiet stood with Nancy Dacus. Stony-faced and now calm, Priscilla went in to change clothes. The others followed. Ed Caldwell and Al Collins drove up. Caldwell was in tears.

"I don't know what happened," he said huskily. "I expected a hung jury at least. I never got them to see Priscilla for what she is, and I should never have let it ride on reasonable doubt—they obviously needed an alternative. I shouldn't have let that cursed phone call into evidence!" He paused for a deep breath. "It's that damned Dan White verdict, that had to have an effect. But still, I don't understand how they could find second-degree murder. It's so inconsistent—a compromise, obviously. I'm going to find out. I'm going to call every one of those jurors and ask."

"Will you appeal?" someone ventured.

"Of course we appeal! Letting Blinder's testimony in on Munchausen Syndrome was preposterous." Ed looked murderous.

"What about her sentence?" Jim asked.

"We won't know for a month. At least Burke continued bail. She'll be sentenced under the old indeterminate sentencing law. That's five years to life for second degree."

"Oh, my God!" Jan Doudiet cried out.

"But she could get straight probation if she gets a favorable report from the probation department. It's not unheard of. The P.O. should interview her friends before he prepares his report. You can all help," Ed went on.

"Of course!"

"Whatever it takes!" They were buoyed now, relieved that they might make a difference, that they could act.

After awhile, Jim Hutchison slipped out and drove home. Priscilla had emerged pale and composed from the bedroom, and Jim had watched her friends close in around her, all of them holding onto her, soothing her, bathing her in support.

Later that afternoon, a reporter from the *Independent-Journal* caught up with Jim.

"What does the church think of the verdict, Reverend?"

Jim hesitated only momentarily: he had prepared an answer. "Well, I suppose the members of the church have reacted like the community at large," he offered. "There are three general categories: those who believed in her innocence and still do; those who were confused and decided to await the trial's outcome; and those who considered her guilty all along. There was tremendous restraint in the congregation, and those who considered Priscilla guilty from the beginning have expressed sympathy for her mental condition," he added.

"You know, there's been another case of this Munchausen Syndrome by Proxy recently. A Houston mother went on trial in April. Josh Thomas mentioned it just now in an interview," the reporter confided.

"Really?"

"Yeah. And supposedly the pediatricians never suspected a thing because of the close bond between mother and child. One doctor said the mother became an expert on immunology—knew as much as some specialists. The *I-J's* carrying an article in tomorrow's edition."

"Amazing." Jim turned away and watched as the reporter moved off. He remembered the stretched and flattened acreage of Bahia Cemetery in Novato where they had buried Tia twenty-seven months earlier. In the midst of a two-year drought, the day had brought rain.

* * *

"Tia has gone to Heaven and told God to send down rain," little Erik had announced at the graveside service that had followed by a day the memorial service at Aldersgate. They had all smiled through their tears.

Like all services for children, Tia's had been difficult for Jim. It was hard to understand the death of a child. He had preached to the overflowing crowd on the topic of: "What I do now you know not, but ye shall know," the statement Jesus had made to the Disciples on the eve of his crucifixion. Jim found the theme to be comforting, as it underlined the divine purpose in all that happened. Who knew what purpose little Tia's death might ultimately serve, or who might benefit from it? Perhaps others would learn about Munchausen Syndrome by Proxy; perhaps other infant lives would be saved. The purpose might not become clear for some time, but that did not deny its existence. The cross, after all, had become the resurrection.

Meanwhile he faced the problem of how to deal with Priscilla now that she stood convicted. The church had helped to raise money for her defense fund. Jim, despite reservations, had allowed the church post office box to be used for collections because he believed that no one should be denied the best possible defense. But now what stance was appropriate? Could he in good conscience support a convicted murderer? Would support, in the end, even help her? He could not sit on this uncomfortable fence much longer. But for now, he needed to gain a sense of proportion, and he needed to pray.

2

Shortly before ten on the last Friday in June, Priscilla appeared once again before Justice Louis Burke of the Marin County Superior Court for sentencing. In addition, Burke was to rule on the motion for a new trial that Ed Caldwell had filed. In the event this motion failed, Priscilla would file an appeal.

In the sparkling summer air, Priscilla was weighted with spent emotion and dread. For the last month, a San Mateo County probation officer had been preparing a report that the judge would use for sentencing. The Marin County probation department had ruled that it would be a conflict of interest to become involved, as both Steve and Priscilla were well-known in the department and Steve's job involved daily contact with it. Consequently San Mateo had been called in. The same man who had interviewed Priscilla in county jail following her arrest—and whose recommendation for OR had been ignored at that time—had been reassigned to handle this presentencing report.

On this report hinged Priscilla's future. Probation Officer Richard Mallon could recommend straight probation, perhaps with stipulations as to psychiatric treatment or reduced community involvement for Priscilla. He could recommend ninety days' observation for psychiatric evaluation at the California Institution for Women in southern California—an evaluation that was usually followed by a department recommendation for probation. He could recommend county jail, with sentences on each charge to run either concurrently or consecutively. If he chose to be harsh, he could recommend state prison with sentences to run consecutively.

Priscilla had hoped desperately for a recommendation of straight probation. Barring that, she thought she could withstand confinement in a nearby jail, where she could see the boys regularly and often. Perhaps she might be released early on a work-furlough program. There was none in Marin County as yet—although one was expected to start soon—but Oakland had such a program, and Oakland was only forty-five minutes away.

Mallon had prepared a detailed report. He had interviewed Priscilla and Steve and Marietta. He had telephoned Priscilla's sister Louise, and talked with Dr. Satten. He had interviewed Ted Lindquist and Josh Thomas. He had read and quoted in his report the many letters from Priscilla's friends expressing outrage at the verdict and urging leniency. He had considered circumstances in mitigation and circumstances in aggravation. Finally, on the last page of his twenty-three page report, he had made his recommendation.

Richard Mallon recommended that criminal proceedings against Priscilla Phillips be suspended until a ninety-day evaluation and report could be provided by the Department of

Corrections. He further recommended that the Marin County probation department submit a suggested probation program to be considered by the court when sentencing was imposed following the ninety-day observation at the California Institution for Women at Frontera, San Bernadino County.

If the judge followed the recommendation, it meant a three-month separation from the boys and Steve. Priscilla had resigned herself to that. But Judge Burke was not bound by Mallon's report; he might still sentence her to straight probation, or to state prison.

"Ed, will I have to go to jail right after the hearing?" Priscilla asked Caldwell the night before sentencing. "Should I bring the boys to court so I can say good-bye to them?"

"No, that's not necessary. No matter what the sentence, I plan to ask for you to have this weekend at home. I'm sure you won't have to report until Monday if you're sentenced for ninety days. I'm going to request bail pending appeal. And, though I doubt it, we may even get a new trial on the basis of that fireman's experiment."

It was not uncommon for attorneys on both sides of a case to call the jurors following a verdict and ask for their opinion on strategy or question them about which arguments or witnesses had been most convincing. Although such calls could not, as a rule, help their clients, the information could be beneficial in other cases. Both Ted Lindquist and Ed Caldwell had telephoned the jurors after Priscilla's verdict was announced. And with his call to Jerome Polizzi, the defense attorney had hit pay dirt.

The San Francisco fireman who lived in Novato had been polite. He and Ed had chatted for a few minutes.

"There's one thing I wanted to ask you," Ed probed gingerly. "Yeah?"

"The DA offered no evidence to show how Mrs. Phillips might have transported baking soda to the hospital. All her handbags were examined by the FBI, as you heard, and were found to contain no traces of baking soda. That has always seemed like a big hole in the DA's case to me."

"I don't think so. There were a lot of ways she could have done it. She could have brought it in her hand. She could have dissolved it in some water and brought it in a bottle. I know she could have done that because I did a little experiment myself one night: I mixed some baking soda in a glass of water and it dissolved completely. You couldn't tell it wasn't pure water."

Ed paused and gulped as the adrenaline surged. "When did you do that, Mr. Polizzi?" he asked, his voice a careful neutral.

"Oh, I don't remember exactly. Awhile ago. I was reminded of it when we started deliberations because one of the exhibits was a box of baking soda, and it was the same brand we have at home. That made me remember the experiment."

"Listen, could I come talk to you about this—maybe tomorrow?"

"Well, I'm working tomorrow. I'll be at the firehouse if you want to come out."

"I'll be there." Ed hung up and let out a shout of excitement. Then he explained to Priscilla the significance of Polizzi's experiment.

"Jurors are not allowed to consider any evidence that has not been presented to them in the courtroom. Burke explained that the first day. They cannot perform experiments on their own."

"But it's such a nothing experiment," Steve said. "Everyone knows baking soda dissolves in water."

"It doesn't matter. If the experiment tainted that juror, then Priscilla didn't have twelve unbiased members on her jury. And if he mentioned the experiment to others, maybe he tainted them all. We might get a new trial out of this—we just might." He had added juror misconduct to the other grounds for a new trial. Now the moment had arrived to see how the judge would rule.

Judge Burke began the hearing by addressing the motion for a new trial. There were two somewhat conflicting affidavits that had been submitted in the Polizzi matter, one prepared by the defense, one by the prosecution. After meeting with Polizzi, Caldwell had forwarded to him an affidavit that purported to describe what the fireman had done. But the juror refused to sign it without prior consultation with his lawyer, and in the end he did not sign it at all on the basis that it contained information that falsely suggested that he had conducted his experiment during jury deliberations. In fact, he said, he had conducted it earlier. The second affidavit had been prepared by the district attorney, and this Polizzi signed. In it, Polizzi swore that he had indeed conducted the experiment but maintained that he had not discussed it with other jurors.

In the courtroom, Burke now asked for and received

arguments on the issue. Priscilla watched in silence as Ed Caldwell and Josh Thomas argued and counterargued. Polizzi had clearly passed beyond the scope of a juror's proper activities during trial; that was indisputable. But whether the experiment had been prejudicial, and if so, to what extent, was at question now.

Burke finally ruled that Polizzi's experiment was not prejudicial enough to warrant a new trial. The decision shook Priscilla, and although Steve took her hand and pressed it, she had to grit her teeth against the apprehension that twisted her stomach.

The lawyers moved on to a discussion of the probation report. Josh Thomas brought up the polygraph test Priscilla had taken months before. The polygraph expert was in court and ready to testify, Josh said coyly. Perhaps Mr. Hart could shed some light on sentencing issues by testifying about the results of the test.

It was a dirty trick and Priscilla stared at Josh in fury. Mr. Hart had never even submitted a report to Gary Ragghianti, who had been her lawyer at the time. Her polygraph had not been an issue during the trial; indeed such tests were not admissible even if they exonerated a suspect. Obviously the district attorney already knew that the test results had been inconclusive; she had admitted as much, in fact. But Josh Thomas was not above that sort of tactic: Priscilla had seen him try before. Late in the trial, Josh had attempted to draw an inference from an X ray Priscilla needed following a fall from a ladder, implying that Steve had beaten her. It had disgusted Priscilla then, as did this underhanded trick now.

But the judge saw through the ploy.

"I doubt that at this stage of the proceeding it would serve any purpose to open that matter," he said firmly. Then he sat back, his small, alert eyes full on Priscilla, ready to pass sentence.

"By reason of the unique nature of the crimes, I believe that the objectives of sentencing could be listed as the following: one, punishing the defendant because of the serious nature of the crimes; two, protecting society; three, encouraging the defendant to lead a law-abiding life and to deter her from future offenses."

Priscilla turned in panic and whispered frantically to Steve. "He's going to send me away! Call my mother—get her to bring the boys here so that I can see them."

"Pris, you've got plenty of time. Ed will get you till Monday if—"

"Steve, just do it! Please!"

"Okay." He squeezed past her and whispered to a friend to make the call.

The judge meanwhile was in full stride as he laid out his reasoning for the sentence he planned to pass.

"I have given serious thought to the matter of probation in this case but rejected it, although it might be considered an unusual case that in fact permits the court to grant probation. It's legally possible because of psychological problems not amounting to a defense, and psychiatric treatment could be required as a condition of probation.

"However the court is not convinced that any such treatment would succeed. The defendant has steadfastly maintained her innocence. Her defense was that she did not commit the crime and that she was sane. The expert witnesses all testified that she was normal and not mentally ill.

"Normally, for a person to benefit from therapy, she would have to acknowledge wrongful behavior and attempt to gain an insight into why she committed the acts, so that upon her return to society she would not constitute a danger to others. Here, there is no indication that the defendant has ever admitted, even to herself, that she committed these acts. Perhaps if she were to do so, she would find it very difficult to live with herself. So consequently she continues, perhaps, to block out any responsibility for these crimes.

"Although the probation officer recommends suspending sentencing pending completion of a ninety-day observation, in my opinion, this would accomplish nothing. It would just delay the eventual date because she has been thoroughly examined by her own experts, and those examinations failed to disclose any mental illness. Furthermore, such a referral is usually a prelude to a grant of probation, and I have concluded that I cannot in good conscience grant probation in this case under any conditions. The substantial evidence of her guilt was clear and convincing. I personally believe she was proven guilty beyond all reasonable doubt.

"The defendant is hereby sentenced to state prison on count one for the murder in the second degree of Tia Phillips. Because the crime was committed before the change of law, it is an indeterminate term—specified as five years to life—with the actual term to be fixed later by the Community Release

Board. The possible ranges for count two—child endangering—are sixteen months, two years, and three years. I have chosen the median term of two years. And because of the defendant's good record in the community, her lack of prior violations of the law, and her obvious devotion to her natural children and to her husband, the court orders the sentences to run concurrently.

"The defendant is remanded to the custody of the sheriff for delivery to the state Department of Corrections. Her bail is exonerated."

Priscilla slumped in her chair, her face waxen in defeat. The worst had happened.

"Your Honor?" Ed Caldwell was a dim figure on his feet at her side. "I have a request to make on behalf of the defendant. As I understand it, the transportation to Frontera will not take place until at least Monday of next week. I would ask that the order of the court be stayed until Mrs. Phillips reports to the sheriff's office on Monday for transportation to CIW."

"We would oppose that motion, Your Honor," Josh Thomas said at once.

"Well, I think under the circumstances that motion should be denied. Ample opportunity will be provided by the jail, and the court will so order, for visitation with the members of her family."

"Your Honor, in that case I would like to ask the court—and I understand it is discretionary—to allow the release of the defendant on bail pending appeal. She is no danger to the community and the financial hardship is obvious." Ed was fishing now, but he knew such bail had been granted in other cases.

"The motion for bail on appeal is denied. And parenthetically, I intend to recommend to the Department of Corrections that if the defendant should come to believe she might be aided by psychiatric assistance, the Department of Corrections should see that she gets it. You can't force it on a person; to do so serves no purpose. But if a person believes that she could be aided in any way by psychiatric or psychological assistance, I believe that this is a case where that assistance is indicated. All right, gentlemen, that concludes the matter."

The court reporter rose and began to collect her equipment. Priscilla grabbed frantically at Ed's coat.

"The boys are on their way—please see if the judge will let me see them for a minute before I go. The Visiting Room at the jail has those awful phones and the glass partition—I won't be able to hug them—" Her voice rose in a hint of hysteria.

Burke had heard. "Yes, that will be all right. There's a room across the hall. Bailiff, get a matron. Someone needs to be present."

"Yes, Your Honor."

"Thank you, Your Honor," Ed said. He turned to Priscilla. "I'm sorry."

"You did the best you could." She was back in control. "But it's not fair. The judge's reasoning—" she began bitterly.

"I know. A real Catch–22, isn't it? The only way you can get leniency is by admitting you did it, showing remorse."

"It's just like this whole case, with everything twisted against me. All the things we've been taught about truth and justice and honesty turned and used against me. If I'm loving, that means I'm after attention. If I join community activities, I'm crazy. If I protest my innocence, that means I should be punished more severely. It's not fair!" She was crying now.

Ed took her arm. "I know, damn it. But here are Erik and Jason." They were running down the hall, Marietta in tears behind them. They all crowded into the little room the jail matron showed them.

"I have to go away," Priscilla managed to say. "But it won't be forever. I want you to remember that."

"Will you be home for my birthday?" Jason asked.

"Oh, son—" Steve threw his arms around the six-year-old.

"No, Jason. But I'll write you a special letter, with something in it just for you."

"Pris—"

"Steve, I can't stand it! I can't! I've already lost two of my children and now they're taking the rest away—"

"Pris, we'll see you at the jail, and then we'll come down to Frontera—you know that."

"I'm sorry, but she'll have to go now," the matron said softly. She put a hand on Priscilla's arm and firmly guided her from the room. Priscilla, in a blur of tears, did not resist as she was taken down to the elevator and across the narrow strip of roadway to the county jail.

ii

She was given the same cell as before, but this time she was not confined there. In the six days before her transfer, she was allowed to visit the canteen and mix with the other prisoners, and every day she crossed to the exercise yard for a game of volleyball.

Almost at once she found a friend. Judy, a woman she had known slightly from AAUW, had been imprisoned for kidnapping—a woman so withdrawn that she had talked to no one since her arrival. Priscilla spent most of her time with this prisoner, trying to draw her out. She became Priscilla's special little project, her focus at the jail, and the staff was pleased when the woman began to talk to Priscilla.

The rest of the time Priscilla spent trying, as much as possible, to plan her future. She learned that she would leave on Thursday, July fifth, but she did not know how she would be transported or what possessions she would be allowed. Nor did she know what to expect when she arrived at CIW. It was the only state prison for women, and she had visions of San Quentin, with its cages and tiers and noise. None of the inmates at Marin County jail had been to CIW, so Priscilla finally asked one of the officers for help, and she was able to find an old list of items permitted there.

The list indicated that prisoners could have no jewelry valued over fifty dollars, so Steve bought Priscilla a plain gold wedding band to replace her diamond and gold wedding set. Priscilla drew up her own list, which she gave to Steve. He and Marietta packed a box of supplies for her to take.

The trip to Frontera devastated her. She was terrified, inexperienced, and alone, and everything they subjected her to over the next two days enhanced her fears.

First the sheriff's officer examined her box of supplies, dumping it on the floor. Then he wrapped chains around her waist and handcuffed her to the chains. It was the first time she had ever been chained and she began to cry. Across the room, a probation officer whom Priscilla knew slightly saw her and turned away in tears as well. This appeared to enrage the officer in charge. He began looking through Priscilla's box, pawing at her belongings. Then he stared at her.

"Who do you think you are? You can't take all that stuff—all that jewelry. Take it off."

"But—"

"Take it off!"

Priscilla removed her ring and chain; the officer stuffed them in an envelope that he put with her box. Then she was hustled to tiny Gnoss Field in Novato, where she was led to the plane.

It was a six-seater, and it contained one other woman-prisoner and four rough, sweating, stinking men. Priscilla was shoved between them. Instantly they looked her over.

"Where ya going, lady? Whatcha in for?"

Terrified and unwilling to answer, she shrugged away from them. If they knew her crime, they might hurt her; she knew that much.

The tiny plane took off raggedly. Bucking from municipal airport to rural field, it skipped in a haphazard tour around the Bay Area on its route south. At each airport, prisoners clanked off in a shuffle of chains and sweat to be replaced by new convicts. Priscilla was given nothing to eat or drink. When she asked to use the bathroom, she was refused. She had departed Marin County in the early afternoon, but the sun had set in a froth of lavender by the time the plane stopped for the night in Visalia.

Visalia's jail resembled something from the set of *Cool Hand Luke*. The holding cell where Priscilla was put for the night reduced her to tears. Bugs scraped along the floor, and smears decorating the walls gave testimony to the earlier fate of other insects. The metal toilet, which was built into the wall along with an attached metal sink, smelled of old excrement. Priscilla was forced to strip, and her clothes were taken from her. They insisted she remove her contact lenses. She was given jail clothes, a pallet, and a blanket that stank of disinfectant.

The cell was crowded, and as evening dragged into night, more residents appeared. Drunks were pushed hastily through the door. One of these vomited throughout the night; another was afflicted with diarrhea. A fat woman squeezed in and perched all night long, teetering gently, on the metal table. The woman laughed and talked in a street vernacular Priscilla did not understand. The noise was constant and assaultive; after her early bout of tears, Priscilla sat stoically, a headache building. She retreated to a corner finally, and crouched there, her head in her hands.

Bag lunches were passed around. Priscilla was hungry, but she couldn't eat; she could not force down the inedible-looking food. She wondered if CIW would resemble the Visalia jail, and how, if it did, she might endure it.

At four A.M. a blare of country music burst from the loudspeaker system and the lights came on. A line of men chained together was brought in. Breakfast at five was soggy and nauseating. Priscilla refused it numbly. She was given her clothes and told to wait since the tiny airport was fogged in. There was always morning fog in the central valley, and she waited a long time.

At last, handcuffed again, she boarded the small plane once more. The trip was again long and circuitous as they zigzagged to the coast and then back, loading and unloading passengers. Finally they arrived at the Chino airport, a few miles from Frontera. Priscilla had not been to the bathroom all day and was in agony.

"I have to go—please, I can't stand it!" she said to the woman-officer. Grudgingly the guard led her to the bathroom, but she unlocked only one of Priscilla's handcuffs. Priscilla struggled a long time with her pantyhose while the guard stared at her with indifference.

Perhaps the Department of Corrections deliberately made transportation to Frontera unpleasant, it later occurred to Priscilla, because when she finally arrived at the California Institution for Women, she thought she had gone to heaven. She did not notice the smell of the dairy farm down the road, nor the chain-linked fence topped by barbed wire, nor the guard towers. All she saw was the green grass—acres of it—the neat cottages, and the clean administration building. And trees.

She was taken into the reception center and her chains were removed. In a few minutes a guard brought her soup and a grilled sandwich and left her alone to eat. It was silent and clean, and after what she had been through, completely bearable.

. She was processed and taken to her room in the reception center. Every new and returning inmate spent her first weeks in the RC. Priscilla's room resembled a college dorm and possessed a wooden door rather than bars. She tried the bed. Then she closed the door and lay down. She thought she had to stay in her room. No one explained the rules to her. No one told her she could go into the yard anytime she wanted, or down the hall to watch TV, or play Ping-Pong in the recreation center. No one mentioned the pool. And no one thought to tell her that closing the door to her room automatically locked it.

Priscilla missed dinner her first night at CIW because she could not get out. She was finally able to attract the attention of another inmate who came to release her.

"Well, you've missed dinner, but in the future you can order food from the canteen and have it in your room, as long as you do it by Saturday," the girl told her, smiling. She stayed with Priscilla for a while, explaining some of the rules. Priscilla was impressed by the amount of freedom inmates were allowed. And the girl seemed nice. But later that evening, another inmate stopped by to talk.

"Don't you hang around that girl," she advised seriously. "She's got a bad reputation. Watch what you say around her."

Priscilla swallowed. There was a game here, and rules to be learned; she saw that clearly. This girl was all right, that one bad. Don't talk about your crime; don't be honest. Watch yourself.

Priscilla soon would learn something else about prison. It was something Ted Lindquist could have told her. Everybody there was innocent.

3

On Thursday, October eleventh, Steve and Ed Caldwell flew PSA from San Francisco to Ontario Airport to attend Priscilla's serious offender hearing. In July, shortly after her departure for CIW, the Community Release Board had set Priscilla's term of imprisonment for Tia's murder at the median term of six years. This was automatic in converting an indeterminate sentence to the determinate sentences now in force. But because this was a murder case and in addition involved more than one count, it was also automatic to hold an enhancement hearing to determine whether the sentence should be increased to the maximum—in Priscilla's case, to seven years.

This was Steve's third visit to Frontera since July. He and Marietta and the boys had driven down shortly after Priscilla's arrival, camping at the nearby Prado State Park campgrounds. And they had returned, after Marietta's departure for North Carolina, the last weekend in August. By then Priscilla had expected to be moved from RC to Campus, which was the main part of the facility. But August found her still in the reception center. Because she was a superintendent's case—assigned, due to the nature of her crime and the publicity attached to her case, to the superintendent personally—her transfer to Campus had been delayed. Since visiting at the RC was much less appealing and open than at Campus, with visitors confined to a small airless room without food-vending machines, the boys had soon grown irritable and restless. The visits had also proved difficult for Steve.

He did not want to burden Priscilla with his problems, though he had many. After her departure, Steve had switched to night shift at juvenile hall. Each night, before reporting to work at eleven, he brought Erik and Jason to the Doudiets to sleep. At seven, he returned there, retrieved the boys, took them home, and readied them for school. He slept until they came home. It was the only way he could find to spend time with the boys but it was hard on Jan and Jim, he knew, and it was beginning to tire him to the point of illness. He was smoking heavily and felt depressed and out-of-sorts. On top of that, the boys—and particularly Jason—were taking the separation from Priscilla very hard. Jason had suddenly forgotten how to read. But Steve didn't want to mention this to Priscilla. She had enough troubles of her own.

At Ontario Airport, Steve and Ed rented a car for the forty-five minute drive to Frontera.

"How was Pris doing the last time you were here?" Ed asked.

"She was reporting some hassles because it's a child-related case. She was working in the kitchen, she said, and some inmate started pointing at her and holding her nose and talking about the rotten odor, that it smelled dead—stuff like that."

"How's she handling it?"

"Who knows? She's so naive about things. She thought if she just told people she was innocent, they wouldn't hassle her. She told me that the ones who go after her the most are the ones who feel guilty about their own kids, not the ones who are loving mothers. But she's starting to learn the institutional lingo. Calls everybody girls. You know they turn everybody into children in institutions. Makes them easier to deal with."

"But no one's actually threatened her right out?"

"Some lady in the kitchen who was in for a knifing got burned at her for something and started pointing Pris out to all her friends. Pris felt pretty threatened by that!" Steve shuddered and his voice hardened suddenly. "Christ, why don't they leave her alone? She's a better mother than any of them."

Ed lifted a hand from the wheel and patted his arm. "Steve, I know," he said. "What about you? How are things going?"

"Oh, I'll make it. I mean, as you know, I've got a net worth of minus thirty-three thousand dollars, monthly expenses of over twelve hundred dollars, and a salary of fifteen hundred dollars. Not to mention the forty thousand dollars I owe you in fees and costs. You know, one time I told Dr. Satten I'd be satisfied to come out of this with my family intact, that the rest didn't matter. Now I don't even have that."

"Well, the defense fund is still in operation." Caldwell raised a finger from the steering wheel to tick off a point. "And one juror—that old lady-librarian—is even contributing to it! We've also got this new attorney, Jonathan Purver, to handle the appeal for a new trial, and he's supposed to be a bright, capable guy." He raised another finger. "And personally I think Burke's denial of our request for Pris's release pending appeal will be overturned." A third finger came off the wheel. "Then there's this Syntex thing: that could win us a new trial."

"Right!" Steve was animated for the first time. When th news about the formula recall for chloride deficiency had broken in August, everyone had called Steve in excitement. Syntex Corporation, a drug and baby formula manufacturer, had withdrawn two of their baby formulas due to chloride deficiency, he learned. It had been an innocent mistake, apparently. With all the new linkages between sodium consumption and heart and arterial disease, Syntex had decided to reduce drastically the amount of chloride in its formulas. No government standards existed for baby formulas; no agency tested them. No one realized that certain levels of chloride were essential for infant growth until babies began to get sick. Then a doctor in Tennessee, Dr. Shane Roy, had tracked down the problem to the chloride-deficient formulas manufactured by Syntex.

But what was significant to Priscilla's case was that the two formulas recalled were Neo-Mull-Soy and Cho-free. Both Tia and Mindy, and particularly Tia, had been on Cho-free for months. Maybe that had caused their problems.

Ed was working on this new development, Steve knew. He was in touch with Dr. Roy. And so was Josh Thomas. So far nothing definitive was known. Syntex wasn't talking, and there was disagreement about which lots of formula had been affected. A number of lots manufactured in 1978, and probably other lots sold as early as 1975, had certainly been deficient.

Steve did not know how this might affect Pris. There seemed
to be no correlation linking decreased chloride with increased
sodium levels, but Ed had found that decreased chloride in a
formula could lead to increased bicarbonate levels. Many
times over the course of her illness, Tia had exhibited elevated
carbon dioxide levels, and those were a reflection of bicarbonate. Still, although there had been one or two exceptions, her
chloride level had not been decreased. Also, she had been
receiving food other than Cho-free some of the time, while it
appeared that the babies who had fallen sick from the formulas
had been younger and consequently had been given no other
food. There was another difference: although these chloride-
deficient babies had not thrived, they had not suffered from
diarrhea.

The investigation into the formula was only preliminary, but
Steve thought it might well suggest an answer. At the very
least it would throw up considerable doubt, and Steve was
confident that the appellate court would be forced to grant a
new trial on the basis of this new evidence.

Another forty-five minutes elapsed. Finally the correctional
officer behind the glassed-in section that looked out on both
the Visiting Room and the Waiting Room called out, "Priscilla
Phillips."

Steve and Ed were buzzed into the brightly lit Visiting
Room that resembled a train station with its line of vending
machines and its TV bolted high on one wall. Still, Steve
thought, train stations did not have guards in one corner who
insisted that visitor and inmate embrace only in front of them,
and who refused to allow an inmate to handle the change
visitors were permitted to bring in for the vending machines.
Priscilla was not even supposed to push the machine buttons
for her selection.

Then Steve saw her coming in through the back door,
pulling down and adjusting her clothes unselfconsciously from
the search, and when she looked up and smiled and started to
run to them, Steve had to blink hard. He missed the hell out of
this lady—that was the worst of it.

4

Exactly five weeks later, Priscilla returned in the six-seater airplane from CIW via Visalia to Gnoss Field. She hadn't wanted to make the trip, agreeing only at Ed's insistence. "You have to be here for your bail hearing; I can't emphasize that strongly enough," he had said.

"But I can't stand another trip like the last one. You know how terrible it was. Can't I just wait down here, and then if Burke decides to release me on bail, I'll just walk out of here?"

"No, Priscilla. I want you to be here. Grit your teeth and bear it. I want that judge to see you."

"Everyone here says there's no way he'll grant bail—they're all laughing at me and my optimism."

"Most people don't get out on bail pending appeal. But you know the appellate court ordered Burke to reconsider his decision. I think you've got a good chance or I wouldn't subject you to this."

"Okay." She had packed her belongings: her clothes and the clock radio and her Bible. She had said good-bye to some of her new friends—among them Kathy, who was in on a child-abuse case; Laura, a Beverly Hills socialite; and Wendy Yoshimura, who had been captured with Patty Hearst. Wendy had left the RC for Campus the same day as Priscilla, and her enhancement hearing had also coincided with Priscilla's.

Ed had been eloquent at the enhancement hearing the month before. He had cited Priscilla's impeccable record, the support of her many friends and family, and the possibility that the Syntex formula recall would affect the findings in her case. The board had voted unanimously not to enhance her sentence. It had been a victory, and it meant that Priscilla's sentence could be as little as twenty months. And assuming good behavior, her maximum sentence would not exceed four years. Priscilla had no doubts concerning her behavior, but she was beginning to acknowledge that her time would not be easy, that it would not be simple to avoid trouble.

Problems began, in fact, as soon as she moved from the reception center to Harrison Cottage on Campus. Harrison was known as a rough cottage, and because it was the last cottage on Campus, its inhabitants had the longest walk to meals or to the canteen or the pool, and this was to prove significant.

All the newcomers to Campus passed through an initial period of double-bunking before receiving their own rooms. Priscilla achieved single-room status sooner than most because an inmate moved suddenly to Wilson—the prerelease cottage—freeing her room for Priscilla. Hers was one of the nicest rooms on Harrison B, with extensive wood paneling. But by the time Priscilla moved in, someone had deliberately gouged long scratches in the wood. It foreshadowed Priscilla's reception at the cottage and on Campus.

It was only later that Priscilla realized she was being set up for persecution. Priscilla's assignment to work as a clerk for Mr. Williams, the counselor at Harrison, required her to order housekeeping and office supplies for the whole unit. She was responsible for picking up the supplies from the warehouse and bringing them to the cottage. But before she could turn the supplies over to the cottage staff, the inmates clustered around her, taking whatever they wanted from the boxes. She soon understood that the cottage inmates were hoarding the supplies; then they would come to her for more. It was nothing more than stealing; within a few weeks, they were taking things directly from the office, daring her to stop them. The code she was fast learning required Priscilla's silence, if not her cooperation. But one day a girl reached into the box containing Mr. William's own supplies.

"No," Priscilla told her in exasperation. "That box is for Mr. Williams. Take it from this one."

The girl snarled back at her. It had been the opportunity, Priscilla discovered later, that this inmate had sought. From that time on, she was Priscilla's personal persecutor, taunting her with shouts of "Baby killer!" Others tormented Priscilla, too. Once a group of women called Priscilla over.

"You're Priscilla, the baby killer, right?" asked one conversationally.

"That's my name, but I'm no baby killer."

"Well, no killer is fit to use that name, so don't let me hear you use it again."

"It's my given name, and I'm going to use it," Priscilla snapped in return, and she walked away, her back tight against the abuse the group hurled at her. At least they had not offered physical abuse, as they had to Kathy. Priscilla was thankful for that, and for her friends on Campus and in her cottage who warned her and tried to protect her.

"Don't go in the pool without some of us being around," they told Priscilla. "We've heard people talk about trying to drown you."

"I'm a good swimmer," Priscilla insisted.

"Yeah, but you haven't heard about what's going on around here. Somebody threw shit in a child abuser's room awhile ago, and there's all kinds of wild rumors about you. One girl said your husband had been killed in Vietnam and you had adopted Korean kids and killed them just to get revenge."

Priscilla laughed. "Oh, come on!"

"Really! And there's another one that you're really a man and had a sex-change operation and you murdered the kids because they weren't yours!"

Priscilla tried to ignore the abuse, even after mud was thrown through her window, but her problems came to a head shortly before she left for her bail hearing.

The first week in November brought early darkness to the prison grounds. One night after dinner, Priscilla delayed returning to Harrison because she wanted to talk to a friend. When she was ready to leave, she found her usual group of companions had left, and she began to worry about whether she should walk back alone. Finally, dressed in a light Windbreaker, she started off, her muscles bunched against the fall chill and the threat of darkness.

They were waiting for her. A group of girls appeared suddenly and fell in behind her.

"There's the one who killed that Korean kid! Let's get her!"

Priscilla's blood stopped dead in her veins. She peered ahead and made out two dim figures. She rushed up. They were from Harrison and she knew them slightly: one was a huge black woman, the other a thin little white girl.

"Please, can I walk with you?" Priscilla was trembling.

"Why, sure, girl. You come right on." The black woman pulled her between them. Behind them, the others were still following, taunting.

"Dirty kid killer!"

"You deserve to die!"

"Wait till we catch you alone, baby killer!" Without warning, they were right behind Priscilla.

"How's that feel?"

It was burning her and Priscilla screamed. Then they were all throwing it at her. The boiling coffee drenched her shoulders and back, the heat slicing through her thin jacket. Some of the liquid flecked the black woman and she turned on the pursuers in fury.

"You burned me, too, you bitches! Get outta here!" she screamed. And in a moment the others were gone, shrieking with laughter.

Priscilla was sobbing as they led her to the cottage. She ran to her room and collapsed on her bed. Soon her friends began gathering.

"It's so ugly. Where does all this ugliness come from?" Priscilla cried. Somebody told the officer on duty and he summoned Priscilla.

"You know who they are?"

She nodded.

"Want me to lock them up?"

Priscilla recoiled in horror. It was the worst thing she could do.

"No, no," she said. She knew she would soon be leaving for her court appearance; it was only a matter of surviving the next few days. And she was fortunate, as it happened, because the ringleader behind the incident had a court date herself that week, and she never returned to CIW.

The Air Security return flight to Marin County was only slightly more palatable than before. Priscilla was the sole woman on the flight; even the guards were men. She could have demanded the presence of a matron or refused to go, but she would only have hurt herself, and so she said nothing. At Visalia she was again placed in a filthy call, but at least she was alone. With the bizarre logic she now saw as routine in the prison system, the officers at Visalia agreed as a special dispensation to allow Priscilla to keep her book, but they insisted she remove her contact lenses so she could not read it. At Gnoss Field, they handcuffed her hands tightly behind her back, and after a few minutes she was in such pain she thought she would cry. The Marin County jailers released her from the cuffs but they had no clothes that would fit her. The jeans were not even close to her size, and the sweatshirt they gave her to wear was so stretched she was embarrassed to appear in it. Still, she was back in Marin County. She was home.

The next day the courtroom at the Civic Center that had been selected for the bail hearing was filled with Priscilla's supporters. Some clients were there, the Doudiets, and Dr. Satten. Pat Wrigley had driven over from Vallejo. She and Harry and their two older children had taken a trip to southern California the previous weekend and had dropped by CIW unexpectedly to see if they could visit Priscilla. She wondered how quickly the officials would have denied visiting privileges had they realized the Wrigleys were Mindy's new parents.

Today's bail hearing afforded Priscilla her first glimpse of Jonathan Purver, her new appellate attorney. Ed had felt he should not handle the appeal for the new trial himself, that he was too close to see the issues clearly any more. In any case, financial expediency had finally forced Priscilla to request a court-appointed lawyer. They had been lucky with Jon Purver, Ed assured her. He was a respected appellate lawyer with considerable experience and some good results. He was studying the four-thousand-page transcript for grounds upon which to appeal.

"You look terrific, Priscilla! You look like you've lost some weight and I like that new hairstyle—it's softer somehow," Ed told her.

"I guess prison agrees with me," Priscilla tried a feeble joke. Around her, her friends laughed. Only Steve looked grim. Priscilla knew how he felt, how much this meant to him. She could not think beyond the plane ride: if she had to go back in that smelly plane, she didn't know if she could bear it.

The bail hearing was short. Josh Thomas appeared and spoke passionately against granting bail pending appeal. He drew attention to all of Priscilla's supporters in court.

"She thinks she's some kind of modern Marin Joan of Arc and a victim of circumstances," he said scathingly, gesturing around him. "No one who believes her guilty can doubt she is a threat to the community."

Ed Caldwell had prepared the application for release pending appeal: a bound document the size of the Marin County phone book. Now he argued that if denied this release, Priscilla would undoubtedly be eligible for parole before the appeal could be decided.

"In effect, Your Honor, this would deny Mrs. Phillips the right to appeal. In addition, there is new evidence that may find that the formula consumed by Tia and Mindy Phillips was improperly prepared by the manufacturer and not spiked by the defendant."

"Mr. Thomas?" Judge Burke turned to the district attorney.

"While it is true that some of the formula has been recalled by the manufacturer, as Counsel well knows—or should have found out—the lowered chloride content was not instituted until after Mindy's formula was contaminated," Josh Thomas argued in rebuttal. [Although early reports indicated that the defective formula had been manufactured solely between March 1978, and August 1979, more recent data suggest that the formula may have lacked sufficient chloride as early as 1968. Syntex resumed sales of Cho-free and Neo-Mull-Soy in January 1980, with the chloride deficiency corrected. A class action suit against Syntex is currently in litigation.]

When both prosecution and defense had finished their arguments, Judge Burke paused for a moment and the courtroom stilled. Then he rendered his decision. He began by recounting some of the testimony that he said proved Priscilla Phillips had repeatedly poisoned her two daughters.

"However," he noted, "there are no infants presently in the Phillips household. Mrs. Phillips has always manifested strong family and community ties, so I cannot believe she is a threat to flee. I have read and strongly relied on a report submitted by the psychiatrist at the California Institution for Women, Dr. Roh. As did many of the psychiatric experts who testified in the trial, Dr. Roh found no evidence of mental illness in Mrs. Phillips.

"Furthermore, as to the grounds for the appeal, this was a very complex case. I feel the issues are without merit. The jury verdict was sound. But I cannot say the appeal is frivolous. The points raised are seriously argued—they are not simply for purposes of delay. And they are debatable.

"In the light of these circumstances, I cannot say that she represents at this time a potential danger to society. For that reason I'm going to admit her to bail. Bail is fixed at five thousand dollars. The defendant is remanded to the custody of the sheriff while bail is rendered."

Priscilla burst into tears. All about her, people leaned and hugged, surrounding her. Ed's face split in a monstrous grin. The bail was a token only. They had all expected a much higher bail—perhaps a hundred thousand dollars or more—if the judge agreed to release her at all. It was a demonstration of such leniency in the face of what Priscilla had considered extreme severity at the time of her sentence, that Priscilla was shocked almost into speechlessness.

Within an hour, Priscilla was released. Jim Doudiet put up

five hundred dollars and a bondsman the balance. Cyndy Hamilton offered her house as collateral for the bondsman.

"We'll get lunch—"

"Yeah, McDonald's—"

"Right, and meet you at the house," said Steve. "It's gonna be the biggest damn party Terra Linda's ever seen! C'mon, Pris, let's get the boys. The principal will let them out early!"

Later that afternoon, Priscilla called CIW. "I'm out! I'm out!" she cried over and over as her friends came on the line.

That evening, Steve sat comfortably in the family room with his arm around Priscilla.

"How do you feel now, honey?" he asked.

"Like I'm human again," she said. "After five months, I'm a person."

Steve stroked her shoulder and neck, his fingers soft on the scars of her old burn.

"You're never gonna go back there, Pris. I can sense it. We've turned the corner," he said.

5

Steve shifted slightly, so weak that the movement required an effort of will equal to any he had ever been called upon to make. He opened his small brown eyes beneath their straggly black brows and tried to focus. There was nothing to attract his attention beyond the limp tubing of the IV and the peaks of white sheet stiff beneath his chin.

Then Priscilla was there, smiling down at him.

"Are you feeling any better?" she asked. He made an attempt at an answering smile.

"Now that they know what it is," he whispered. Then he closed his eyes. He still might die. He was dangerously ill, Dr. Werschky had told him.

"You're in here for a month, kiddo, on an IV with a constant drip of antibiotic right to the bloodstream. That's thirty days and you don't get out a day sooner," Werschky had said.

Steve had accepted this without argument. He was conscious mainly of a feeling of relief. He had started feeling lousy within two weeks of Priscilla's release on bail, the beginning of

December. He could put the pieces together now that he knew what was wrong.

But for a long time no one had suspected the cause of his worsening health. Steve had attributed it to heavy smoking, poor eating habits, and worry. When his condition deteriorated, everyone assumed he had the flu. So did he. In any case, there were too many other things to worry about after Priscilla was released on bail. Finances continued to be a chronic problem. Priscilla had realized immediately that she needed to find work, but she did not want to leave the boys so soon after her return. And she worried about what sort of job might be available because everyone knew who she was. Problems and tensions continued.

Steve dragged himself from work to home to work again. There was Christmas to prepare for with its endless rounds of festivities. After the holidays, Priscilla applied for a part-time job at Fotos 'N' Films, which had a drive-in booth at the Northgate Mall in Terra Linda. To its advantage, the job offered work during school hours, but the hourly wage of $3.25 was not going to do much to solve their financial problems. Still, it was a start.

Steve had been damned proud of Pris. She had waltzed into that place, told the woman who was doing the hiring exactly who she was, and the woman had admired her honesty and hired her on the spot.

The job itself had scarcely been challenging, he knew. But within a few weeks, Priscilla was running the place, training other employees, enjoying the selling and the communication with the public. She had applied for other jobs more consistent with her training; one in particular she was hoping to get was in Social Security. But the application process was long and drawn-out. She continued studying the job openings, sending off applications to the Firemen's Fund, which was known for a hiring system that did not discriminate against ex-offenders, and to a convalescent home in Mill Valley. She was almost hired at the home, but in the end her criminal record prevented it.

On March 7, 1980, Steve finally landed in the hospital. In January his health had deteriorated to such a degree that Priscilla began insisting he see a doctor. By then he had lost thirty-five pounds.

"Look, they're going to say I'm doing something to you! I

just get home and you start getting sick! You're looking worse and worse. You've got to be checked out," she said.

But they didn't have a doctor. On January first, they had switched from Kaiser to Blue Cross; that had been the earliest they could accomplish the transfer of coverage. But Kaiser had supplied their medical needs since 1968, and they hadn't needed—nor did they know—a private doctor.

Finally Nancy Schaefer arranged for Steve to see Dr. Werschky. Because Nancy knew the general practitioner, she obligingly told him about the background of the case, easing the awkwardness of the entire situation. Steve had been frank with Werschky.

"You gotta find it, doctor. If I die, they'll accuse my wife. She'll be right back in jail."

"We'll figure it out."

But it had taken Werschky two months. Steve had improved at first when an ear infection had been diagnosed and antibiotics prescribed. But as soon as the course of medicine ended, his condition worsened again. Blood tests and an extensive physical were normal. But finally some strep showed up and Werschky hit upon the truth.

"You've got a bicuspid heart valve instead of a tricuspid, Steve," Werschky had said.

"Yeah, I know."

"Been to the dentist lately?"

And that had been the solution. Steve's heart condition had surfaced ten years before; because of it he followed standard routines before visiting the dentist. When his teeth were cleaned all sorts of bacteria were released into his bloodstream and could cause serious heart infections in people with heart abnormalities. Steve always began a course of antibiotics before dental appointments. But apparently the protocol had changed. This time his precautions had been insufficient.

"You've got a heart infection, Steve. We don't fool around with those."

Within a week of hospitalization, Steve was much improved. He began to eat, sit up, and receive visitors. One of the first to come was Jerry Dodson.

Jerry was one of the best things to happen in a long while: Steve knew that. He was good for Steve and even better for Priscilla. They had met Jerry and his wife at Christ Presbyterian, the church they now attended. They hadn't seen Jim Hutchison since June, right before Priscilla's imprisonment, when they had a final parting of the ways. Steve would never understand what motivated that man, what caused him to withdraw his support and then pretend he hadn't. Marietta had seen through it; Steve admired her for that.

One day in June, Marietta had gone alone to Aldersgate, where she had been a loyal parishioner for months, and in the portion of the service during which the congregation shared its joys and concerns, she had stood to lambaste the congregation for its lack of support for her daughter.

"Only God and Priscilla know whether she's innocent, but that is not the point. You should support her," she had scolded. Jim Hutchison had not been present, but as always when he missed service, he had listened later to the tape recording that had been made. Then he had written a long letter to Marietta—addressed to her North Carolina home so she would not receive it while she was in Terra Linda—all filled with some sort of mumbo jumbo about the prodigal son. Marietta would never let Steve read it; she was afraid it would set him off. Just hearing about the letter had been enough for Steve. He had called the bishop to complain about Hutchison, and followed his call with a formal letter of complaint. At least— and Steve had been grateful for that small favor—Priscilla was no longer making excuses for Hutchison. She saw him for what he was. Steve had no doubts about what the man was doing: Hutchison wanted that church built up on the hill on Kaiser land; he had always wanted that. He'd do anything for it. As far as Steve was concerned, that was going to be the church that Pris built.

The congregation and minister at Christ Presbyterian had welcomed Priscilla and Steve. They had even contributed to the defense fund. And Priscilla much preferred Reverend Dave Steele's style in church. The church, after all, was a congregation and its spirit, not the minister or the building. That was something Priscilla recently had come to realize about Jim Hutchison, that to him the building was paramount. Steve agreed with her. And to his mind, Reverend Steele was less conservative a preacher. You could hear guitar music in his church. The Doudiets attended, and Nancy Dacus—now Nancy Greenfield since her divorce—was talking about joining. And that's where they had met the Dodsons, who had just returned from Germany. Jerry was an army psychiatrist who had been stationed in Frankfurt.

"It was absolute hell over there," he told Priscilla and Steve.

"I was the only child psychiatrist in the whole region. The pressure was unbelievable. And then when Sue got cancer, I thought I'd go off the deep end. You know the thing that attracted me to you was that you were the only people I could find who had had a worse year than I did!"

Sometimes it was hard being around the Dodsons, of course. Steve acknowledged that. Jerry and Sue had a daughter just Tia's age—the memories were bitter. But their friendship was worth that because Jerry offered some invaluable reality testing. He hadn't known Priscilla before her arrest; he didn't have any preconceived notions about her. Yet within a few months he was telling her she wasn't crazy, and she wasn't a child abuser.

"Look, the more I get to know you, Priscilla, the more certain I am that you don't have this Munchausen's," he said one day in his whispery Texas drawl. "I've really started reading up on the syndrome. Frankly I'm intrigued. But nothing I've read leads me to conclude you've got it. The literature I've read indicates that once a Munchausen loses the proxy, she starts showing the symptoms herself—and you haven't done that. You're sound as a bell! The only thing I can possibly imagine is some sort of multiple personality, but there's absolutely no evidence of that. And the people around you would know that even if you didn't. There's just no way to disguise that sort of a thing."

It had been damn reassuring, Steve thought. For Pris, too. Dodson knew what he was talking about: he treated adults as well as children. And he was young and sensitive and kept assuring Priscilla that he wasn't likely to be attracted to child killers. He had been a big help while Steve was in the hospital, too.

Dr. Werschky released Steve from Marin General the first week in April.

"Try not to put that weight back on, Steve. You're right where you should be. And no more cigarettes."

"Right, Doc. I don't need the damn things anymore anyway. We're gonna take care of business now."

"You know I got a call from a doctor who had been asked to call me by a Detective Lindquist," he said. "He just thought he'd fill me in on who you all were, in case it affected my diagnosis."

Steve gave a bitter laugh. "Lindquist thought Pris was poisoning me, right?"

"I guess he thought it was a possibility. I told the doctor we had it under control."

"Pris calls that sucker an avenging angel. Lindquist seems to have made us his personal little vendetta. He got what he wanted; you'd think he'd leave us alone to live our life—what's left of it."

"What's the status of the appeal?"

"No news."

"What about the Syntex thing? I saw *20/20* just had something on it."

"Yeah. Our lawyer's following up on it. The family that's got our little girl now, the mother wrote in for a transcript of the program. Her older adopted boy was on that formula, too, and she thinks they may have some cause for a lawsuit. There's some kind of class action suit being filed by a lawyer in Chicago. She's investigating that for Mindy, too."

"What about you? Did you ever consider a suit against Kaiser for malpractice?"

"Yeah, we talked about it once. But what do we sue them for? Failure to spot sodium poisoning? That would be admitting Pris had done it, and of course she didn't. Our lawyer or somebody said they'd just turn around and countersue us for the money they spent on Tia and Mindy. I heard one estimate that Tia's treatment cost Kaiser half a million dollars." He shook his head.

"And for what?" he added softly.

6

Nine and a half months later, on a cold and rainy January day, Priscilla's case came up for oral argument at the state court of appeal in San Francisco.

Priscilla dressed carefully for the session. The judges would not know she was there, Ed had told her. It was unusual for the appellant to be in the courtroom; most convicted murders were in jail during the appellate process. They were to meet Ed there, but Al Collins would not attend. Ed had told Priscilla that the two attorneys were no longer on speaking terms: their friendship a casualty of the case. But he would never tell her the details of the schism.

Priscilla was shocked to see Josh Thomas and Ted Lindquist in the courtroom. The district attorney had no say at the appellate level, as it was the state attorney general who handled the respondent's brief and court appearance. And the only reason for Lindquist's appearance could be personal interest.

"They just can't stay away," Steve muttered when he saw the two seated in the rows of spectator seats. "They'll be at our funerals if they live that long."

Priscilla knew that the court's request for oral argument was a positive sign. In most cases the panel relied solely on the briefs prepared by the attorneys for appellant and respondent. But if a case interested the justices—or if they were sharply divided in their initial impressions—they called for oral argument. At that time the two attorneys who had prepared the briefs appeared before the three-judge panel and were given strictly regimented periods of time to present and rebut arguments. In Priscilla's case, the judges had requested that argument be focused on one of the three grounds of appeal: Judge Burke's failure to present diminished capacity instructions to the jury *sua sponte*, even though the defense had not requested such instructions and had, in fact, actively opposed any motion that they be given. The defense, after all, had been based on the supposition that Priscilla was completely sane.

Ed had told Priscilla that he believed the best grounds for her appeal lay in another direction. Burke's decision to allow Martin Blinder's testimony on Munchausen Syndrome by Proxy *when the defense had not raised the issue of Priscilla's mental state*, was unconscionable, Ed felt. And Jon Purver, in the appellant's brief, had discussed this issue at length, as well as what he believed to be Juror Polizzi's prejudicial experiment. But Purver had insisted—and apparently with some justification, as the panel had ordered argument on this issue—that Priscilla's best ground for a new trial rested on the failure to give diminished capacity instructions. He had found some cases to support his opinion that the judge, *on his own*, should have issued such instructions.

In the months since her release on bail, Priscilla had regained some of the confidence she had lost at CIW. Jail infantilized prisoners and played on their helplessness and dependency; indeed this seemed to be a conscious method of control. But Priscilla's understanding of this process had not shielded her from its effect, and when she emerged from five months of imprisonment, to some extent she had to relearn how to function independently and with her old assertiveness.

Her experience at Fotos 'N' Films had been significant. At the beginning of the summer, after six months with the company, she had been called in and offered the position of supervisor in the San Francisco office.

"I know you've had some legal problems, but we're not concerned about that. What we're looking at is your job performance," Mr. Cossman said. "Are you interested?"

Priscilla accepted the position. Although the salary was not high and she would incur the additional expense of commuting to the city, she had been offered the use of a company car during working hours. This would be invaluable as she was expected to travel to the various Bay Area stores. More than anything else, though, the promotion boosted Priscilla's confidence. Now her job more nearly suited her background and knowledge. She would be on her own and expected to deal both with the public and with company employees. Management believed in her. At the end of sixty days, Cossman approved a raise. Then he offered her use of a car and gas money during nonworking hours. After another sixty days he raised her salary again. She began receiving discounts and then commission. What a change it was.

Steve's illness had been hard on Priscilla, but even more difficult for the boys. Suddenly they lost the one person on whom they had been totally dependent. Erik was old enough to remember that members of their family who went into the hospital did not come home again. And to make matters worse for all of them, while Steve was in the hospital, the dishwasher collapsed and the roof began to leak. But Priscilla managed and Steve recovered, and now, suddenly, it looked as though nothing could go wrong.

Priscilla came to the oral argument, then, with the same optimism with which she had faced each stage of the proceedings. When Jonathan Purver, casually dressed for court in dark pants, blue shirt and tie, and a light tan corduroy jacket, rose and took his place before the panel, she leaned forward, her lips pursed in concentration, to listen to her attorney.

As he had been instructed, Purver limited his discussion to the issue of diminished capacity instruction. Presiding Justice

John Racanelli acted as timekeeper and did not speak during Purver's initial presentation. But Justices Joseph Grodin and Norman Elkington questioned Purver closely.

"As a tactical maneuver, the defense attorney did not ask for diminished capacity instructions," Elkington pointed out. "Was this not an admission that Priscilla Phillips was not suffering from diminished capacity?"

"I believe that's irrelevant," Purver replied. "I cite *Cedeno*."

"If the defense attorney had been reasonably competent, he would have asked for diminished capacity instruction," Judge Grodin added. "Since he didn't, he obviously didn't want it. If the court gave such instructions when the defense attorney didn't want it, wouldn't *that* have been grounds for appeal?"

"I believe the judge has the obligation to give those instructions *sua sponte* when there is evidence of lesser and included offenses," Purver replied.

Judge Elkington broke in. "In *People* v. *Newton*, it was established that unless a distinct tactical purpose appears to the contrary, the trial court is bound to instruct on lesser and included offenses. But if a tactical purpose existed, as in this case, that's all that's necessary."

"Well, the defense attorney was in a difficult position because the state introduced the defendant's mental condition. The attorney has to be consistent in his defense."

"I don't see why he couldn't have asked the judge *in chambers* to issue diminished capacity instruction, then," Grodin said.

"You've used up your time, Mr. Purver."

Linda Ludlow, a lawyer with the attorney general's office, stood for her presentation. A woman in her forties, with her hair pulled back into a severe bun, tortoise-shell glasses, and no makeup, she looked like a spinster school mistress in her camel suit and dark turtleneck. Her first remark drew a scathing response from Judge Racanelli.

"Priscilla Phillips was not suffering from diminished capacity at the time of the crime," she began.

"What about Dr. Blinder's testimony that anyone doing such a thing would have to be emotionally ill?" Racanelli interrupted angrily.

"Obviously a person is abnormal to do this," Grodin commented gently.

"Everyone always makes the point about curious and bizarre

crimes that a person would have to be crazy to commit them," Linda Ludlow responded evenly.

"Poisoning an infant is evidence of mental disease," said Racanelli, his voice hard with emphasis.

"I believe that Munchausen Syndrome implies that you know what you are doing; that is part of the syndrome itself. A diminished capacity instruction would not be applicable because the nature of the syndrome is such that the poisoning is intentional," Linda Ludlow answered.

"Don't all crazy people act intentionally? That does not affect their craziness," Racanelli retorted. "Your time is up, Miss Ludlow," he added, after some further argument. "You have one minute for rebuttal, Mr. Purver."

Joe Purver rose and took his place behind the podium facing the judges.

"The jury could have convicted on lots of things, but they chose to convict on the least offense possible—the least except involuntary manslaughter, that is—and they could not convict on that because no diminished capacity instruction was given. Obviously the jury was taking the defendant's mental state into mind. Thank you."

It was 10:48 and the oral argument was over. Priscilla took Steve's arm as they made their way out of the courtroom.

"What did you think?" Steve asked.

"I think that one judge, Elkington, has made up his mind that Ed made a tactical decision against asking for diminished capacity. So he's a negative vote. But the other two—I couldn't tell," Priscilla said.

"I'm optimistic. You can never predict the outcome of oral arguments, of course, and I don't like to try. But I think Jon did a good job. I think we have a reasonable chance," Ed said. He did not add that he had been sitting directly behind one of the law clerks and had seen the proof sheet on Priscilla's case. If they affirmed, Priscilla would be back in prison to serve out her term. But he had seen the preliminary decision: it was to reverse her conviction.

7

The Riverside freeway was clogged with morning commute traffic. Steve swore loudly as a car darted in front of his VW camper, cutting him off. Beside him on the high seat, Priscilla checked her watch.

"He *would* have to say nine o'clock. If only he had said twelve or one, we wouldn't have had to struggle with all this," she said angrily.

"Take it easy, Pris." Steve reached for her hand. She was tense and hadn't felt well for months. Her problems had started last summer during the visit with the Dodsons, who had moved to Idaho. Jerry wanted a quiet private practice in a rural, small-town setting, and he had found an ideal situation in Pocatello.

Priscilla had come down with stomach flu while they were there. Jerry thought it was aggravated by stress. Pris had diarrhea that just wouldn't quit and she couldn't force down enough fluid. All of a sudden she had landed in the hospital on an IV suffering from dehydration.

"Priscilla, it's all right to be upset," Jerry soothed, certain that her medical problems reflected her emotional state. "Things are pretty precarious for you right now."

"But I'm worried about being sick. If Josh found out he'd say it was Munchausen's, that I'm doing it to myself."

"That's nonsense," Jerry said. "It's okay to lose control of your body once in awhile. It doesn't mean you have Munchausen's. If you go through life dreading illnesses because you think it's a symptom of Munchausen's then you're going to be in real trouble. I've seen you in every sort of situation, Priscilla. You and Steve and the boys. I know how you relate. I know what sort of person you are. You don't have Munchausen's—I'm sure of it."

Steve had been reassured—Jerry did that for you. Still, Pris did not get well. They had come back from Idaho at the end of the summer and she had returned to work, fighting the low-grade fever that apparently persisted no matter what she did. Dr. Werschky could find nothing wrong.

"I'm going to put you in Marin General for some tests," he had finally told Priscilla a couple of weeks ago. Steve agreed.

"Keep it quiet," he told the doctor and their friends. "We don't want Josh Thomas or Lindquist hanging around." If they knew, they'd say it was deliberate, the timing coming as it did. But the test had showed no cause for the fever.

The camper picked up speed. It was brand-new; the old one had finally collapsed. They had debated whether to buy a new van or look for something more affordable. Finally, they had decided to go ahead with a camper: they might have to live in it one of these days. They were going to have to sell the house soon to pay their debts. The house had a third mortgage on it now, a move they had made to assure eventual payment to Ed. The three of them had finally settled on a figure. They had pretty much plucked the sum out of the air. It didn't approach the true amount. Ed had poured hundreds of free hours into the case. His clock had stopped months ago now.

"Hurry up, we'll be late," Priscilla said.

"We'll get there, hon."

"Hey, Dad, there's the campgrounds."

"That's right, Jase." The boys were holding up, at least, though they were tired from the hectic Thanksgiving and then the hurried weekend trip down to Disneyland.

"There's the country store."

"Yeah, I see it, son." Steve turned right at the corner. Nothing was marked around here. If you didn't know where you were going, you'd never find the place. But there, finally, was the entrance. Steve checked his watch.

"Report at nine," the judge had said. Well they had made it. Priscilla had never missed a court appearance, never been late, not even to jail. Steve stared at the high chain-linked fence topped with barbed wire that ringed the California Institution for Women.

Priscilla had lost the appeal.

EPILOGUE

1

Reverend Jim Hutchison always dated his final break with Steve and Priscilla Phillips from the time of Marietta's diatribe at Aldersgate United Methodist Church in June 1978.

Despite Marietta's criticism, he believed that he and the church members had in fact been as supportive of Priscilla as they were able. Any lack of support was due to their failure to understand how to proceed. She was accused of no mere traffic violation, but of murder.

Jim had suddenly realized the contradiction in his own behavior since the arrest, and what he had to do. He remembered the parable of the prodigal son, and its key statement: that it was not until the son *came to himself* that he could acknowledge his sin. Unless Priscilla reached such a point, support would not help her. Jim's insight carried its own problems because as a pastor his duty was to help and care for people, but he believed that to continue aiding Priscilla would be to reinforce her act of denial. He could not do it, despite some pressure from friends of the Phillipses. If he had to lose several parishioners, so be it. Acting on a suggestion from his district supervisor, he talked with Reverend Dave Steele of Christ Presbyterian Church and asked Steele to take in the Phillips family.

In September 1981, Jim returned to school to study for a Ph.D. in Medical Ethics at the San Francisco Theological Seminary. He continued, as before, to counsel and minister to the congregation at Aldersgate. The work on the new church went forward as scheduled.

On the afternoon of December 19, 1982, the new Aldersgate Church on top of the hill was dedicated by Bishop Wilbur Choy. The modern, pentagon-shaped church with its vaulting, beamed ceiling of rust-colored wood, was filled with worshipers. Outside in the clear sunshine, the church grounds afforded a three-hundred-sixty-degree view of Terra Linda. On one side, directly below the church, was Kaiser Hospital, which had donated the flowers for the first service.

As Jim reminded the congregation on this opening day, Kaiser could claim responsibility for the debt-free condition with which Aldersgate began its service in its new site. Without Kaiser assistance, there would have been no church.

Jim expected imminent transfer. His appointment to Aldersgate exceeded what was customary. The new church was built and dedicated, and it now seemed right to move on. He still thought often of Priscilla Phillips and he believed himself to be part of her Christian life despite her incarceration. When her parole board met for the first time in April 1982, to consider setting a parole date, Jim learned that Steve had been soliciting supportive letters from the community—to be mailed to the board—urging Priscilla's early release. Jim felt compelled to write a letter counteracting the positive mail. Although his was the only negative letter received, apparently it helped to achieve its desired effect. The parole board had not set a date, ordering Priscilla to present herself again in a year.

Priscilla Phillips would not be salvaged until she came to herself. Jim knew that absolutely. Back in the arms of family and friends who would reassure her and soothe her, she would have no reason to face what she had done. Perhaps in prison the realization would be forced upon her.

2

Priscilla Phillips's conviction marked the rise of Ted Lindquist's star in the San Rafael Police Department. He received a commendation and the congratulations of the chief. Soon afterward he was promoted to the position of detective in charge of crimes against persons.

In 1980 he developed an interest in the Police Association and was elected vice-president. The next year he was made president. Within months he was embroiled in a losing battle to pass a binding arbitration initiative for the police and fire departments.

In 1982, he ran unopposed for a second term as president of

the PA and became involved, this time more successfully, in another long labor dispute with the city. In September 1982, Ted won a 19.6-percent salary increase for the police department plus an agreement by the city to pay $180,000 in back wages. He was equally successful in department matters, helping to solve a complicated murder-for-hire case involving a man with bizarre medieval fantasies about taking over Marin County. Six months later, Ted was promoted to sergeant and transferred, by departmental regulation, to patrol duty.

As for the Phillips case, Ted had not forgotten it. He knew Priscilla Phillips saw him as some kind of black-robed avenging angel, but this he disputed. What she had done was terrible—the ultimate betrayal, even—but Priscilla herself? Priscilla had been overdue and he had caught her, that was all. Protestations of innocence meant nothing to Ted. He had seen too many of the guilty sincerely explaining away the evidence left by their bloody handprints to take such assertions seriously.

In addition, Ted saw deep-rooted, repeated insincerity in Priscilla. Although she claimed repeatedly that her prison sentence primarily punished her sons, in fact she often courted the limelight, opening old wounds and subjecting her children again and again to renewed publicity. She had granted one newspaper interview after her release on bail—in which she detailed the harshness of prison life—and another on the eve of her reincarceration. She seemed unable to let the story die.

Ted never doubted Priscilla Phillips deserved her punishment. He knew it would not bring back that little girl buried under the Japanese plum tree in Novato.

3

Sara Shimoda and Evelyn Callas remained in practice at Kaiser-San Rafael. Sara continued to see patients as before. After awhile she ceased to speak of the Priscilla Phillips case and it was clear to everyone that she did not wish to be reminded of it.

In March 1983, Evelyn began her sixth year as Chief of Pediatrics. Shortly after Priscilla Phillips's trial, she and Jim had moved across the road into a large sprawling house on wild county land.

Evelyn continued to follow the literature in the medical journal relating to child poisoning and Munchausen Syndrome by Proxy. More and more cases were reported and the syndrome became a recognized phenomenon, although the third edition of the *Diagnostic and Statistical Manual* still did not mention it, listing only Munchausen Syndrome, which itself did not rate a separate section but was indexed under the category of factitious diseases. In the spring of 1981, a Concord, California, woman was arrested and charged with causing her daughter's near-fatal seizures by injecting bacteria into the child's IV. The hospital involved was Kaiser-Walnut Creek.

In 1982, Roy Meadow, the British pediatrician who had initially named the syndrome in the English publication *Lancet*, wrote a follow-up article for *Archives of Disease in Childhood*. Evelyn Xeroxed and saved the article that detailed nineteen case histories of Munchausen Syndrome by Proxy. Meadow provided some new and interesting statistics on the families involved. Most of the children in his case studies had been examined by numerous doctors, often in different hospital settings.

In every case Meadow listed in his update, the mother was behind the fabrication. Interestingly, half of the seventeen British mothers involved possessed some nursing training, although only one was fully registered. Most of the mothers had histories suggesting that they either suffered from Munchausen's Syndrome themselves, or had histories of symptoms similar to those they fabricated for their children. Most of them either lived in the hospital during their children's illnesses or spent most of their time there. In general, Meadow also found that the father was the passive partner in the marriage, and in most of the families there was a greater than usual discrepancy in social or intellectual level between the parents, with the wife at the higher level. In two families, a second child fell victim to Munchausen Syndrome by Proxy, with a high probability in yet a third family that an older sibling's mysterious illness was another case of Munchausen's.

Evelyn no longer doubted that Priscilla Phillips did indeed suffer from Munchausen's Syndrome by Proxy. The label was helpful because it allowed Evelyn to stand back from Priscilla Phillips, to accept her—as all her life she had learned to accept medical aberrations—in what she called the Christian spirit. She viewed Priscilla Phillips with repugnance and distaste but not with hatred.

4

After Priscilla's imprisonment in November 1981, Steve was relegated to the background at Marin County juvenile hall. While once he had dreams of promotion to superintendent, now he saw no future at the job. The community knew his identity and that of his wife. He was kept from the public as much as possible. His supervisors, initially supportive, started proposing schedule changes that would cut into his weekend time with the boys. He recognized the signs and started looking into other careers.

In the fall of 1982, he put the house up for sale; it was the only alternative to declaring bankruptcy and neither he nor Priscilla wanted to go that route: they owed too many friends. He hoped to move back South. His sister and brother-in-law were urging him to come and friends there had lined up a few job possibilities.

Priscilla did not want him to move as long as she remained jailed, however, and that posed a problem. Sometimes Steve thought he had three children once again, two at home and one in prison in southern California. He believed Priscilla was weakening in prison, not hardening. Less and less often she talked about early release or work furlough, while to him those were all that mattered. Once she had been a fighter; now she expected the worst. She had experienced trouble with visiting rights after her return to prison, and for a while that conflict gave her some reason to be assertive, but once the issue was settled, she seemed to give in to the paralysis of prison life.

Part of it, Steve knew, was that her constant illness had depleted her. It was the prison environment. Status in women's prison depended largely on little outward signs: how often the family visited, how much money they sent, how often they wrote. Priscilla was always scolding Steve about these things. Once the flowers he sent for Mother's Day had arrived late, and she, thinking he had forgotten, mailed off a blistering letter. Her life consisted of waiting expectantly for the next box from home or for the delivery of the food orders from Wendy's or Taco Bell that the inmates were allowed to place from time to time. Since her illness she was not allowed to hold a prison job. And doing time in the Psychiatric Treatment Unit, where the new superintendent had assigned Priscilla and other protective custody cases—as well as the mental cases—was limiting and restrictive. Priscilla had dreaded the psychiatric unit, but her assignment there had not come as a surprise. Her friends at CIW had warned her that she would probably be placed in PTU instead of Campus because there had been some problems with child-related cases since her last stay at CIW. But now she was resigned to the unit, as she was resigned to everything about prison life. That frightened Steve.

Steve looked forward to little in Terra Linda anymore—only to leaving it. Many of his friends had moved away: the Schaefers lived in Novato now, the Dodsons in Idaho, and finally the Doudiets had relocated recently to Indiana. Nancy Greenfield remained a faithful, dogged friend to both Priscilla—whom she wrote daily—and to Steve, but many of the people who had supported them prior to the trial and verdict—Debby Roof, Maria Sterling, Marilyn Hansen—had drifted away. His support system, so carefully constructed, threatened to crumble.

Still, Steve coped better than during Priscilla's first imprisonment. The boys were older, more independent and more capable. They could be left alone. And Steve now knew he could manage. It was just a matter of hanging in there, doing what had to be done to survive, until Pris returned.

Steve tried to let the past sift away. He stopped visiting Tia's grave. The sixth anniversary of her death passed unobserved. He did not want to go up there and he did not want to remember. It was one of the things he remained bitterest about: Josh Thomas and Ted Lindquist and the rest had taken away the beauty that was Tia's life and replaced it with ugliness, injustice, and anger. He would never be able to forgive them for that.

He removed Mindy's photograph from the hall. It was too savage a reminder and evoked too many questions from visitors. The flowers painted on the pieced strips of raisin-drying trays remained on the living room walls, though, the natural lines of blossom and stem and fence still broken and distorted by the spaces between the slats.

5

Priscilla was hospitalized in the prison infirmary three months after her arrival at CIW, and in April was transferred by ambulance to Riverside General—chained to a gurney—in hypertensive crisis. She spent several days in Intensive Care, alone except for her guard. Her doctor finally asked that she be released from the cuffs holding her to the bed so that he could more easily examine her. In keeping with prison policy, no one contacted Steve, afraid that he might try to break her out. After a few days the doctors released Priscilla, but they had not cured her.

When the prescribed medications were ineffective, others were initiated. At Riverside General, Priscilla saw whichever resident was on duty; she had no regular doctor and there was no continuity of care. In her weekly ten-minute phone call, she and Steve discussed calling in a private doctor, but the red tape involved was immense, and the idea was finally dropped. Sometimes she improved for a while only to deteriorate again. By June she was passing out regularly; once she struck her head during a blackout. She suffered from repeated kidney infections that the doctors said were related to the high blood pressure.

Priscilla became increasingly concerned that she really had contracted Munchausen's Syndrome. In an ironic moment she wrote to a friend that perhaps Josh Thomas had even "given" it to her by some strange power of suggestion. Everyone tried to reassure her. She had suffered from high blood pressure before, when she was pregnant with Jason, someone reminded her. It was only natural that during this time of stress, the problem should recur. Jerry Dodson wrote her that he believed her hypertension stemmed from her sudden loss of control over her life. He suggested once again that she had a right to be sick. Other people made different points. The medical personnel at CIW told her that she was emotionally unstable and could not deal with stress. That was the cause of her high blood pressure. She did not believe that because she had always dealt well with stress, but when she pointed this out, they informed her she was denying reality. The prison minister, a black fundamentalist, told her that her blood pressure would only come down if she "gave it all to God." She stopped attending services.

In September 1982, ten months after her return to CIW, she was again hospitalized at Riverside. This time she spent eight days there. Her medication was changed once more. She wrote frantic letters to her friends, raging at her illness, at how her body was failing her. Still her blood pressure soared.

But if her health remained poor, at least, after the first shock of adjustment, the Psychiatric Treatment Unit did not prove to be the sinister place of its reputation. True, she was denied many on-site facilities, training, and educational programs automatically extended to Campus residents. The unit was reserved for misfits of one sort or another; there were women there with emotional problems so severe they were constantly drugged, and there were protective custody cases such as Priscilla, whose crimes put them at the lowest end of the rigid totem-pole system in prison. But there were compensations: particularly an incredible sense of closeness within the small group. The women there were special, separate—almost specially sinned against. That was how they felt. Every night, before bed, they hugged and kissed and smiled at one another to support their isolation.

Priscilla settled into a routine. On her calendar she marked the six-week intervals that separated each visit by Steve and the boys. She instructed Steve to bring her sewing machine and she made curtains for her room. After a time she was allowed her first Family Living Unit visit—a weekend for the inmate and her family alone in a private room on the prison grounds. She enrolled in a creative writing course by correspondence and began another journal. She took up painting. When it became mandatory for all prisoners to hold a prison job, she was assigned work as a clerk for the lieutenant.

In March 1983, the doctors finally found a blood pressure medication that worked. Priscilla's health improved dramatically. In that same month, the hearing officers representing the Board of Prison Terms met for the second time to discuss her release date. The previous year the Board had refused to grant her a date, urging her instead to see a prison psychiatrist, and she had agreed to do this, fuming. There was only one psychiatrist for a thousand inmates. Even if there was something wrong with her, and she knew there wasn't, she doubted he could see her more than a few times. There was nothing he could do. Soon even he was gone, to be replaced by a psychologist.

Steve was counting heavily on an early release date. He had started another letter-writing campaign. If that proved ineffective, he was planning a trip to Sacramento. He had met some people there who might help. He had it in mind to contact a southern senator if all else failed. But he really believed the board might release Priscilla immediately; she had served the minimum time already. However she had marked on her calendar the last possible release date, assuming good behavior: December 10, 1984.

On Monday, March 14, 1983, the hearing officers called Priscilla in. They had read all the letters but one. Dr. Satten had spent a long time constructing a highly favorable letter, which he had sent by special messenger the week before. Strangely, although the receipt for the letter had been dated Friday, the prison administration claimed never to have seen it and it was not read by the hearing officers. What they did consider was the report from the newly hired psychologist, who had administered the Minnesota Multiphasic Personality Inventory to Priscilla, a standard psychological profile test used universally by psychologists as a diagnostic tool. The psychologist's report indicated that Priscilla Phillips had been diagnosed at the time of her trial as suffering from Munchausen's Syndrome by Proxy—a misstatement of Dr. Blinder's testimony—and that tests indicated that Priscilla tended to overvalue her family. It also stated that the prisoner's future behavior was impossible to predict. On the basis of this report, the hearing officers refused either to grant parole or to set a release date.

6

In September 1982, Sarah Wrigley entered a regular kindergarten class. Because of her excellent progress in the handicapped class, her teacher had pronounced her ready for "mainstreaming."

At five, Sarah already could read. Cytomegalovirus had left its mark on her, however. Her motor coordination—particularly the fine coordination of hands and fingers—was impaired, so that although she could form all her letters, she could not write in a straight line. Her speech handicap was severe, and it was very difficult to understand her. Half her face was paralyzed and one eye was turned in so completely that she was functionally blind in that eye; the other eye was very far-sighted. Sometimes her life was frustrating enough to cause tantrums. But in kindergarten Sarah began working with a teacher for the visually handicapped who started her on an electric typewriter. Within a few days Sarah had mastered the keyboard because although she could not see without twisting her head and staring closely at the keys, she was able to memorize their position. It was impossible to give her standardized tests so the teachers planned to convert them to large-print format. But it was evident to everyone that Sarah Wrigley possessed a very high IQ.

Both Joey and Sarah Wrigley were members of the class in the class action suit that had been filed against Syntex, and the Chicago lawyer handling the case had asked Pat Wrigley to obtain Sarah's Kaiser records, still being held in the clerk's office at the Marin County Civic Center. At the same time, Pat hoped to retrieve the photographs of Mindy as a baby that had also been entered as evidence. Sarah had often stared at the baby pictures that had been taken of her brother and sister, but the records of her own past were barred to her by the criminal justice system. It would be difficult—requiring a court order, Pat discovered—to recover that evidence from the Marin County clerk.

Meanwhile, every once in awhile, in an effort to keep memories fresh, Pat Wrigley sat down with Sarah to retell the story that had become as familiar to the little girl as her nightly prayers. It was a story that from the beginning Sarah could participate in.

"Once upon a time there was a little girl in Korea who had a foster mother. And the little girl's name was—?"

"Seo Yun Kim," said Sarah.

"And her foster mother loved her very much. Then the little girl came to America and lived with the Phillips family. And her name was—?"

"Mindy Leanne Phillips," Sarah supplied.

"And she had two brothers named Erik and Jason. Now her name is—?"

"Sarah Kim Wrigley."

"Yes, and she has a mommy and daddy and a sister, Becky, and a brother, Joey, and they love her very much." Pat looked down at the little girl beside her—the most affectionate and expressive of her children. Then she ended the story as she always did.

"And all her mommies and daddies and brothers and sisters have loved her very much."

ABOUT THE AUTHOR

NANCY WRIGHT, a native of New York, was graduated from the University of California, Berkeley, and subsequently taught high-school English in Richmond, California for ten years. *A Mother's Trial* is her first book. With her husband and two children, she recently moved to southern California where she is now working on a screenplay.

We Deliver!
And So Do These Bestsellers.

DON'T MISS
THESE CURRENT
Bantam Bestsellers

☐	23639	**THE GOLDEN AX #1** Eric Nielson	$2.50
☐	23924	**THE VIKING'S REVENGE #2** Eric Nielson	$2.50
☐	24368	**IRON HAND #3** Eric Nielson	$2.50
☐	24541	**THE WAR GOD #4** Eric Nielson	$2.95
☐	24244	**GAME PLAN** Leslie Waller	$3.50
☐	23952	**DANCER WITH ONE LEG** Stephen Dobyns	$3.50
☐	24257	**WOMAN IN THE WINDOW** Dana Clarins	$3.50
☐	24363	**O GOD OF BATTLES** Harry Homewood	$3.95
☐	23823	**FINAL HARBOR** Harry Homewood	$3.50
☐	23983	**CIRCLES** Doris Mortman	$3.50
☐	24184	**THE WARLORD** Malcolm Bosse	$3.95
☐	22848	**FLOWER OF THE PACIFIC** Lana McGraw Boldt	$3.95
☐	23920	**VOICE OF THE HEART** Barbara Taylor Bradford	$4.50
☐	23638	**THE OTHER SIDE** Diana Henstell	$3.5(
☐	24428	**DARK PLACES** Thomas Altman	$3.5(
☐	23198	**BLACK CHRISTMAS** Thomas Altman	$2.95
☐	24010	**KISS DADDY GOODBYE** Thomas Altman	$3.50
☐	24561	**THE VALLEY OF HORSES** Jean M. Auel	$4.50
☐	23897	**CLAN OF THE CAVE BEAR** Jean M. Auel	$4.50

SPECIAL
MONEY SAVING
OFFER

Now you can have an up-to-date listing of Bantam's hundreds of titles plus take advantage of our unique and exciting bonus book offer. A special offer which gives you the opportunity to purchase a Bantam book for only 50¢. Here's how!

By ordering any five books at the regular price per order, you can also choose any other single book listed (up to a $4.95 value) for just 50¢. Some restrictions do apply, but for further details why not send for Bantam's listing of titles today!

Just send us your name and address plus 50¢ to defray the postage and handling costs.